# Yoga Consciousness in Ancient Mystery Religions

## Cinderella Sutras

# Yoga Consciousness in Ancient Mystery Religions

## Cinderella Sutras

**Tony Butcher**

JANUS PUBLISHING COMPANY
London, England

First published in Great Britain 2006
by Janus Publishing Company Ltd,
105-107 Gloucester Place,
London W1U 6BY

www.januspublishing.co.uk

British Library Cataloguing-in-Publication Data
A catalogue record for this book is available from the British Library

ISBN 10: 1 85756 622 X
ISBN 13: 978-1-85756-622-2

Cover Design: Michael Hopson

Printed and bound in Great Britain

# Contents

# Foreword

In this important new study, Tony Butcher presents an intriguing analysis of the real meaning of what is commonly called the 'fairy tale'. Selecting examples we have all grown up with – Cinderella, Snow White, Lucky Hans – he argues that such stories are not just fanciful works of the imagination designed to entertain children, but potent allegories that teach of nothing less than life's quest: the journey to spiritual enlightenment.

Unlike previous travellers through this enchanted territory, Butcher's guiding signposts are not the modern theories of psychoanalysis, but the teachings of the Wisdom Schools of the ancient world. Each tale is shown to be an account of the soul's journey home, in terms of the venerable mystery religions of Egypt, Greece and Rome. Such a thesis is saved from being a merely academic exercise by detailed reference to the most contemporary, and accessible, incarnation of this perennial wisdom: the teachings of Maharishi Mahesh Yogi, the guru who brought Transcendental Meditation [TM] to the West.

In other hands, such a profound subject could weigh heavily, but it is here treated in a thoroughly readable manner, enlivened by the author's enthusiastic and unpretentious tone. Like a good meditation, this book provides deep and nourishing refreshment, allowing one to see the world with different eyes.

Alistair Shearer.
*October 2006*

Author of *One Equal Light* and *The Spirit of Asia*. Founder of the Neeleshwar Hermitage Retreat Centre in South India.

# Preface

Transcendental Meditation (or TM) has transformed my life in a big way since I first learnt it in 1968. Five years later came the blossoming of an ability which has given me a great deal of pleasure ever since and has made the reading of 'fairy stories' and myths such a joy. I would like to share this with you because it has expanded my awareness and opened my mind to many new insights.

One afternoon in 1973 I was sitting in my classroom listening to a fourteen-year-old read. He had reading difficulties. I put myself out to hear him read every day and give him lots of support and encouragement. At that time there was a shortage of reading material suitable for adolescent children. He was reading a so-called fairy story when I had an unusual experience.

Whilst he was reading, I had an unexpected cognition that suddenly flashed into my mind. I knew what this story was really about and this new meaning was radically different to the familiar version of the story with which everybody is familiar. I began to recognise the story on two very different levels. Whilst the story retained its familiar version, simultaneously, it also transformed itself into a vertical form that was really new to me and tremendously exciting.

For the first time I actually knew what the story was about. Rather than carrying on in the usual literary horizontal form I had known since childhood, it came to me as a series of highly charged symbols, each of which had many levels of meaning. The meanings came instantaneously and I am hoping to convey these to you.

The language of symbolism was the norm until Descartes claimed to have made a radical separation between mind and body. Since then the written word has been analytical and discursive like human reason. Whilst this is eminently suitable for scientific thinking and giving practical and factual accounts, it is also limiting and less supple.

Symbolism is not exclusively intellectual and develops a person's natural synthetic and intuitive abilities. It is also indispensable in receiving intuitions from higher planes of existence. Lacking the language of symbolism, many people have dismissed genuine spiritual experiences as make-believe because they do not sound convincing when constrained by the strongly analytical and taut parameters of discursive language.

This was the start of a new and exciting phase of my life, which considerably added to my understanding and enjoyment of the world. It was as though I had been presented with the secret tools of decoding a long-lost language.

As this came about through a revelation I was worried about it being taken seriously but as time progressed I realised that I had stumbled upon an ancient yogic tradition that is still in use. In Yogananda's version of the Bhagavad Gita, he cites the entire epic of the Mahabharata as an allegory of the battle between good and evil in everybody's journey on the path to enlightenment.

In this great epic the five Pandava brothers represent the divine qualities in man and the Kauravas the materialistic inclinations of the individual ego represented by Bhishma. Whereas the devotee Arjuna always follows the advice of Lord Krishna, the higher self, the Kauravas are always prone to the miscalculations of the blind sense mind Dritarashtra. This same method of symbolism is also used by Swami Satyananda Saraswati in his book about the Chandi Path[1], which is a *puja* allegorising the systematic purification of an individual by the goddess Chandika.

The purpose of writing this book is to bring alive a tradition that has slept peacefully amongst us for so long. Whilst the versions of the stories that have been passed on to us are common knowledge, their real import has been lost because the symbolism they all use has been forgotten. I would like to share this 'lost language' with you.

At first I had no idea that these tales consigned as being only fit for the nursery would be connected with the hidden teachings of the Ancient Mystery Schools that flourished all over the ancient world, particularly Egypt, Greece and Rome. I found that link later, when I realised how well the three phases of initiation into the ancient Mysteries corresponded with the three main tasks of the folk-tale hero. I noticed that some symbols turn up time and time again so I began to examine them and found many more links with the Mystery Religions.

Some of the ecclesiastical authors of the classical period mentioned the use of formulas or symbols in the mystery rites. In some cases they had obtained first-hand accounts from some of the participants but they reported that the symbolism used by the initiates led to great difficulties in interpretation.

I would not like to give the impression that I have completely grasped all aspects of this symbolism. This would be far from the truth because there are certain picture images that still escape me. Often discoveries are made simultaneously, so I am hoping that some readers with an interest in this would like to help me further this work.

The opening lines of this preface may have given the impression that this book is about Transcendental Meditation. Whilst this is not so, it did have some part to play in this study. Just as the technique opened my awareness to the transcendental field of consciousness, at the source of the mind, sufficiently to understand the symbolism in the stories, Maharishi's definition of the seven states of human consciousness provided me with a useful framework with which to interpret the symbols relating to the progressive evolution of consciousness.

I also drew on his knowledge of the so-called paranormal powers of the heroes in the chapter on the *Yoga Sutras*. We have long been used to the tradition in folk tales of people with the ability to fly in the air or to make themselves invisible. This apparently is based upon fact. There is a particular chapter in the *Yoga Sutras*, dealing with the acquisition of these powers on the path to becoming a fully developed human being.

As a matter of interest, there was a particular yogi interviewed during the recent Channel Four television coverage of the Kumbha Mela in India in 2001. He was called Pilot Baba. He was given that name because he used to be a pilot in the Indian Air Force. One day he was flying his jet when he was overtaken by a yogi sitting in the lotus position. He marvelled at the sight. It inspired him to want to become a Sadhu, or holy man.

Earlier in my life when I was grounded in the mechanistic scientific theories of the West, I would have scoffed at this as being impossible. However, following a personal awakening, I took up Transcendental Meditation and the TM-Sidhi programme, part of which is the 'flying sutra'. Whilst nobody I have seen practising this is remotely near the standard of the yogi that inspired Pilot Baba, there are aspects of it that certainly lift the experience out of the mundane. Whilst not yet rising high into the sky or even hovering, there is definitely a surge of energy which makes the execution of this sutra effortless. There is no doubt that it is easy to rise up and move forward and bounce around. This movement is accompanied by a great wave of happiness.

However, returning to the subject of the *Yoga Sutras*, there are at least two stories in this book entirely relating to the so-called supernormal feats.

# Introduction

Throughout recorded history, a handful of distinguished thinkers have stood out like beacons of light from the mountain tops of their amazing achievements, whilst the rest of us flounder about, squabbling over trifles on the plains of life.

Such men as Pythagoras, Socrates, Plato, Christ, Rumi, Copernicus, Giordano Bruno and Isaac Newton are just a few of a long and illustrious list. It always seems odd that during their own lifetime they were often shunned, reviled, persecuted and even killed because their knowledge was so out of kilter with the times and orthodoxies in which they lived.

They plainly thought that their fellow citizens were sadly wasting their lives, rushing about after an illusion when the truth was under their noses all the time. Although these great men lived in different times, they all shared one thing in common. They were all enthusiastic members of the Mystery Religions, originating in ancient Egypt, and continuing through the empires of ancient Greece and Rome, down through trade crafts such as the cathedral builders of the Middle Ages, to the Rosicrucians and Masonic secret societies nearer our own times.

Both to protect themselves and the knowledge which united them all, these early Mystery Schools had to find a way of keeping that knowledge safe. They had to keep it away from the prying eyes of their relatives, friends, neighbours and, of course, people in authority. Hiding it, or going underground, always arouses suspicion. So there was only one answer – make it freely available to everybody without people realising its significance.

They wisely encoded their knowledge in symbolic form in myths, stories and playing cards. It would then be both protected and regarded as harmless fun or a form of entertainment in the hands of storytellers. Just as the symbolic pictures on Tarot cards are only intelligible to the initiated, to anybody else they are simply degraded down to card games, for gambling and divination; to most people the folk tales would be impossible flights of fancy into a world of make believe.

Sir Isaac Newton was a testimony to this. Following an unbroken line from the hermeticists of the Hellenistic and Renaissance periods, he believed in a primordial tradition that was transmitted through fables and stories and myths, which was largely inaccessible to the profane. It is interesting to note that Vedic scriptures say this primordial tradition goes back further than humanity.

Most people view him as the father of modern science. What is not so well known is that he devoted himself to the study of alchemy from 1668 to 1696. He was eager to prove the hermetic axiom of 'as above so too below', and so strove to unite the molecular world with the cosmological order.

Thus, the transmission of knowledge through symbols has worked so well down the ages that most people have copies of this priceless knowledge in their homes. Today, we even read the stories to young children, but we don't recognise the significance of what we are reading. The stories are alluring, memorable and full of magic. Most people remember at least a couple all their lives. They are popularly known today as 'fairy stories', even though there are seldom, if ever, fairies in them.

But what was the nature of this precious knowledge? We have far more disciplines of knowledge, systems and forms of analysis in the twenty-first century than the ancient world ever dreamed of – so what kind of knowledge did they so cherish? They obviously had something that we have either overlooked or don't have.

At this point it would be interesting to hear what Mircea Eliade has to say on the subject of the gains and losses of modern man as opposed to his ancient counterpart. He regards modern man as asleep, unconscious or infantile because he no longer functions as a whole man. Although still nourished in part by a deeper level of consciousness, modern man is not able to attain a proper religious experience or vision of the world because his private mythologies never rise to the ontological status of myths.

Another difference is that modern thought processes tend to be mainly discriminative; thus we mainly isolate a small part of the subject and exclude the rest. Some critics speak deprecatingly of the methods of modern scientific thinking as a method of 'knowing more and more about less and less'.

Ancient teachers of the Mystery Religions did the opposite. They used universal symbols, which communicated the teaching in an integrated and comprehensive manner so as to nourish and reinforce the initiates understanding. Thus, any natural object in the everyday environment, such as a tree, a hill or a mountain was both a means of connecting earth and heaven in their minds and also a ladder of ascent from the ever changing temporal world in which they lived and moved, to the unchanging transcendental sphere of life which was their goal. This was why symbolism was so important in communicating the breadth and depth of the teaching of the ancient Mystery Religions.

Although initiates into the Greater Mysteries were sworn to secrecy, to the point of death, so as not to reveal their knowledge and rituals, some were so moved by the blissful nature of their experience that they committed it to words. Apuleius had a vision of the goddess Isis at his initiation. He wrote, 'I was bound by a debt of gratitude so large that I could never repay it.' Plato was similarly moved by the experience, and thereafter would 'perform the holy rites and consort with pure men in a state of bliss'. They obviously had discovered the art of being supremely happy. What we call happiness is often an evanescent, bitter-sweet thing. We have lots of things that make us happy whilst we are engaged in them but they are all part of the flux of change and soon pass.

The source of happiness of such initiates such as Apuleius and Plato lay inside them. It was part of their being. They had attained a state of inner happiness and well being, by undergoing a long process which transmuted their minds and nervous systems so they could support higher and more blissful states of consciousness. By so doing they also answered the sixty-four thousand dollar question of why we are here on this lovely earth.

Where did this priceless knowledge come from and when? According to modern experts on the Mystery Religions, it came originally from ancient Egypt and was very much part of the fabric of life in the ancient cultures of Greece and Rome. Much of it is attributed to Thoth in the shape of the Hermetica and most experts think it dates back about five thousand years. Some researchers say it is much older. James Churchward was convinced that he had deciphered stone tablets proving that Thoth founded the first Mystery School about eighteen thousand years ago.

The Hermetica is a series of instructions written in hieroglyphics by Thoth after receiving a complete revelation from God on how to make a gross human being divine. It was believed to be the origin of the ancient science of alchemy, which is often called Hermeticism. It is not surprising to find many references to alchemy in the stories we will later be examining. Many modern experts only date the appearance of alchemy to the Middle Ages. However, the clue about its Western origins comes from the word *Khem*, the ancient name for Egypt. Alchemy has also been in existence in India for many thousands of years, but there it is subsumed under the general heading of Ayur Veda and the Tantra

Many legendary ancient Greeks, such as Pythagoras, went to Egypt for initiation and spent many years there. They came back so profoundly moved that, on returning to their homeland, they set up their own Mystery Schools. Herodotus said the Egyptians 'are meticulous in everything which concerns their religion', but it was obviously not possible for the Greeks to be quite so assiduous.

Thoth, known as Hermes by the Greeks, predicted that Greek was an unsuitable vehicle for such wonderful knowledge, and the translation into Greek 'will distort much of the meaning of the secrets and all possible measures should be taken to prevent these holy secrets from being corrupted'[2]. As the centuries passed he was obviously proved right because many Greek sages found the need to import some of the profound spiritual techniques from India to revivify their own Mystery Schools.

It was fortunate for me that they did. I was sufficiently proficient in the Vedic knowledge, brought to the West by Maharishi Mahesh Yogi, to realise that the transformations of the hero or heroine in many fairy tales were really about different states of consciousness. Maharishi has always said that it is very important to satisfy both the heart and the head. The experiences one can have whilst practising spiritual techniques, such as the TM technique and TM-Sidhi programme, certainly satisfy the heart but if the head doesn't understand what is happening, anxieties and doubts will certainly arise. An explanation of higher states of consciousness follows in Chapter 3.

Most people consider that the superhuman feats of characters in fairy tales are make-believe. Until recently we have scoffed at the possibility of flying through the air, becoming invisible, understanding the speech of birds and animals, and stupendous feats of strength and the like. However, after Maharishi's interpretation of chapter three of the *Yoga Sutras* by Patanjali, and the practice of some of the *Sidhi* techniques he has given out, these feats now seem feasible rather than impossible. We will go further into the rationale of the *Yoga Sutras* in Chapter 4.

There is no way of knowing how old the stories are, but it is possible to distinguish an underlying template. They were constructed around the same essential elements so they could be altered to accommodate changes in time and place. For example, the story of *Cinderella* always has the two step-sisters; a wish-fulfilling aspect in the form of a tree or an animal; the three transformations or appearances at court, a ball or festival; and the fitting of the shoes. Thus, the same story can be told to suit the geographical and social conditions of very different places on the earth without damaging the fundamental message encoded in the plot.

It is also impossible to date them because they were part of an oral tradition. Some of the motifs are not only ancient, they are also very well travelled. The motif of the golden ball falling into a well is at least five thousand years old. We know this because that is the widely accepted age of the Mahabharata. The same motif appears in European versions of *The Frog*

*Prince*, such as Iron Hans, featured in this book. It appears in the ancient Indian epic when the five Pandavas first meet their weapons guru Dronacharya.

The earliest written version of *Cinderella* can be traced to the ninth century AD in China. The story of *Cupid and Psyche* was written in the characteristic fairy story mode by Apuleius in the second century AD, and was the prototype of *Beauty and the Beast*, but experts believe he was retelling a much older Greek folk tale.

It is impossible to say how far oral traditions go back, except to say they were highly esteemed. The ancient masters did not have the same respect for reading and writing as we do. Whilst we regard literacy as the sign of a highly developed civilisation, they regarded its introduction with some disgust. They took it as proof that an age of ignorance had dawned upon the earth and an inferior type of human being was incarnating. To them, the need to teach reading and writing was a sign that a race of people with diminished intellects and poor memories was incarnating.

Whether these tales originated from remote periods of ancient history or from the classical civilisations of the Near and Far East, there is no doubt in my mind that the originators of the folk tales wanted to pass on the importance of transcendence in relation to spiritual growth and higher states of consciousness, leading to the complete enlightenment of an individual.

Plato once said that there are four levels of knowledge that can be extracted from any work. I have covered the most spiritual aspect of the stories called *mythos*. This is not the only interpretation, however. The next level down was called *dianoia*, and is concerned with teaching people how to think and to act effectively. A famous Indian book called the Panchatantra dealt with this level of storytelling. It was said to be written by a great teacher called Vishnu Sharma, after he had succeeded in educating the three ignoramus sons of a famous king in six months. Previously, the three sons had shown themselves to be completely averse to education and had always set their faces against all aspects of learning. The key to Vishnu Sharma's success lay in the fact that the knowledge came incidentally in the course of discussing the fine points brought out by his stories.

The next level down is that of *pistis*. Essentially, pistis means faith. At this level thoughts or opinions are shaped in us by imitation. They either feel right and are not investigated intellectually or we just absorb them from the ethos and values of the society in which we live. This is the level of social conditioning covered by Jack Zipes. He sees folk tales in the past, primarily as a medium of social control to condition people to accept their position in life and not to seek to rise above it.

Finally, the most gross level is *eikasia*, which represents a total absorption of the images and actions of the outer world. We could always assign this to be the pure entertainment level of the story.

Whilst this may be generally true, it does not paint the complete picture. It can be seen that the stories have a life of their own, irrespective of the aims and motivations of the storyteller. The level at which the listener both enjoys and evaluates the story depends upon his own level of spiritual evolution and intelligence.

I have limited my study to some of the familiar tales collected by the Brothers Grimm. I have chosen their collection because they were collected from authentic storytellers, who would be part of a long oral tradition and, as such, kept the stories they told much nearer to the original. These storytellers would have carried on their family trade long after the original meanings of the stories had been lost. Although each storyteller would treat a tale in a different way, he would retain the original version in his memory as a standard he could deviate from or embroider according to the character of a particular audience.

The onset of the industrial revolution in Europe brought about vast changes in the way of life of the people. This seems to have coincided with the time when the popularity of the storyteller was diminishing. As is often the case, the demise of the storyteller brought about a renewed interest in the tales as a literary vehicle.

Charles Perrault and his contemporary Madame d'Aulnoy both gained a high level of prestige in retelling some of the best-loved tales in an imaginative literary style, aimed at impressing the VIPs of their time. At that time, the term 'fairy tale' was unknown. In fact, the term came about inadvertently. Madame d'Aulnoy published her *Contes des fées* in 1698. It was translated into English the following year as *Tales of the Fairies*. By the middle of the eighteenth century 'fairy story' had become an established term.

Although most people have heard of the Brothers Grimm, their collection does not, probably, contain the versions with which you are familiar. The tales we have been brought up with are the work of Charles Perrault. He lived from 1628 to 1703. Although he rewrote many of the most modern folk tales with great imagination and flair, he unfortunately altered them beyond recognition from the original. In the case of *Cinderella*, he invented the Fairy Godmother, the changing of a pumpkin into a coach, the white mice into horses and the two frogs into livery men.

When you read the version of *Cinderella* in this book you will be surprised to see how far he departed from the original. Original may not be the best term to use. Researchers such as Anna Rooth found over seven hundred variations of the story of *Cinderella*, with many versions coming from Indo-China, the Near East and Eastern Europe.

In this book I have retold the Grimms' version of the tales in a slightly condensed form.

I respect the view of the Grimm brothers, who thought these tales were not allegorical. This is a natural conclusion to draw from the evidence they had to hand at that time; however, I am sure they would have changed their minds if they had had the benefit of Maharishi's knowledge of the seven states of consciousness and the *Yoga Sutras* at their disposal.

Without this knowledge the question of an allegorical framework would be a thorny one because the situations and characters are not a straight swap. Taking *Cinderella* as an example, all the characters in the story are aspects of the same person. The father symbolises the mind and intellect generally; Cinderella represents the illumined *buddhi* or that part of the intellect awake to spiritual growth; and the two ugly sisters are the surface aspects of the mind and senses respectively.

Aurobindo says that the Eleusinian and Orphic mysteries follow the same tradition of the Rig Veda. That is, they used the outward trappings of everyday life to tell one aspect of the story and employed the same terms as symbols of a deeply hidden psychological quest. The two aspects hang together as one garment and cannot be easily separated from each other.

Despite the excellent work of other commentators on 'fairy tales' by encyclopedic writers, such as Joseph Campbell, the full complexity of their meaning has yet to be unfolded. However, Joseph Campbell was well on the way to discovering the complete truth. He said that

> The fall was brought about by the machinations of the separate human ego, which tirelessly promotes the interests of the I and mine above the living creative process of which we are individual expressions. Thus we become estranged from the process, and we anxiously try to direct the course of the river of life rather than yielding to its innate wisdom and power.[3]

Great stuff and very perceptive. If he had stumbled upon Maharishi's seven states of consciousness, I am sure he would have written a book similar to mine. The lack of Maharishi's teaching caused him to draw heavily upon the psychoanalytic school of thought for his information. Whilst this is interesting in itself, the roots of this school of thought are deeply embedded in abnormal states of mind based upon the complex world of obsessive and neurotic behaviour. It does not have a clear conceptual framework of the growth of the evolution of consciousness. This is the purpose of this book. I am sure that I have fresh evidence proving that many of the mythic tales are really allegories of the stages of achieving enlightenment.

Many are allegorical stories of the spiritual traveller, who continues to perfect his own nervous system until it is able to fully reflect the pure light of Consciousness at the source of his being. There the traveller through time stops travelling because he has found enlightenment, happiness and peace. He has found his true home. In the case of feminine heroines, such as Cinderella, the allegorical marriage with the king or prince only occurs after the complete spiritual evolution of the individual has taken place. This is called Unity Consciousness. Similarly, in the case of male heroes, the marriage of the hero and the princess takes place when the individual is fully evolved.

The relationship between the devotee and his higher self is that of the bride and the bridegroom. During the courtship, the vibration of the lower self is raised gradually by degrees until it reaches that of the higher self and becomes united into a single enlightened being, never to be separated again.

Maharishi Mahesh Yogi, the founder of the Transcendental Meditation and TM-Sidhi techniques, has revised a wealth of material from a long-established oral tradition dating back many thousands of years. My main sources are Maharishi's seven states of human consciousness and his rediscovery of the meaning of the *Yoga Sutras*, particularly chapter three – the supernormal or perfection Sidhis.

The early chapters of the book are principally about the Mystery Religions because much of the literature of their beliefs and methods of self-development bear a striking resemblance to present-day Indian techniques of achieving the spiritual goal of life, particularly the aphorisms of the *Yoga Sutras*. The existence of the Mystery Schools dates back, at least, to the earliest days of the ancient Egyptian civilisation. Perhaps it goes back even further – nobody knows. They remained entirely secret for many thousands of years.

So many of the great names of ancient Greece and Rome, whose ideas laid the basis of our modern civilisation, were initiated into the Greater Mysteries. They were under an oath of secrecy, consequently we cannot be completely sure of the methods and the teachings they employed but there are many clues to enable us to put together a road map outlining their aims and objectives.

Some further chapters on the Mystery Religions, their states of spiritual development and the structure of their encoded stories follow the chapters on the Seven States of Human Consciousness and the *Yoga Sutras*. These early chapters form the basis upon which this current interpretation of a selection of Grimms' fairy tales begins.

[1] Saraswati, 2001, 6
[2] Scott, 1997, 106
[3] Campbell, 1991

# Part I

# Chapter 1
# The Gospel According to Hermes

The origins of all the Mystery Religions in the West can be traced back to Thoth. He is believed to be the ancient and original author of the Hermetica, which was written in hieroglyphics. The ancient Egyptians attributed their forty-two books of the sciences to him. These included astrology, astronomy, geometry, arithmetic, medicine, grammar, logic, music and magic.

Thoth was depicted as the ibis-headed god in the ancient Egyptian pantheon. The ibis is a bird with a long beak, which enables it to catch its prey in deep water. With water being symbolic of consciousness, Thoth was able to make contact with the source of the mind – namely God. The basis of the Hermetica was his enlightenment as a result of a revelation by God. He was chosen to pass on this knowledge to all who would benefit from it.

According to James Churchward, Thoth founded the Mystery Religion of ancient Egypt sixteen thousand years ago[1]. Ancient stone tablets say that Thoth was an Atlantean priest, who fell in love with the daughter of King Kronos of Atlantis. This match was not approved and Thoth was actively pursued for several years before he finally landed at Sais and founded the Nile colony.

These dates are a little hard to swallow in the light of the prevailing view of time and the span of human civilisation. However, Churchward substantiated his claim by referring to a stone tablet found by Heinrich Schliemann at Maycarne in Crete. The tablet says that 'the Egyptians are descended from Misor, the Son of Thoth. Thoth was the emigrated son of a priest of Atlantis. He built the temple at Sais and taught the wisdom of his native land.'

The starting point of Hermes/Thoth was his own transformation through a revelation by God. As a result of this he was instructed by God to be a spiritual guide in his own lifetime, and to carve in stone the mysteries of life and death in a secret sanctuary. This would keep it safe for the time when a future race of people would seek it out. God's main message was for the individual to seek his spiritual salvation. This was one main aim of the

1

Mystery Religion. The other was to keep the teaching pure by keeping it hidden from people who would abuse it, or were not ready for it.

With startling accuracy, Hermes, prophesied a time such as our own, when the wisdom of ancient Egypt would be shunned. He foresaw that the wonder of God's marvellous creation would give way to mechanistic theories; knowledge of the immortality of the soul would be scoffed at; and, finally, nothing would be left of the true wisdom of Egypt but a few piles of old stones.

It is as though he understood the cyclic nature of time, as brought to light from the Puranas by Sri Yukteswari. This posits a twenty-four thousand-year cycle by the sun, round its dual star. During the course of this revolution around its dual, the sun has another motion by which it revolves around a very spiritual part of the universe called Vishnuabhi. He concludes that the proximity to this very spiritual part of the universe determines the general mode of behaviour of the people on the planet. When the sun is close to Vishnuabhi, people are good and very spiritually inclined.

According to Yukteswari, the last time the sun was nearest to Vishnuabhi was in 11501 BC. This would have been a time of great spirituality upon the earth – a so-called golden age – but as the sun continued on its course it moved further and further away from this centre of great spiritual magnetism. By 499 AD the sun was a hundred and eighty degrees away from this centre and marks the birth of the so-called Dark Ages. This was apparently the lowest ebb in spiritual life generally but there will always be exceptions in every age. Whilst we are now well past that low, there are still many thousands of years before the sun returns to the most spiritual part of the universe.

New knowledge by Robert Cox reveals a slightly different time span but a similar message[2]. He posits a thirteen thousand-year cycle from the beginning of one golden age to another. Most importantly, he is convinced by knowledge he gained using advanced spiritual techniques that the onset of the next golden age is imminent – within the next decade or two.

No record has been found of the original work of Thoth/Hermes, written in hieroglyphs at the beginning of the last golden age. He maintained that it will remain hidden until such a time in the future when worthy seekers of wisdom will rediscover his original hieroglyphs hidden in an underground chamber. According to the sleeping prophet, Edgar Cayce, the great pyramid was not a mausoleum but a hall of initiates called the 'Great White Brotherhood', built by an influx of people from the advanced civilisation of Atlantis. He also predicted that a smaller pyramid, situated somewhere between the Great Pyramid and the Sphinx, houses a hall of records of the sunken continent and should have been discovered by the end of the twentieth century.

The main versions of the Hermetica known today came from Alexandria and were written in Greek. The Greeks identified Thoth as identical to their Hermes.

First and foremost, Hermes saw creation as a trinity of God, Cosmos and Man. The soul is always one with God. It is also a part of God. In fact, there is only One soul. God first created the Cosmic Mind, which in turn gave rise to the physical cosmos. Man is an image of the physical cosmos. His mind is lit by the Mind of God.

The gods, or powers, saw this as a danger to the smooth administration of the cosmos. The misuse of such a potent tool as the unenlightened mind could give rise to a great many dangers.

In order to curb the destructive mind of man in its unfettered form, God placed man under the auspices of the goddess Destiny. She was characteristically dressed in the dark robes of the night sky, with the various constellations of stars as her sequins. Destiny rules over the unchanging fixed constellations of the zodiac. Her main administrators of this are the sun, moon and the five visible planets of our solar system. They were seen as the administrators of our destiny. Consequently, each individual was thought to be governed by the effects of the gods on the twelve houses of the fixed stars at the precise moment of an individual's birth. To be more exact, the individual soul takes on the qualities of the gods presiding over their time of birth.

The gods correspond with the seven days of the week. The sun brings joy; the moon, sleep; Mars, struggle; Mercury gives wisdom; Jupiter, peace; Venus, love; and Saturn defines the limits of the wheel of necessity and justice. Thus, the nature we display in everyday life is conditioned by how strong or weak the qualities of the gods appear at the moment of our birth.

If our disposition is predominantly joyful it is because the sun was very prominent in our birth sign. If, on the other hand, we are inclined to be gloomy and foreboding, this was thought to be the influence of Saturn at the time of our birth. It is easy to see the influence of astrology in the ancient world and also the considerable interest it holds for us in the present time.

The soul is always endowed with superlative intelligence. However, before it incarnates it is already wrapped in a spiritual sheath. The deeper or more dense the gross matter it descends into, the more limited the horizons of its intelligence become.

Hermes says that the individual before birth is horrified at the thought of being imprisoned in matter. As soon as a soul incarnates it takes on the qualities of the gods most influencing its time of birth. All knowledge of its true nature is forgotten. Some recent research has shown that some children below school age remember some aspects of their most recent life, but only until they start school. After that they forget it altogether.

However, God only wanted to limit the destructive power of the mind prior to enlightenment, he did not want to limit mankind altogether. He wanted to make it not only possible but a priority to escape the restrictions placed upon the human individual. This was the essence of the secret teaching that he revealed to Thoth, whom the Greeks called Hermes. This was the secret teaching at the heart of all the Mystery Religions.

The body being born of the cosmos is always changing. We start off as a baby and as the years pass our body changes to that of a child, a youth, a young adult, middle age and finally old age. The dweller in the body doesn't change but the size, shape and look of the person does. Hermes taught that death is merely the discarding of a worn-out body, followed by a period of rest before taking on a new body.

So even death is part of the cycle of ceaseless change. Thus, Hermes exhorts us to seek out the permanent reality underlying the field of change. By so doing we will escape from the wheel of necessity and also all the sorrows of manifestation. Hermes proclaimed that 'every person has the power to know God. The greatest error he can make is not to take advantage of this great gift.' Hermes continues: 'when a man is truly reborn, is not when he has a new body but when he is at one with God'. To achieve this he has to experience the Mind of God. In order for this to happen he must allow God to come to him in silence and tranquillity and transform him.

Thus, Hermes became enlightened by adopting a passive attitude to the will of God. A fitting summary to the teaching of Hermes is: 'An enlightened man does not need to have opinions about God – he is God.'[3]

---

[1] Churchward, 1965, 307. See Also Churchward, 1959, 155, and Cox, 255-266
[2] Cox, 1997, 13-19 & 24-26. New knowledge by Cox posits a 13,000 year cycle.
[3] Scott 1997

# Chapter 2
# Mystery Schools

Reading the Hermetica is both an inspiring and uplifting experience and it certainly increases the desire in an individual to tread the spiritual path through life. However, the most important ingredients are missing – namely the techniques or practices which allow the spiritual regeneration to take place. It is rather like reading one of the six main systems of Indian philosophy today – the entire school of thought is laid out in an orderly, logical and coherent manner. In fact, everything is there except the means of realising that wonderful knowledge. Just as thinking or reading about food will never satisfy your hunger, neither will reading the Hermetica bring about a spiritual transformation.

The Hermetica was the knowledge aspect of the teaching. It was the force that lit the torch of the mind of an ancient aspirant, and motivated him to find an enlightened teacher or master. The vital experiential practice or technique was obviously passed on by a master at the initiation, in the same way as it is today by modern gurus. The techniques which brought about the inner transformation of the individual were obviously given out individually by the teacher and the steps along the way to enlightenment, personally monitored by him. Thus, the mystery and purpose of life lay in the hands of the teacher – hence the name Mystery Religion. Each master had his own Mystery School.

Mystery Schools were a feature of the ancient world and were no doubt the bedrock of the remarkable ancient cultures of Egypt, Greece and Rome. All the great dignitaries of those periods, including Socrates, Plato and Pythagoras, were initiates. Indeed, the Mystery Schools were the major inspiration of our modern Western culture because they laid the foundations of mathematics, astronomy, philosophy, theatre, the arts, music and the Olympic Games. This may seem a little strange to us today because these are now all secular activities, but they all had their birth in ancient mysticism.

It is thought that the teachings at the heart of the Mystery Schools combined essential elements consistent with the widespread religious beliefs of the indigenous culture fertilised by the spiritual techniques of India. Many of the great Greek philosophers are known to have visited India and to have come back deeply impressed with their profound spiritual practices.

There were essentially two kinds of sacred mysteries – the Lesser and the Greater Mysteries. The Lesser Mysteries were available to everybody. These included access to all of the temples, all religious festivals, plays and worship of the gods. The Greater Mysteries were secret and only open to an elite group of people who had experienced an inner calling from the Great Goddess herself. In the case of the ancient Egyptian mysteries this would be Isis; in ancient Greece, Demeter; and ancient Rome, Juno.

Like the spiritual techniques brought to the West by Maharishi Mahesh Yogi at the present time, the Mystery Schools were able to elevate the consciousness of the individual by direct experience of that transcendental field underlying our limited sense of personality. In fact the Mystery Schools, like the *Yoga Sutras*, revealed that the everyday sense of 'I', who we erroneously mistake ourselves, is the true source of all our suffering in the world. They considered that the limited sense of personality was no more than a mask, which hides our true identity. They went even further than this – they taught that the higher self is locked up or imprisoned in the physical human body like an oyster within a shell.

The initiates learned that their life on earth was meant to be a journey of spiritual awakening, which took many twists and turns of transformation before finally realising their oneness with God.

It is obvious that a large part of the spiritual illumination and purification of the ancient initiates of the Greater Mysteries was through the practice of meditation. At the outset of their inward journey everybody who had received the calling of the goddess had to become a *mystae* – which meant seeing with closed eyes. In other words they had to travel in their minds to the transcendent. Contact with the transcendent would both purify and awaken them to their true selves.

They were also purified further by following a strict vegetarian diet, the recitation of sacred texts and by watching the dramatic unfolding of the great myths. Every sacred site in ancient Greece had its own theatre. Sophocles likened the cathartic purging of his emotions whilst watching these plays as almost as powerful as his own initiation into the Greater Mysteries. The most famous of these was the sanctuary of Eleusis just outside Athens.

There were two celebrations of the Eleusinian Mysteries each year. The first was in February. This was for the new initiates to the Lesser Mysteries, known as the *Muesis*. This took place at a temple just outside Athens. In February the initiation of the neophytes – called the 'newly sown' – took place and in September the Greater Mysteries were held in Eleusis itself. This title was well chosen because both the Lesser and the Greater Mysteries were based on the *Hymn to Demeter*, the grain goddess. An outline of the myth is as follows.

Kore, or Persephone, was out with her mother. She was picking flowers with some of her immortal friends. Her attention was on the beauty of the flowers. She wandered away and became separated from Demeter and her friends. Suddenly she saw a beautiful narcissus. She was captivated by its beauty and stooped to pick it. At that point the earth split open and out rode Hades, the king of the Underworld, on his chariot pulled by immortal horses.

He snatched up Persephone into his chariot and drove swiftly back to the gloomy depths of the Underworld, oblivious to her screams and entreaties to her mother to save her. In truth, none of the other gods had seen or heard the incident because it had been planned by Zeus. Hades was his own brother. The chief of the gods had arranged that the beautiful Persephone would be the queen of the gloomy Underworld.

Demeter went looking for her daughter. She learned from Helios, the Sun, about the connivance between the two gods. In disgust she left Olympus and dwelt in the farms and cities of mankind in disguise. Many saw her but none recognised her. One day, sad at heart at the loss of her beautiful daughter, she sat under the shade of an olive tree near the Maiden Well, where the young maid-servants of the royal household came to draw water. Demeter refused all food and drink until Iambe, an old serving woman employed in the household of the King of Eleusis, cheered her up with some lewd jokes.

Soon she was welcomed by Metaneira, the Queen of Eleusis, who offered her a glass of red wine. Demeter declined. Instead she asked for *kykeon*, a drink made from barley groats and water, mixed with pennyroyal. She told Metaneira that she was seeking domestic work. The Queen offered her the post of child nurse of her youngest baby son, Demophon. She accepted the post. She loved the little baby and set out to make him immortal. She did not feed him human food. Instead, she both fed and anointed him with ambrosia. He flourished under her care and had the air of one of the gods about him. At night she would lay him in the flames to purge him of his mortality.

The royal parents were astonished by both his god-like

7

appearance and the mien he showed for one so young. They became a little curious about how the new child nurse achieved these marvellous results. One night Metaneira hid and kept watch. She saw her son being placed amongst the flames by the child nurse. She screamed out and struck her thighs mindlessly. Demeter was astonished. She withdrew the child from the flames and threw him at Metaneira's feet.

Demeter was furious: 'Humans are short-sighted, ignorant of the share of good and evil which is coming to them. You, by your foolishness you have hurt him beyond curing... I would have made him deathless and ageless all of his days and given him imperishable honour. But now it is not possible to ward off death and destruction.

In due season, as the years pass, the children of Eleusis will conduct in his honour war games... I am Demeter, the greatest boon and joy for immortals and mortals. So now let the whole people build me a great temple and an altar beneath it... I will establish rites so that henceforth you may celebrate them purely and propitiate my mind.'

With that she revealed her radiantly beautiful form. Metaneira was speechless. Her knees gave way and she remained on the floor a long time. She did not even remember her own child. She was so shocked that she was oblivious even to the piteous crying of her dear son. Her sisters heard him and leaped from their beds to console the child and wash and comfort him.

All night long the women quaked with fear, propitiating the goddess. In the morning they relayed all that had happened to King Keleos. He immediately summoned his people to build an elaborate temple and an altar on the ridge as Demeter had instructed.

Angry at the stupidity of the human race, she caused a great famine by withholding the power of the grain to grow. Things became desperate on the earth. Not only was the race of people on the earth slowly starving to death but they had nothing with which to honour the gods of Olympus.

Zeus had to do something fast. He sent out one immortal after another to get her to change her mind. However, Demeter was adamant that she would never step foot on Olympus or allow any fruit to grow upon the earth until she saw the eyes of her beautiful daughter again.

At last Zeus sent Hermes down to Hades to try to persuade his brother to lead the pure Persephone out of the darkness into the light to rejoin the deities. He found Hades inside his domain, seated on a couch next to his unwilling wife. Hades listened to what Hermes had to say. He smiled. He did not want to upset his brother. His wry smile meant that he had a crafty trick up his sleeve and he seemed quite unperturbed about the departure of his wife.

Hades quickly gave his assent. Persephone was delighted. She leaped up from her couch in joy and eagerly climbed into the chariot of Hermes. Hades insisted that she should accept a sweet pomegranate for the journey, which he had made potent with a secret rite so that she would not remain with Demeter forever.

Persephone innocently ate the pomegranate on the way. Mother and daughter were delighted to see each other. Persephone told her mother all that had happened; both about her abduction and the pomegranate that Hades had forced upon her.

Hecate came near them and showered a great deal of love on Demeter's lovely daughter. In fact, such a bond was struck that she has been her lady in waiting and attendant ever since.

Zeus was delighted that everything was back to normal. He sent Rhea down with a message. Demeter was welcomed back enthusiastically to the celestial company of the gods on Mount Olympus. The King of Gods also decreed that Persephone would spend one third of the year down in the misty darkness of the Underworld with Hades and the other two thirds with her mother and the other immortals.

In return Demeter revoked her wrath and the earth became fertile and abundant once more and the race of men prospered. In addition she imparted the secret rites to Triptolemos, Polyxeinos and Diocles.

These rites became known as the Mysteries of Eleusis. It is obvious that the story enacted the yearly mystery of the grain cycle. As such it was highly suited to the Lesser Mysteries, which everybody took part in. Ostensibly it was the story of the seasons as perceived by the race of mankind upon the earth. Like Persephone, the grain grows vigorously in its youth; it becomes fair and full, and is cut down and harvested and stored in silos under the earth for the winter. In the spring she returns in all her beauty.

The Greater Mysteries were all of this and more. The myth seems to have two interwoven plots. On one hand there is the story of the abduction and reunion of Demeter and Persephone. On the other there was the process of making the child Demophon immortal by putting him in the flames, which was interrupted by Metaneira. This must have been a very important part of the alchemical process because, after her reunion with Persephone, Demeter went out of her way to bestow the science of agriculture and the secret rites of the Mysteries to Triptolemos, Polyxeinos and Diocles for them to transmit to selected people who would be suitable candidates for the school of their particular Mystery Religion.

The first thing to clear up is the identity of Hades. He is not some gloomy god of the dead in some afterlife location. He is none other than the marauding human ego rampaging about all over the earth. There was a convention in ancient religious literature to portray him as riding in a chariot pulled by five horses, which represented the five senses bolting in all directions in the opposite direction to God. Meditation and deity worship were considered as the way to use the mind to rein in the senses and put them under the control of the divine. Allowing them to bolt and career off in an outward direction would always lead to disaster.

Once Persephone had allowed her mind to be captivated by the beauty of the narcissus – a well-known symbol of self-love – her ego would be in full control of her life.

First of all why did Demeter go out of her way to bestow the science of agriculture? The answer to this is because agriculture has a civilising effect on the masses and the symbolism derived from it would play a vital part in both the Lesser and the Greater Mystery Religions. It meant that whilst the temples they used and the festivals they celebrated would be open to all people, the symbols they employed would have vastly different meanings.

The symbolic nature of the pomegranate is a good case in point. It is a fruit full of seeds and symbolises the periodic return of fertility in springtime and its consequent abundant harvest. This would be the interpretation that would satisfy the masses for it is self-evident – they would see this happening year after year.

However, in the case of the hidden Greater Mysteries, the same symbol had a very different connotation. It still signified a periodic return but of a very different kind – being reborn in another human body – because the mass of seeds inside a pomegranate signified all the unfulfilled desires in a human being, thus guaranteeing his or her eventual return. No wonder that the wily Hades was so compliant in letting his wife – the individual soul – go. As long as she had gained a taste for the fruits of the manifold desires on earth he knew that her parting from him was only temporary.

The other big question is why would a great Mother Goddess lay the baby she was caring for in the flames? This is answered by a quote from the Bhagavad Gita which says: immortality is gained by roasting all the seeds of desire in the fire of *tapas* or meditation, which makes them unable to sprout.

Thus there are two methods: one is to weed them out through meditation; the other is to drink a suitable draft of liquid which had been alchemically transformed and purified to such a degree that it completely purifies a human nervous system and makes it divine.

The other key word to this is myth is the name of the baby – 'Demophon'. In modern times that would be translated as 'the voice of the people', comprised of the meanings of *demo* – of the people, *phon* – voice or speech. To us that would sound both familiar and acceptable, since we live in a democracy ourselves. However, in the time when the Greater Mysteries were being practiced such a term would have been completely unacceptable. *Webster's Dictionary* tells us that *demos* would be referred to as the 'rabble' or 'common people', thus democracy would not have been thought a fit form of government. They would have called 'democracy' the rule of demons. This would certainly be out of step with the hierarchy of the Greater Mysteries and also of the rule of law in ancient societies so we have to look for a hidden cipher.

In view of the long passage of time the myth has been in existence, the number of times it has been told and retold, both orally and in print, makes it not at all surprising that one word became substituted for another.

If instead of 'demon' we substitute 'daimon' we get a totally different state of affairs. *Webster's Dictionary* defines this as literally the distributor or dispenser of destiny, which is exactly the role of the 'inner genius' of every human being as described in the Hermetica. The same role in Indian philosophy is called the *atman*. From this we can deduce that the true meaning of Demophon is the inner voice within everybody. In the myth Demeter would be burning away the impurities which prevent mankind from heeding the word of his higher self.

Rolled up in the separation and reunion of the two immortals is the cyclic nature of things. A soul incarnates, it becomes clad in gross physical matter and then it returns to live with the immortals again, only to be repeated time after time. The ancient mystics called this the Wheel of Grief, which is akin to the Wheel of Karma of the Hindus and the Wheel of Suffering of the Buddhists. This is the cycle of cause and effect whereby the good and bad actions of our past lives are dispensed to us whilst on earth.

Part of the Mystery Religion was death itself. Just as a period of sleep or rest gives way to a new day, so death was seen as a doorway to a new start. The initiate also had to undergo a 'ritual death', which proved conclusively that the identification of himself with his body was really a fiction. From this initiation he learned that in spirit he was divine and, in fact, he was the very image of God. These ritual deaths used to take place at midnight.

On the command of the priest the individual was completely buried except for his head and was taken on a shamanistic inner journey to awaken him to the sublime joys in store for him. It seems that the initiate had what we would call today a near death experience. Apparently, the first part of the rite was horrific. According to Pseudo-Dionysis, who was both a Christian monk as well as a pagan initiate, the rite was delivered in allegories in order to strike terror and awe into a person.

The idea was that the initiate would experience the death of his own body and his rebirth into the light. Following this, the initiate saw the light of God shining like the sun at midnight, which gave way at intervals to visions of gods and goddesses, who were guiding him to his greater spiritual destiny. This greater spiritual destiny must have been the release of the individual soul from the Wheel of Grief and suffering by his becoming immortal through enlightenment.

In the myth the self-love of Narcissus is symbolic of the ego. In Homer's *Hymn to Demeter* it is rather like the Tree of Good and Evil in the Bible. The ego and intellect of a person remain pure as long as they remain within the vicinity of the Absolute, but as soon as they become identified with an object of desire in the relative universe, the ego becomes extroverted and sees itself as separate from its source. Thus, it also becomes bound to the world of illusion and the Wheel of Grief.

## The Myth of Osiris

It would be impossible to leave the question of the basic myths underlying the Mystery Schools without first having a brief look at the myth of Osiris, especially as it was the first. Unfortunately, it has become very confused due to the many translations it has undergone during its long history. The problem is that the spheres of the gods and mortals, bearing the same name, have become inextricably mixed and it is difficult to tell one from the other. Robert Cox highlighted the problem very succinctly when he said 'the golden knowledge the ancient Egyptians once possessed became buried under a thick rubble of myth and legend'[1], not to speak of the many translations it must have undergone.

Here is a shortened, potted version of the main strands of the myth. Since the myth is so confused, I have found it necessary to add a commentary after each section as an extract.

> When the Sun heard of Rhea's intercourse with Kronos, he invoked a curse upon her. He decreed that she would not be able to give birth to a child in any month of the year, but Hermes, being

in love with the goddess, consorted with her. Some time later, playing at draughts with the Moon, he won sufficient time from her to make up five whole days. From that time on the Egyptians called them the birthdays of the gods. The five gods born on those days were Osiris, the Elder, Horus, Set, Isis and Nepthys.

According to James Churchward, the Rhea in question was the daughter of King Kronus of Atlantis and not the goddess of the same name who gave birth to Hestia, Demeter, Hera, Hades and Poseidon. Churchward maintains that Thoth eloped with the daughter of King Kronos of Atlantis and was pursued for several years before he landed at Sais in Egypt and built a settlement there. It is significant that later generations of Egyptians referred to the original seers as the 'builder gods' who originally came from an island. After surviving a great flood they settled in Egypt and created a new world order there.

The days that Thoth won were obviously a discrepancy between the five-season solar year and the lunar calendar. Robert Graves tells us that the ancient Egyptians had five seasons of seventy-two days. In addition to the 360 days they added an extra five festival days on which they worshipped each of the five gods.

> When Osiris was born a voice proclaimed, 'The Lord of All advances to the light,' and a great light he proved to be. One of the first acts of his reign was to teach the Egyptians how to live in a civilised society in accordance with the laws of God. Prior to this they were always at war with each other and practiced cannibalism. Thus, through the efforts of Osiris and Isis, they were educated out of their destitute and brutish way of living and were taught the art of agriculture and how to honour the gods.
>
> Once Egypt had become a land of harmony, Osiris left the ever vigilant Isis in charge of the country and set about civilising the whole of the earth. He travelled far and wide teaching the people of the earth agriculture, giving them laws and teaching them how to honour the gods. In addition the people were won over by his great charm, the potency of his discourses and the wide variety of music he introduced to their lives.

It is very significant that this part opened with a voice proclaiming that, 'The Lord of All advances to the light,' because it signified the onset of a golden age, which comes as a matter of cyclic return every twelve or thirteen thousand years. This tells us that two things are involved here. One is a natural cycle, which coincides with an upsurge in pure consciousness or waves of pure spirituality from the centre of the Milky Way galaxy, by way of the Pleiades; the other is the birth of a highly evolved mortal who later grew up in Egypt and then went on to civilise the whole world. It is more than likely that both the cosmic process and the person were named Osiris, after a very saintly high priest of Atlantis, who was a friend of Thoth before he eloped with the king's daughter.

One of the main problems with the Osiris myth is that the dual strands, which I have mentioned, became twisted into one confused skein and that the original meaning became lost because it was interpreted without any reference to the precession of the equinoxes, which was at its base.

A growing band of modern researchers, such as Robert Cox, Santillana and Dechend and Graham Hancock are sure that the precession of the equinoxes was at the heart of the main myth underlying the teaching of the Mystery Religions, because the originators left clues for later civilisations to decipher. The knowledge of the precession was important to the ancient seers, so they kept copious records of the sky and knew the precise time when each golden age would take place. They also knew when their great hermetic knowledge would become lost and made adequate provision by hiding it in ciphers and in secret vaults beneath the earth.

Without going into too much detail, the precession of the equinoxes is basically caused by a very slow wobble in the earth's axis, very much like a spinning top when it slows down. The earth is not a perfect sphere. It bulges at the equator. The pull of the sun and moon on this bulge has the effect of making it look to the observer on earth, that the celestial sphere is changing. This slow wobble is caused by the gravitational effects of the sun and moon. The rotating axis of the earth moves around in a complete circle once in approximately twenty-six thousand years. By ancient calculations this was exactly twenty-five thousand nine hundred and twenty years. Due to this gyroscopic wobble, the sun appears to move around the zodiac in the opposite direction to its annual path.

One look at the horoscope page in a newspaper sees the signs of the zodiac listed beginning with Aries and going round in twelve equal divisions to Pisces. Our annual trip around the zodiac is rather like the minute hand of a clock. From the perspective of the precession the signs seem to move in the opposite direction. Due to the slow movement it takes about two thousand one hundred and sixty years to pass through each sign of the zodiac. This could be viewed as being like an hour hand, in that it moves much more slowly.

The same tradition also marks the emergence of different religious teachers in the Bible. Moses was originally a shepherd and was obviously the great teacher in the age of Aries. He was most upset when the Children of Israel fashioned a golden calf to worship, as this was the emblem of the previous world age – namely the age of Taurus.

It is also no surprise that the shepherds – the guardians of the age of Aries – were the first people to come to honour the newly born Jesus, whose birth heralded the movement of the precession clock to the age of Pisces. The sign of Pisces is of two fish swimming in different directions. Thus, it is quite natural that the main disciples of Jesus were fishermen.

At this time the slow hand of the precession clock is moving through the few remaining minutes of Pisces into the new age of Aquarius. It is no surprise that the two parallel saw-edge signs of this new age loom large at this time in the world of advertising; namely the tread patterns of most car and aircraft tyres, as well as a sign of fast communication in the world of household telephones and mobile phones.

To recap, Robert Cox informs us that every golden age brings about huge changes every thirteen thousand years upon the earth, when every aspect of life takes on a new and uplifting spiritual dimension. He believes the next one will take place within the next twenty years. A precise timing of a new golden age was not the only reason why the ancient Egyptian seers studied the night sky. The reverse side of this coin was a contingency plan to ward off the possibility of cataclysmic natural disasters, which can often occur as the passage of time, marked by the precession clock, moves from one world age to another.

At this point it is important to add that the increased spiritual impulses of pure consciousness, which Cox calls 'celestial fire', come from the centre of the Milky Way galaxy at the beginning of a new golden age and were the means that gave rise to the expanded awareness of the people of the earth, which caused them to heed the teachings of Osiris.

> Osiris's brother Set grew more and more jealous of his brother and, with the aid of his seventy-two conspirators, he devised a clever plan to rid himself of Osiris forever.

Now we come to the worst kind of confusion. Here the same cyclic cosmic process has become personified as an evil person. It is here that Churchward's charge against the declining awareness of the Egyptian takes place. He accuses them of inventing the devil. The clue to the fact that Set is not the devil or even a person, is the mention of seventy-two murderous conspirators.

This is a well-attested number discovered by Santillana and Dechend in their ground-breaking study *Hamlet's Mill*. Seventy-two is the number of years it takes to move one degree away from the twelve o'clock high peak of the golden age. As each sign of the zodiac occupies thirty degrees, this means that each world age as measured by the precession clock is two thousand one hundred and sixty years long. We are now at the end of the period occupied by Pisces. The seventy-two conspirators have now moved almost thirty degrees and the world awaits as Aquarius moves into the frame.

Thus, the murderous conspirators of Set were the old enemy – Time itself. Time has always been the reason for the eventual loss of the golden age, enlightenment, high states of consciousness and the subsequent onset of ignorance in just the same way as summer gives way to winter. However, the slow cyclic movement through the constellations of the zodiac is also the mechanism which brings about a new golden age.

The precession of the equinoxes is, of course, a very large cosmic cycle and would be known to a very few select people at the time when the Mystery Religions were in full swing. However, the same conclusion can also be drawn from the yearly cycle with which everybody at the time would be conversant. As Robert Graves has informed us, the key numbers in the canon of the ancients were five and seventy-two. Just as the larger cosmic cycle moved one degree every seventy-two years round any given pole star, the greater cosmic year extended for five pole stars: Alderamin, Dench, Vega, Alpha Draconis and Polaris, our present pole star; so the yearly cycle of the sun god passed through five seasons of seventy-two days.

Thus the sun god, whether he is Hercules, Osiris or any other from the host of names, follows the yearly pattern of the grain. He is born in exceptional circumstances in the springtime. He does great things when still very young in the next season. In the third season – mid-summer – he is cut down by his brother, as men harvest the grain, with his scythe. In the fourth season his seed lies dormant in the earth and in the fifth season he comes again. This model of the yearly sun god fits names as diverse as Hercules, Osiris, King Arthur and Jesus.

From this we can do nothing else but infer that there was also a parallel skein to the identity of Set. His name too was a cosmic process as well as the brother of a famous ancient Egyptian king. Perhaps it was the custom at that time to name the five royals at the head of the Egyptian dynasty after the five main deities the ancient Egyptians worshipped.

Also it seems that the perception of Set changed with the passing of time. Dr Seton Williams reminds us that Set was viewed very differently in earlier times. She described him as previously being a very ancient desert god, who was associated with the dark night sky. At one time he was one of the two gods pouring the water of immortality over the king but was later replaced by Thoth. It seems as though the popularity of Set declines in proportion to the loss of knowledge of the golden age; or to put it another way, the decline of pure consciousness of the people causes them to adapt his persona to fit the particular world age they live in.

As thousands of years passed and the knowledge and enlightened thinking of the golden age receded into the background, confusion arose. Once the knowledge of the precession had evaporated it wouldn't be difficult to mix up the roles of humans with a cosmic process.

Once we are talking of mere mortals it becomes feasible for a younger brother who hated his elder brother to want to kill him and usurp his mantle. If we are talking about gods then the whole thing becomes impossible, for they are immortal.

> Somehow Set secretly measured the body of Osiris and had a chest beautifully fashioned and ornamented to the exact size of his hated brother.
>
> When Osiris returned triumphantly from his travels a festival was held in his honour. At the height of the festivities Set announced an amusing challenge. He ordered the beautiful chest to be brought into the hall and announced that he would give it to the person it exactly fitted. It was such a beautifully crafted piece that all the men present desired to have it. Many men tried their luck but to no avail. It was then the turn of Osiris. It fitted him exactly. As soon as Osiris lay down in it the conspirators rushed forward and slammed down the lid. They fastened the lid down with nails and poured molten lead to seal it. Following this, they carried it to the river and sent it on its way to the sea.

There is one other answer to the question of how the Osiris myth became so confused. This was the convention of the Mystery Schools to view the spiritual essence or higher self of a person and his superficial, unenlightened persona as separate. As far as these schools were concerned, from the point of view of the personality, the inner genius is experienced as a separate being.

Plato said, 'We should think of the most authoritative part of our soul as a guardian spirit... which lifts us from the earth towards our home in heaven.'[2] A good example of seeing the persona and the inner genius as separate is in Homer's *Odyssey*. Odysseus saw the shadow of the great hero Hercules wandering about in hell, with an arrow grooved on his bowstring and the dead crying out 'like frightened birds, fleeing in every direction'[3]. This surprised Odysseus, but his guide put him right. The spectre was only

17

'his ghost... Hercules himself delights in the grand feasts of the deathless gods on high'. In Greek literature the journey to the Underworld is a metaphor for the soul's descent into the physical world; for here it lives as a shadow of its true self, which is always at one with God.

In the myth of Osiris it is his persona that desires the beautiful chest so much. Like Persephone with the narcissus, his ego became extroverted with desire and his soul encased in a body-sized prison, sealed with iron nails and molten lead. The latter are significant because iron and lead were regarded by the alchemists as occupying the lowest rung of all metals, and were therefore a metaphor for the basest desires of the body which needed to be purified by their art.

> Isis was distraught. She searched far and wide for her husband. Finally, Isis learned that the chest had been cast up by the sea near a land called Byblos. The waves set it down gently in the arms of a tamarisk tree. The tree grew miraculously to a magnificent size, enclosing the coffer of Osiris in its trunk, and completely hid the chest. The king of that country so admired the tree that he ordered it to be cut down and used as a pillar to support the roof of his house.

Although now living in a body in the Underworld on earth, Osiris is also joined to the Cosmic Tree whose roots are on the earth and its fruit and branches in heaven. The tamarisk tree was always held to be sacred to Osiris, because manna exuded from it. In China it was regarded as an immortality symbol. Its resin was used as a drug to prolong life.

Byblos was an ancient port on the coast of Lebanon. The king wanted the same Tree of Life to support him and his own family and countrymen through the journey of life. It was the *axis mundi* that joined heaven and earth. As such it was the Tree of Life that joined all worlds and planes of existence in the macroscopic world, which has its roots in the transcendental field of life and whose fruit on the earth can ripen into the apples of immortality.

In the individual, it is the spine that is its physical trunk and the means of spiritual ascent is the *shushumna*. The shushumna is a very thin subtle tube running from the base of the spine to the brain. *Prana*, which can be thought of as refined breath, flows up the tube of the shushumna. In an enlightened person the prana flows the whole length of the shushumna, which activates each of the *chakras*, and allows the individual to use the full 100 per cent of his spiritual, psychological and intellectual inheritance.

However, in the case of the majority of people, the passage of prana is prevented from coursing up the shushumna by impurities. The twin aims of yoga and hermeticism is to unblock these subtle channels through specific yoga postures, meditation, diet and other spiritual practices. Gradually, purification takes place and allows the prana to rise. As it ascends it opens one chakra after another, until finally the thousand-petalled lotus at the crown of the head unfolds. This is analogous to the tamarisk tree that supported Byblos. It had its roots in the *muladhara*, or the first chakra, the shushumna is its trunk, which nourishes and supports the thousand-petalled lotus – hence the full Osiris is inside everybody and only needs awakening.

> One day Isis came to Byblos. Dejected and tearful she sat down by the side of the river. As she was sitting there some of the king's maid-servants came down for some water. Isis greeted them very graciously and plaited their hair. The maid-servants were captivated both by her skill in hairdressing and by the wonderfully fragrant smell of her body.
>
> Soon news got back to Queen Astarte of Byblos, who sent for this wondrous lady. The two got on so well that soon the Queen appointed Isis to be her baby son Dictys's nurse. It is said that she gave the child her finger to suck instead of her breast and instead both fed it on ambrosia and burned away the mortal portions of the body in a fire.
>
> One night the Queen, who had been watching secretly, saw the goddess place the child into the fire. The Queen screamed and rushed forward to take her child out of the flames and so deprived it of its immortality. At this point Isis revealed her true identity. The Queen was terrified and knelt at her feet, shaking. Isis demanded the pillar, which the queen gratefully gave her to redress the wrong she had perpetrated. Isis took out the chest which Set had fashioned and gave them back the tamarisk pillar to hold up the roof. From that day it became the most sacred object in Byblos because it once held the body of a god. The King, Malacander, provided her with a ship in which to sail back to Egypt with the chest.

These three paragraphs are very nearly an exact parallel with Demeter in all of their details. Like Demeter, Isis gets taken into service as a nursemaid of the King's son. She burns away the mortality with spiritual fire and is thwarted in her attempt to make the young child immortal by the rashness of the Queen.

Today we would call the 'spiritual fire' pure consciousness. Thus the goddess in both myths employs the same tactic – she subjects the infant to the flames of transcendental pure consciousness where he would be purified. In so doing the outer persona would become one with his inner genius.

The goddess took the chest to the vicinity where her son Horus was being brought up. She hid the chest in a safe place and went to see her son. One night, Set was out hunting by the light of the moon when he chanced upon the chest. He recognised it immediately, opened the lid and dismembered the body into fourteen parts and scattered them all over the land of Egypt.

Isis heard of the terrible deed and went looking for all the parts. She succeeded in recovering them all but his penis but made a replica of it to take its place.

Again, it seems as if we are talking of two separate processes here, one individual and the other cosmic. On the level of the individual initiate it seems likely that there were thirteen separate, secret rites or levels to be enacted before the resurrection of Osiris, or the perfected man, could take place. This would also coincide with the number of full moons in a year. On a cosmic level it would mean that the dismemberment of Osiris took place in thirteen incremental steps of one thousand years, before the whole cosmic renewal of a golden age began again.

Finally, over a long and protracted series of battles, Horus overcame Set. He thus avenged his father's death and claimed his rightful inheritance.

The question of Horus is an interesting one. All the accounts of the myth say he is the son of Osiris and Isis, who eventually conquered Set and thus avenged his father's death. However, one reading of the Hermetica, with its high moral aims and objectives, tells us that revenge had no part to play in the process of spiritual regeneration.

A great deal of the latter part of the myth of Osiris is concerned with the child Horus seeking to avenge his father's death. Bearing in mind that the whole point of the myth is to restore the fallen Osiris, in just the same way as the myth of Demeter restores Persephone to her rightful place amongst the gods on high, there is no need to include Horus in the story at all.

James Churchward tells us two very important facts that he discovered whilst deciphering ancient stone tablets. Firstly, Horus was the name given to the head of the early Egyptian church, in much the same way as the 'Pope' is the head of the Roman Catholic Church today; secondly, at the latter end of a very long hegemony priests of ancient Egypt invented the devil in the form of Set.

Once again two parallel strands emerge. Horus may well have been the son of Osiris the human being, and probably was. It is also likely that they were in conflict for the throne of Egypt. However, there were a host of magical battles over the course of hundreds of years between Horus and Set, which was more likely to represent a protracted battle by the Egyptian high priests for supremacy, which of course they eventually won.

Could not this be the victory of Horus over Set? The recovery of the dismembered pieces by Isis, with the help of the child Horus, and their transformation back to the state of Osiris, could well be the work of the enlightened priests of ancient Egypt. Schooled in the teachings of Thoth, they were able to regenerate any human being through the Mystery School of the god with the head of an ibis. In other words, the high priests became the power behind the throne. They became the guardians of 'wisdom' in a time of diminishing spiritual, intellectual and moral values personified by Set.

This sounds at first to be a very satisfying ending to the saga. It must have been perfect for a few thousand years. However, due to the decline of spiritual and intellectual values, over a long passage of time, everybody was affected, including the high priests. As the high point of the golden age receded further and further into the distant past, the knowledge of spiritual regeneration became lost. Consequently, the pyramids ceased their role of being places of initiation for the king and other highly evolved people and were relegated to the role of being used as elaborate tombs for the rich and famous.

It must be said that many of the ideas enshrined in the myths of Demeter and Osiris are similar, especially the process of making a child immortal by purging his mortal body by putting him in the flames. This must not be thought of as an ordinary fire. In this context, the true meaning of the myth means spiritual fire.

In India this process of being placed in the flames is called tapas. Tapas is a collective noun including all types of spiritual practices, including mantras, pujas, yogic postures, meditation, diet, taking herbs or fasting. To the individual seeker, the practice of tapas represents asceticism in its widest sense. However, his or her presiding deity on the celestial plane perceives the fruit of his labours as heat or spiritual fire and grants him a boon, which is really a reward to indicate that the seeker has made significant spiritual progress.

Whilst on this subject, it is important to say that there was one other means of purification and that was through taking the secret elixir of 'living gold', which was made by the alchemist himself. The adept alchemist or hermeticist did not stop when he had produced gold from a base metal, such as iron. He then went on to make it into living gold, which has the same vibration as human vital energy. Just as iron can be magnetised by passing an electric current through it, so a person can be completely transformed by taking this alchemical medicine.

Once taken, miraculous changes are said to occur. An old, feeble person can gradually become transformed into an active, robust person with a youthful appearance and awesome spiritual powers. One of the reasons why the utmost secrecy was observed concerning the teachings of the Mystery Schools, was that this kind of knowledge would be very dangerous in the wrong hands. Such knowledge would best be preserved in ciphers or symbolic text that only the initiates, who could be trusted, could understand.

It is claimed that the entire tradition of Mystery Schools had its birth in Egypt from Thoth/Hermes and influenced many of the ancient Greek thinkers, such as Plato and Pythagoras.

The myth of Osiris was not just the oldest but also the most misunderstood and the most confused of all the myths. I promise that the folk stories we will be covering later in the book will not be subject to so many alterations and deviations from the normally accepted meaning as this one.

To sum up, it was the common practice of the Mystery Schools to encode their teachings into symbolic form in stories. In the more familiar myths the hero is one of the gods. Thus, Heracles purified the whole of his being – his mind, body and soul – in the process of completing his twelve labours. In the case of folk stories, the hero is 'everyman', because the journey to enlightenment is common to all of us. The obstacles he meets are similar to the ones we all encounter.

In each story an outer journey symbolised an inner transformation. It was through the process of transformation – or re-awakening – that the individual was able to tease out the meaning of the symbols – in much the same way as *koans* are used in Zen Buddhism today.

A classic example of a koan is the raising of the individual's consciousness by practising 'one-hand clapping'. This of course makes no sense at the surface level of the mind because it takes two hands to clap. Then, after much mental wrestling, the mind gives up and the answer spontaneously arises. The regular contact of the mind with the transcendent is the clapping in question here. It is the regular contact of the mind with the transcendent that purifies the central and subtle nervous systems and makes higher states of consciousness not only possible but a day-to-day reality.

The purpose of this book is to tease out the meaning of these symbolic conundrums and so reveal the true import of the teaching hidden within it.

[1] Cox 1997, 18. Also 253
[2] Quoted in Freke & Gandy, 2000
[3] Homer, 1996, 269

# Chapter 3
# Transcendence

Younger children invariably end their stories with 'and they all lived happily ever after'. Similarly, every adult watching a play or film wants the guy to get the girl or the police to catch the villain so that everything turns out happily in the end. Most of us also hold onto the belief that we will all end up perfectly happy in heaven when we die. So there is a deeply seated notion in the human psyche that in the end suffering will eventually be transcended by happiness.

The same aspiration exists in all folk stories. The heroine may sleep in a fireplace and spend her days doing lowly, back-breaking, menial work but eventually the king's son will recognise her true worth and come looking for her. The feeling throughout all the trials and tribulations of the hero or heroine's progress during the story is that suffering will eventually be replaced by happiness.

This too was the aim of the Ancient Mystery Religions. They realised that every individual, except for brief periods, is alienated from happiness by the restless tide of relentless and uncontrollable change in their lives. The first thing to do was to find a safe and reliable shore to land upon. Every person needs to find a stable element with which to anchor their life in a changing world.

The first aim or goal of an initiate into the ancient Mysteries was to learn of the difference between the changing world of the senses and the *nous*, the intuitive factor of higher reason. After the initiation, a person would no longer be subject to the same sense of alienation in life because he would have experienced the very ground of his being. His mind would have made contact with the All.

Maharishi puts it very clearly in modern terminology. He says that there are two distinct spheres of life. One is the ever changing round of relative existence we are all engaged in; the other is the unchanging transcendental sphere of life underlying all forms of activity and the human mind.

Transcendence is the process of going beyond the ceaseless tide of thoughts that occupy the individual mind to a pleasant serenity and stillness, which Maharishi calls Transcendental Consciousness. When the mind and body experience the purity of this state of consciousness it allows the mind and physiology to gradually throw off its abnormalities and evolve so as to be completely cognisant of its source.

There is no better illustration of this truth than the myth of Demeter, which was the mythological structure surrounding the Eleusinian Mysteries. A myth has many levels of meaning, both from the point of view of the evolution of the individual, his society and its history. We are examining it from the perspective of the individual incarnating in a human body and the process of 're-remembering' his or her spiritual home.

After the abduction of Persephone in Homer's famous Hymn, very little of the story centres upon Persephone, except to say that she is not happy in the Underworld and yearns to be reunited with her mother on Mount Olympus, where the immortals live. The immortals live in the transcendental realm of life. The point is that all the efforts to effect the reunification take place from the mother's side. Persephone's role is passive but twofold. She has to keep herself pure and have her attention on the transcendental sphere of life.

The same is true of the abduction of Rama's wife, Sita. In the first of the great epic poems by Veda Vyasa called the *Ramayana*, Sita is abducted by Ravanna, the king of demons, and spirited away to Lanka in his aerial chariot. She rejects all entreaties to become his wife and his promises of a life filled with pomp, luxury, adulation and great wealth. Instead she prefers to sit under a tree in Ravanna's beautiful garden and waits to be rescued by her loving husband Rama.

Rama is an incarnation of the god Vishnu. Aided by his brother Lakshman, Hanuman, the commander of the monkey warriors, and the monkey king, Sugriva, he eventually manages to overthrow and defeat both Ravanna and his minions and take Sita back to their home in Ayodhya. It is important to note that both Hanuman and Sugriva were also related to the immortals. Hanuman was the son of a wind god called Pavana and Sugriva was born of Surya, the sun god.

The same is also true of the ancient Egyptian myth. Osiris, the god who brought the knowledge of cultivating wheat and barley to the ancient world, was cut down and dismembered by his brother Set. Different parts of his body were scattered throughout the land of Egypt. Isis discovered them. She reconstituted them and brought him back to life to rule over the spirits of the dead.

This action of Isis was probably the basis of all the myths similar to the labours of Heracles, where the solar hero has a task in each of the twelve houses of the zodiac before he regains his immortality.

Thus, the same thread runs through all these great myths. That is, all the effort for reuniting the individual mind with the cosmic mind comes from the side of the immortals. The same is still true in the twenty-first century. If we want to maximise our happiness on the earth we have to open our attention to the Absolute and so transcend the relative field of cause and effect. This will enable us to evolve and grow to our full stature.

However, the habits of hundreds and perhaps even thousands of years mitigate against this. In fact, the population upon the earth today is largely made up of Persephones and Sitas who have not only sold out to the earthly counterparts of Hades and Ravanna, but have also no memory or knowledge of the celestial beings or their true home.

We act under the delusion that we are in control of our destiny. We have spent many centuries acting as though we are at war with Nature. Despite the real achievements of our technological way of life we are still ignorant of our true nature. Due to an over-riding viewpoint of thinking that it requires a great effort and privations to become enlightened we turn away from it and pretend that the transcendental aspect of life does not exist.

In modern times the most effective and easiest way to achieve a state of transcendence on a regular basis is through techniques like Transcendental Meditation and the TM-Sidhi programme, as brought to the West by his Holiness Maharishi Mahesh Yogi.

Maharishi speaks of the mind as having a fourfold hierarchical structure, comprised of the senses; the surface of the mind, which deals with day-to-day thoughts and impulses; the intellect, which deal's with decision-making and deeper intellectual and spiritual questions; and the ego. When a person practices the TM technique, an individual is able to transcend these four relative aspects of the mind and enjoy the pure transcendental field of pure consciousness, which is the basis of all our thoughts, feelings and actions.

Maharishi has hinted several times of a very advanced world-wide, Vedic civilisation many thousands of years ago before prehistoric time. Perhaps the importance of transcendence was encoded in stories to preserve the teachings of the high civilisation of that far-off age. Transcendence is so important because it facilitates beneficial changes so as to enhance the evolution of the central nervous system. This means that it is possible to become enlightened in just one lifetime.

Maharishi tells us that the human nervous system is precious and a great gift because it is capable of so much expansion. He says,

The evolution of all other species is fixed. Even the angels are jealous of us. Whilst they start much higher up the ladder of the evolution of consciousness, we can overtake them because our central nervous system can be fully developed to Unity Consciousness.[1]

This is in complete accord with what Hermes says in the tenth chapter of the Hermetica:

> For man is a being of divine nature; he is comparable, not to the other creatures on the earth, but to the gods in heaven. Nay if we are to speak the truth without fear, he who is indeed a man (an enlightened man) is even above the gods of heaven, or at any rate equals them in power. None of the gods will ever quit heaven, and pass its boundary, and come down to earth; but man ascends even to heaven, and measures it; and what is more than all beside, he mounts to heaven without quitting the earth; to so vast a distance he can put forth his power.[2]

It is a sad fact that a majority of our scientists still stick stubbornly to their opinion that the complexity of the human brain produces consciousness, even though there have been over six hundred studies in more than thirty countries showing that transcendental consciousness not only is a fact, but also that it produces a very large range of benefits both to the individual and the society they live in.

---

[1] Speaking at a Global TV press conference on 17/3/04
[2] Scott, 1997, 82-83

# Chapter 4
# The Seven States of Consciousness

As soon as we venture into the sphere of initiations into the ancient Mysteries we encounter the knotty problem of trying to evaluate their method of grading the higher states of consciousness. Each new initiation would bring the initiate to the threshold of a higher state of consciousness, thus transcending the one before. A higher state of consciousness necessitates a much wider band of reference and abilities. It does not merely bring more intellectual knowledge. It necessitates a complete change in the nervous system to support the new range of abilities acquired by the initiate.

Many individuals experience flashes of higher states of consciousness, which can transform their lives. I had one in the summer of 1967 in Regent's Park. I was walking with a friend one summer's morning when I slipped into a very profound state of consciousness which changed my life. I had no idea that life on earth could be as beautiful or sublime.

Suddenly, I had the feeling that I was a part of everything in existence. My mind was tranquil and at peace and I was no longer bound up with my individual worries. I also seemed to have a greatly enhanced state of touch. Even though I was wearing shoes I could feel the grass pulsating on the soles of my feet and although the trees were some distance away I could feel them as though they were physically joined to me. It moved me so much that I wrote the following poem:

*Regent's Park '67*

The place was London's Regent's Park.
The year was sixty seven.
When the Mother of the Universe
Gave me a glimpse of Heaven.

'Twas a morn I'll long remember.
My mental banners unfurled.
An inner sun broke through their ranks
And redefined my world...

I was out walking with a friend,
When some potent inner thrill
Enveloped me in solitude
And bade me to be still.

I stood transfixed. My thoughts changed from
A separate 'I' and 'mine',
To an all-embracing oneness –
Immutable, divine,

Enhancing both my sight and touch,
So that everything I could see
Was set in the same perception –
I was them and they were me.

Each swathe of moving grass I saw,
Each near and distant tree,
Were unified in one large whole
And seemed rooted, still, in me.

I could see the brown-black ruts of bark
That ranged a yonder tree,
And yet feel no sense of distance –
Just the One proximity.

The earth was alive and vital.
All was perfect and complete.
That lively contact with the trees
And the grass beneath my feet

Must have lasted for an instant,
Though Time seemed suspended there,
Amidst the trees and swathes of grass
And the warm fresh morning air.

There is a saying, that the seed
Contains the fully grown tree –
Perhaps the park was a preview
Of what I will one day be!

I felt I had stepped into the shoes
Of the man I'm meant to be –
Somehow the captive inner man
Had managed to break free,

Somehow the peripheral person
Had become the inner soul
And everything was unified
In One live and vital whole.

My shadow had met face-to-face
With the quintessential me.
I put aside my trivial toys
For a greater destiny.

This new-found sense of union –
This source of ecstasy,
Replaced the sense of emptiness
Of Life's futility

With a surge of optimism,
And the joy of feeling free.
It set my feet upon the path
Of spiritual liberty.

Whilst I am still a partial man,
The shadow that is me
Has glimpsed the realm of the source of bliss
In all its entirety

And strives to merge the shadow self
With the vibrant inner Whole,
And Be-at-One with everything –
Life's ultimate cosmic goal.

Whilst this was one of the major highlights of my life, I later found out that this was not such a rare phenomenon. About 40 per cent of undergraduate students who took part in a particular survey of 'transcendental', or 'heightened', experiences of 'nature' had undergone something similar. The name of the book was *Inglorious Wordsworths* because the examples of transcendental experiences were inspired and illustrated by excerpts of Wordsworth's poems, especially from *Tintern Abbey*, *The World is too Much With Us* and *Intimations of Immortality*. The author of the survey found that these kinds of experiences are more likely to take place when walking in the countryside, by the sea or trekking in mountainous areas or areas of natural beauty.

The figures in the USA confirm this. Many surveys carried out there since the 1960s consistently come up with between 30 and 40 per cent of people having had powerful spiritual experiences. A particular Gallup poll in the 1990s reported that 53 per cent of the adults consulted had experienced at least one moment of 'sudden religious awakening or insight'.

However, whilst such experiences may be both memorable and even life-transforming, they do not last very long, whereas higher states of consciousness are permanent. Before we try to shed some light upon the higher states of consciousness experienced by initiates of the Mystery Religions, it would be very helpful to gain a clear understanding of the seven major states of consciousness as defined by Maharishi Mahesh Yogi.

We are used to only three states of consciousness in Western civilisation. These are the waking, dreaming and deep sleep states of consciousness, which are well known to us. They alternate as different patterns of bodily functioning, which affect us daily. However, they are very different from each other empirically, biologically and mentally.

In deep sleep the body benefits by having deep rest but we have no awareness of what is going on. There is some subjective awareness taking place when the body is dreaming but much of this proves to be illusory when we regain the waking state of consciousness. In the waking state we have what we regard as the full range of our mental, perceptual and emotional life, even though we actually only usually use 5–10 per cent of the full potential of the brain. As a matter of interest, Ramana Maharshi, the great sage of Tiruvannamalai, regarded the waking state to be as illusory as the dreaming state.

Maharishi Mahesh Yogi, the creator of the TM and TM-Sidhi programmes, also regards our present state of development as abnormal compared to the ancient Vedic tradition of knowledge, which he draws upon as his source. Maharishi's technique of Transcendental Meditation comes from this ancient tradition. It both expands the mind in the modern sense of the word and also brings about a fourth major state of consciousness, which is the bridge to three higher states of consciousness.

When a person practices the TM technique he or she becomes aware of a growing sense of well being. This is called Bliss Consciousness. The physiological functioning of the body slows down during meditation and gains a very deep state of rest. As the breathing becomes less, the thinking process becomes more alert and refined.

The vehicle that naturally takes the mind to quieter and quieter levels of functioning is called the *mantra*. A mantra is employed because it has no obvious meaning to the meditating individual and is therefore a suitable vehicle to allow the individual to explore deeper and deeper areas of his or her own mind. This very deep exploration of the mind leads the individual to experience increasingly pleasant areas of charm and well being. Mantras can only be chosen by a fully qualified teacher of Transcendental Meditation.

Once an individual has elected to learn Transcendental Meditation he is given his own personal mantra and is taught how to use it properly. Following this instruction the meditating subject sits down in his comfortable chair, closes his or her eyes and begins to repeat the mantra quietly and effortlessly. As the mind quietens down one is able to experience finer and finer levels of the sound until at last the sound is transcended and the subject remains wide awake with no object of perception. This is called Transcendental Consciousness.

Transcendental Consciousness is characterised by psychologists and physiologists as 'restful alertness' because, whilst the body is fully rested, the mind has gained maximum alertness. There have been over six hundred scientific studies showing the beneficial effects of Transcendental Meditation physiologically, psychologically and behaviourally, which are outside the remit of this particular study.

At first, due to the inflexibility of the central nervous system, a meditator can only experience one level of reality at a time. A new initiate into meditation moves from the surface value of everyday thought and experience, through increasingly deeper levels of thought until he or she experiences the Absolute, unmanifest, unmoving aspect of life. Whilst in the field of action he experiences the ever changing aspect of relative creation. In order that transcendental Bliss Consciousness is lived at all times it is necessary for the mind to become so familiar with unbounded consciousness that it is never lost, even in the midst of the field of action. Maharishi calls that field of universal consciousness underlying the relative aspects of the mind the 'Self' in order to differentiate it from the limited sense of 'self' we call the ego.

At first, the mind of the seeker lacks that degree of flexibility and can only experience one aspect of consciousness at a time. In meditation he experiences transcendental consciousness and attenuated aspects of his own thought processes; but when he is engaged in normal activity he experiences the waking state, dreaming and deep sleep states of consciousness.

However, as the practice progresses, some of the qualities gained in transcendental consciousness are maintained. Thus, vestiges of transcendental consciousness are seen to exist alongside the waking state. By degrees this grows until the individual is aware of his expanded sense of Self all the time. This means that his own sense of expanded Self awareness is never overshadowed by the object of perception in the field of action. This state of consciousness is called Cosmic Consciousness.

In Cosmic Consciousness the whole of the mind is fully developed. No longer is the individual using only 5–10 per cent of his full potential. In this state of consciousness he uses all 100 per cent of his mental potential. Perhaps the main benchmark of Cosmic Consciousness is that the Self is always found to be separate from the field of activity.

That is to say, the subject maintains his or her awareness for twenty-four hours of the day. He or she no longer loses that state of awareness, even in sleep. The body sleeps and continues to benefit from sleep. The mind still dreams but the awareness of the individual is not dimmed. He can now enjoy his sleep and his dreams, not just enjoy the effects of it. In other words he gains the ability to experience himself sleeping.

Cosmic Consciousness is the full development of the mind. Thus, there is a duality inasmuch as the Self is always found to be separate from the field of activity. That is to say, although the mind has risen to its full development, the senses through which we perceive the world have not. Thus, there appears to be a separateness between the realised Self and the world of activity.

The full value of the objective world can be appreciated when the growth of consciousness unfolds on the level of feelings and intuition. We call this the growth of the heart.

We know from science that the material world is made up of many levels, such as the molecular, the atomic and the sub-atomic, and that all these are evanescent manifestations of an underlying unified field. A so-called 'normal' person in the waking state of consciousness is only able to see the surface value of an object. However, on the journey from Cosmic Consciousness to God Consciousness the organs of perception become purified so that perception can take place on finer and finer aspects of the objective world through our senses.

The organs of perception continue to develop until it is possible to perceive the finest level of the objective world. This is called God Consciousness – so called because one is able to perceive the whole range of our environment, including the ability to see and hear the full range of beings in the celestial realm. Devotion to a particular aspect of God is the limb by which Cosmic Consciousness is transformed into God Consciousness.

I would like to quote a little from Maharishi's poem called *Love of God*, in order to convey a little of the flavour of what it is like to be in the state of God Consciousness:

> In the love of God, the lover of life finds expression of the inexpressible. Cosmic life gains expression in his activity. The thought of cosmic life is materialised in his process of thinking. His eyes behold the purpose of creation; his ears hear the music of cosmic life; his hands hold on to cosmic intentions. His feet set the cosmic life in motion; he walks on earth, he walks in the destiny of heaven. Angels enjoy his being on earth; this is the unity born of love.[1]

The seventh and last state to develop is called Unity Consciousness – so called because everything that is perceived is seen as part of one's self. Although everything stays exactly as it was in the waking state of consciousness it is nevertheless accompanied by the knowledge and experience that everything is joined together in a unity at its fundamental level of our being. Apparently there is nothing for the individual to do at this level for the transition from God Consciousness to Unity Consciousness is automatic. Everything that is perceived visually in Unity Consciousness is through the medium of a golden glow.

From God Consciousness onwards the heart and mind operate together. Every thought and perception are appreciated in their infinite sense. Thought and feelings are no longer separate and fragmented, but operate in their most integrated and expanded form. Thus, such an individual lives the life of a human being with the mind of God. This means he is able to appreciate everything in its infinite value as a part of himself.

It is interesting that these levels of consciousness defined by Maharishi in modern times, correlate with those of Elizabeth Haitch in a book called *Initiation*, in which she remembers her life as an initiate into the priesthood in ancient Egypt.

She refers to the state of development of most people upon the earth as the 'average man', who shares many of the attributes of the animals, including emotions, drives, desires, sympathy and antipathy, but is above

35

them by virtue of his intellect. Man's intellect places him one octave above the animals because he is able to think consciously. It is significant that the word 'man' is derived from the Sanskrit word for mind – *manas*.

A giant step above the average man is the one who displays his 'inner genius', or his real Self. Such a person is no longer buffeted about by the effects of the stars or the daily catastrophes brought to us by changes in our environment. He now operates in the world of causes and is able to draw upon the divine source of life. He is able to use his intellect to express his experiences on a higher plane of consciousness in art, music, dance, poetry and sculpture.

There is one proviso – when we are speaking of art, we mean sacred art. Art for its own sake was unheard of in the ancient world. In fact, art as we mean it today, emerged out of the new thinking of the Renaissance. Prior to that, all art was dedicated to the divine – especially in relation to the Mystery Schools.

As far as I can tell, the definition of Elizabeth Haitch's inner genius seems identical in all respects with Maharishi's Cosmic Consciousness.

The next step up the ladder of spiritual evolution, according to Elizabeth Haitch, was 'prophet'. This also seems to be in complete accord with Maharishi's God Consciousness. It is interesting that this very high state of consciousness culminates with the full development of the heart and emotions. It is also significant that Maharishi says it is not possible to be fully devotional until the seeker has realised the state of Cosmic Consciousness. That is not to say that a person will not be of a devotional disposition but that he or she cannot be fully devotional whilst any trace of the separate ego exists.

Elizabeth Haitch says that a person achieving the status of a prophet not only displays all the forces of the preceding levels of consciousness, but is also conscious too of the next level above him – namely universal love. She is careful to differentiate universal love of the sixth level of consciousness from the 'love' on the animal plane, which is for the propagation of the species. The difference between the two is that, whereas animal love involves the need to embrace, kiss, hug and possess the body, universal love springs from the primordial unity of the Divine. A person who has attained this level of development does not feel the need to possess anybody because they already feel in complete union with all the beings in the celestial world.

Finally, the seventh and most complete manifestation of God in human form she calls 'god-man'. Only at this level is a person fully conscious. All the previous levels of consciousness are only partial revelations of God. She defines a god-man as: 'a person who manifests God – his own divine self – completely and perfectly through a perfect consciousness; one who experiences and radiates the divine creative forces in their primordial, untransformed vibrations and frequencies. He is supremely conscious; no part of him is unconscious.'

As far as I can understand, this again is completely consistent with Maharishi's Unity Consciousness. This is why the Mystery Religions have something important to say to us in the world today. Whilst we have many tools, techniques and technologies the ancient world neither predicted or possessed, they did have one major advantage over us – namely the means to make a person completely whole and divinely happy.

---

[1] Yogi, 1965

# Chapter 5
# Parallel States of Consciousness in the Mystery Religions

Without Maharishi's map of the full development of an individual it would be virtually impossible to accurately gauge the different degrees of an initiate into the Mystery Religions of the past. It is also useful to know that modern science, Maharishi and Elizabeth Haitch all agree that people in the past had the same mental, physical and perceptual apparatus as we have today, so we are not dealing with an altogether different kind of being. This makes it easy to generalise and extrapolate the different states of consciousness as defined today with those of the distant past.

Many esoteric Western descriptions of man, and certainly all the Eastern ones I've read, say that he is a tripartite being. Thus we inhabit three bodies. Yogananda calls them the physical, the subtle and the causal – similarly Aurobindo names them the physical, the vital and mental bodies.

Yogananda concurs with the Hermetica. He points out that the soul is invisible and can only be distinguished by the presence of its body or bodies. 'As long as the soul is encased in one, two, or three body containers, sealed tightly with the corks of ignorance and desires, he cannot merge into the sea of the Spirit.'[1] He says, 'the three bodies are held together by the glue of unfulfilled desires'. Physical desires spring from egotism and the pleasures of the senses, and are much more powerful than the desire force connected with astral or causal perceptions.

Astral desires are centred in terms of vibration. Apparently astral beings can hear the ethereal music of the spheres and are 'entranced by the sight of all creation as exhaustless expressions of changing light', which they can also feel, taste and touch. Causal beings see the whole universe as realisations of the dream-ideas of God and can materialise their desires immediately.

In line with his tripartite being, the hero or heroine of many tales has to accomplish three extra tasks to establish his supremacy over the three worlds. In some of the more recent structure of stories, such as *Cinderella* and *Allerleirau*, this was symbolised by three appearances at the court ball.

Similarly, the King's son in *The Six Servants* and the old soldier in *How Six Men Got on in the World* had to perform three tasks to win the princess. Another hero had to extract three hairs from the head of the giant; and Jack, in *Jack and the Beanstalk*, had three forays to the giant's castle before overcoming him altogether.

Thus, an initiate into the Greater Mysteries was conceived as having three births.

The Mystery Religions symbolised individual birth and creation as the splitting of a large golden egg. This idea parallels the scattering of the *Purusha*, when the birth of all beings took place at the beginning of creation. Guenon tells us that the two halves of the World Egg become, respectively, heaven and earth.

The closeness of the teachings of the Mystery Religions of the West to Indian mystical thought and spiritual practices can be seen from their World Egg equivalent, the *Hiranya-Garbha*. This has been translated as the 'golden womb', 'golden seed' or 'golden egg'. It is said that Brahma, the Hindu creator, lived inside this golden womb for one of his years and then divided it into two parts, one male the other female. It was conceived that we are all inside one hollow eggshell of the earth, with its many lands and oceans, looking up at the vast, spectacular, inverted dome of the heavens, containing the moon, the sun and the stars.

The concept of the World Egg or Hiranya-Garbha contains another important symbolic element – that of the golden seed, or the germ of life. It is often depicted as a golden egg enfolded within the coils of a serpent. From this viewpoint it is the *kundalini* housed in the muladhara chakra at the base of the spine, waiting to be aroused. The ascent of the kundalini symbolises the awakening of the individual from his sleep of forgetfulness of the 'average man', to rise to his full spiritual status. Pilot Baba tells us that kundalini is a new word; the old word was *jagadamba*. *Jagat* means the universe and *amba* is mother; the mother Energy of the Universe. The same energy from which heroines such as Cinderella get separated.

Expressing the same idea from a different viewpoint, the golden seed gives rise to the World Tree, whose trunk is the world axis and, as such, passes through the centre of each state of being and links all of these states with each other. It is also the wish-fulfilling tree in the story of *Cinderella* and the tree which bears the golden apples of immortality in the garden of the Hesperides, whose acquisition was the eleventh labour of Heracles. It also appears in this study as the tree bearing golden apples, in a folk tale called *The Golden Bird*.

However, back to the symbolism of the World Egg and the different initiations into the Mystery Religions. Rene Guenon informs us that the splitting of the World Egg into two halves corresponds to two caves – one on earth and one in heaven. The cave representing the earth is the place of the second birth into the Greater Mysteries, which took place at midday. The third birth took place in a cave at midnight. This third birth was seen as the gateway to the supra-individual states – a birth to the realms of heaven beyond the cosmos.

Guenon believes that the second birth is that of psychic regeneration and was concerned with developing the subtle potentialities latent in man. This seems to accord very well with Maharishi's description of Cosmic Consciousness through to God Consciousness, especially as the second birth was seen at the culmination of an individual. That is why the initiation took place at noon – the time of the culmination of the visible sun.

The third birth almost certainly corresponds to Unity Consciousness. This initiation took place in a cave at midnight because it was seen as the culmination of the spiritual sun and thus took place in complete darkness. Apparently, the initiate made his final exit from the cave through a vent in the highest part of the dome above his head.

This signified two things. In the case of the human microcosm it corresponded with the *Brahmarandhra* at the crown of the head, the place of illumination of the thousand-petalled lotus. It also both symbolised the fruition of the World Tree and the final destination of the rising kundalini. More than this, it also renewed the connection of the individual with the pole star, which symbolised the throne of the hidden Central Sun of the Universe – the unity which underlies all diversity. The pole star was symbolic of the fixed point in the universe, which was always still and unmoving.

The pole star was always imbued with paramount importance in the ancient world because it stamps its character on each world age, or thirty degree shift in the precession zodiac. The present pole star is Polaris but its position is not permanent. It was preceded by Alpha Draconis and will eventually be succeeded by Alderamin. In each world age the pole star transcends the zodiac, which the hermeticists called the ring of necessity. It also transcended the lives and fortunes of the ordinary person on the earth, as reflected in the ever changing houses of the constellations of the zodiac, forever visited by the gods and imbued with their powers and qualities.

At this point it is important to go deeper into the mechanics of the rise of the kundalini. The awakening and rise of the kundalini, or golden seed, at the base of the spine awakens and activates the chakras. These are said to be a series of five non-physical organs running up the spine, with the sixth one in the third eye position in the forehead between the eyebrows and the seventh is the Brahma chakra, often called the thousand-petalled lotus – where *Samadhi* is realised. Chakra is the Sanskrit word for wheel. They are

41

wheels of radiating cosmic energy and are said to be at the basis of all psychic abilities.

The awakening of the chakras can be said to be the milestones on the road to enlightenment. Yogananda says that the ordinary person is like a fifty watt lamp that has access to the billion watt power of the cosmic universe. The awakening has to be both a gradual and natural process. Through regular spiritual practices conferred by an enlightened guru or teacher, a person's subtle body can be transformed.

These practices cause the life energy to revolve upward and downward around the six spinal chakras of the astral body: the cocygeal, sacral, lumbar, dorsal, cervical and medullary plexuses. Due to polarity, these resolve into twelve inner constellations revolving round the inner spiritual sun in the heart, and are interrelated to the physical sun and the twelve constellations of the zodiac.

When the life force permanently resides in the heart chakra, the initiate has realised the state of Cosmic Consciousness. This point in spiritual evolution corresponds with the time of the second birth in the Mystery Religions. It took place at midday because that was seen as the culmination of the physical sun.

The full perfection of the human state took place when the full psychic integration of the mind and senses had been realised. This is when the life force resides in the chakra corresponding with the third eye. This is sometimes referred to by Maharishi as refined Cosmic Consciousness, and corresponds to what we know as God Consciousness. It is also identical with Elizabeth Haitch's definition of prophet.

Finally, the third birth takes place at a point of illumination, when the cosmic energy stored up in the crown of the head blossoms into the 'thousand-petalled lotus' and opens the doorway of the infinite possibilities open to the fully realised individual. This is synonymous with the fulfilment of evolution – the reintegration of the individual with the primordial state. It marks the transition from the solar to the polar phase of life and is identical to Unity Consciousness.

According to Maharishi, once God Consciousness has been achieved, the transition to Unity Consciousness is automatic. Thus, in the case of *Cinderella*, probably the most well known of all folk tales, the prince comes to find her, signifying that no further effort is required on her part to achieve Unity or marriage with the divinity.

One of the main assumptions I have made in this study of fairy tales is that the three ball gowns worn by heroines, like Cinderella, symbolise the end of the three phase transitions, or spiritual births of the Mystery Religions, which are synonymous with Cosmic Consciousness, God

Consciousness and Unity Consciousness.

I think we have to take it that this first dress was symbolic of Cosmic Consciousness -- when the full development of the mind is achieved. The two later dresses were not explicitly described in actual materials, only in superlatives of supreme breathtaking beauty, so we must assume that these related to the even higher states of God Consciousness and Unity Consciousness.

It was a silver and gold dress accompanied by a pair of dancing slippers embroidered with silk and silver. Gold was a metal symbolising divine perfection because of its lustrous beauty, its resistance to rust and its malleability. Consequently it was the goal of the Great Work and thus enshrined many symbolic qualities of human refinement including spiritual enlightenment, harmony, wisdom and love. Similarly, silver was associated with refinement, purification of the soul, chastity and eloquence. It is known that Janus was the god of initiation into the mysteries. He was depicted as carrying two keys with him -- one of silver for the Lesser Mysteries and one of gold for the Greater Mysteries.

Whilst the secret ceremonies of the Mystery Religions are all but hidden from us, Aristotle gives us an illuminating insight, which links the initiates with modern saints. He says that although an initiate was greatly affected and changed forever there was nothing intellectual about it. It was not just his mind but his whole being.

Initiates into the Mysteries took part in three rituals when they were sufficiently purified. They were called: *legomena*, which meant 'things recited'; *deiknymena*, 'things shown'; and *dromena*, 'things performed'. The deiknymena was experienced in a sanctuary full of visual images, including many great holy works of art.

I can personally testify that the same three things still happen today in a spontaneous and natural manner. I was on my first trip to India in 2001, when I visited the Hanuman Temple in Allahabad. The main temple has three altars, each with one of the aspects of the deity. The main centre altar is dedicated to Hanuman, the monkey god. To the left of this was one dedicated to Lord Ram and Sita. On the right of the Hanuman altar was one I did not recognise. For some reason I lingered at the second shrine and became separated from the rest of the group. They were already listening to the tour leader's discourse about the deity in the third altar.

I walked towards where the group was gathered and looked at the image even though I was some distance away – that was enough! My heart was filled with love for her and I prostrated myself on the floor in reverence. Simultaneously, as my heart filled with love, I spontaneously chanted a stream of Sanskrit verses even though I had no conscious knowledge of Sanskrit. I learned afterwards that it was an image of the goddess Durga.

I had never prostrated myself before, and was amazed how proficient I was in the etiquette of worshipping. It seemed to go all by itself with my intellect sidelined as a mere observer. My behaviour seemed both natural and instinctive. It was as if a part of me knew exactly what to do on those occasions.

The same instinctive or inner knowingness gently informed my awareness that I could not leave and would be there for some time. I would have to go outside and tell the group leader to go on without me. That Hanuman Temple is very large and goes back a long way. I knew it would be disrespectful to turn my back on the goddess, so I walked backwards all the way to the doors, relayed my message and went back to her.

In retrospect, it seems that my experience exactly matches an authorative account of one of the main initiations. First came the seeing – the deiknymena. Simultaneously, the recitation (legomena) began whilst I was performing the spontaneous acts of worship – the (dromena). Today we would call it a *darshan*, when one is completely transformed by a look from an enlightened person or a divine being.

Any written account would lead us to believe these three aspects to be separate and sequential because this is a feature of the written word, whereas in an intuition every aspect of its detail is perceived as a unity or wholeness. There is no sequence – they happen at the same time.

Unlike the experience I had in Regent's Park, which came and went like a wake-up call, these three aspects have remained. I am still full of love for Durga every time I look at my image of her. I still recite Sanskrit verses, both learned and spontaneously, and I still worship her every day with a puja.

However, there is no outward sign that I have changed in any way. I don't think I look any different. I still work, cut the lawn, take the dog for a walk, drive a car etc. The main change is on the inside and has affected the way I think and feel about many things. I don't know anybody else with whom to compare experiences, though I am sure that some readers will think I had that kind of experience because my head was full of Mystery Religions and suchlike. They would be wrong though because that experience took place in February 2001. At that time I knew nothing about Mystery Religions. It has taken over four years for the penny to drop before I could see a parallel.

Aristotle was right to say no traditional learning takes place. In fact, the intellect takes a back seat in that situation. It largely remains in that back seat because the experience was so all-embracing that there is no element of doubt to ponder over.

---

[1] Yogananda, 1972

# Chapter 6
# The Yoga Sutras

It is well known that folk tales contain abundant supernormal feats. In them we step into a world in which people can fly through the air, perform magical feats, or become invisible by putting on a cape of invisibility. Others have the ability to understand the language of birds and animals, display tremendous strength, and even to easily be comfortable in violently extreme ranges of temperature.

This, however, is the world of the fairy tale. They just aren't true. These things can't happen in the real world of the twenty-first century – or can they?

There was a period in my life when I would have heartily agreed with these sentiments. That was before I learned the TM Sidhis. After learning these techniques one has a different perspective on these things. All inventions, such as aeroplanes, cars, telephones, television, computers etc., would have seemed to be equally far fetched and ridiculous not much more than a century ago. Yet now they are part of our everyday life.

It seems more likely that whatever sphere of life the best minds in any civilisation put their attention on they achieve results. Our present wave of civilisation concentrates on the material aspects of life. Hence, we have more material possessions than at any other time in recorded history. Not only this, a lot of our time and effort is centred upon acquiring more of them.

Therefore it must be equally possible for a more spiritually orientated civilisation to place its emphasis upon spiritual development. My own experience can testify that the practice of a particular selection of Sidhis, or supernormal powers, can considerably speed one's spiritual development. However, we are not talking about possibilities here, we are talking about facts. Whilst it is true that you can't buy them readily packaged from your nearest local convenience store, they did exist in the past, they still exist in the present and they work well.

The most well-known interpretation and organisation of the theory and practice for self-development is called the *Yoga Sutras*. It comes from a long-established oral tradition of spiritual masters, which was reorganised in the third century before Christ by Maharishi Patanjali. It is a work in four chapters. The first two deal mainly with identifying the goal of life and the impediments preventing an individual from achieving unity with the Absolute and the adoption of certain behaviours that enhance it. The third chapter deals with techniques which speed up the process of spiritual evolution – the so-called supernormal powers, and the fourth deals with the achievement of the goal.

The *Yoga Sutras* is a deep and intrinsically fascinating work and requires intensive study in its own right. However, for the needs of this work I will write a thumbnail sketch of it.

Yoga, in its fullest sense, is not just a varied set of postures or asanas. It is the quest to regain our true nature, and consists of specialised techniques, which help us arrive back at the place from whence we all started our journey. The physical exercises prepare the mind and body for the process of meditation. The true meaning of *yoga* is that the mind is yoked to a state of silence and unity with the deepest aspect of itself, which underlies all thoughts and phenomena. All the great spiritual masters of the past and present have emphasised that it is the loss of this real self that underlies the human mind as the source of all suffering in life.

Every culture passes down stories of its own hero such as Christ, Moses, Mohammed and the Buddha. The hero receives the calling to the fullest aspect of life and embarks on a journey that is both difficult and arduous and meets many difficulties on the way and involves many transformations of himself on the journey.

This particular study is not focused on the cultural hero but everyman. Thus, the steps of all our journeys are encoded in story form. Inevitably many 'fairy stories' are allegorical and are concerned with leading the individual in the objective world from a life of wretchedness and suffering to a life of eternal happiness. Each hero begins by being chained to wretchedness and servility by the Wheel of Necessity. He or she then becomes awakened to the deeper spiritual reality. The hero or heroine enters into the service of a master; and, finally, through deeper initiations into higher states of consciousness, attains eternal bliss or happiness.

True happiness comes when the mind has become united with its simplest form of awareness – our true nature – Transcendental Consciousness. Normally our true nature is overshadowed by the activity of the mind. The individual ego, having lost contact with its transcendental roots, wanders lost in the forest of the mind.

The *Yoga Sutras* lists five types of mental activity that may cause an individual to suffer. These are understanding, misunderstanding, imagination, sleep and memory. Normally, in the waking state of consciousness the mind is in an extroverted mode, in that it is always in thrall of whatever is going on in the world. This subservience to the outside world makes the ego think of itself as the author of all its actions and thus denies any great universal process from which all actions arise. In so doing the mind of the individual becomes deluded.

The twin fetters that bind us to ignorance are our attachment to pleasure and our aversion to pain and suffering. They represent the two opposite poles of the mind in that the liking for one thing produces an aversion to something else.

The yoking of the individual mind with the transcendental self can take place through meditation, as is the case with the TM technique, or it can be purified through the breathing techniques inherent in *pranayama*, such as Yogananda taught, and by chanting Sanskrit hymns. In very rare cases an individual may be born with a perfected mind. The mind can also be purified by herbs or by spontaneously experiencing the state of Samadhi, the settled mind.

In the chapter on Transcendence it was mentioned that the individual does not have to do anything more than to open his or her awareness to the transcendental field of life on a regular basis. That experience of the transcendent gives the body and mind great rest and so removes the natural obstacles to Samadhi.

There are nine major obstacles to Samadhi. These are illness, fatigue, doubt, carelessness, laziness, attachment, delusion, the failure to achieve Samadhi and the failure to maintain that state.

The failure to achieve or maintain the state of Samadhi is due to the presence of a legion of impressions lying deep within the mind as latent desires. Like seeds they lay dormant until favourable conditions for their fulfilment present themselves. At that time they come to the surface of the mind and sprout into a desire whose fulfilment requires an action.

Thus, the mind is chained to an eternal wheel of cause and effect, with many of the desires lying latent from a previous lifetime. It is not as though there is anything intrinsically bad in having desires. It is the loss of eternal freedom that is the greatest loss. Maharishi says that a person should have 200 per cent of life. He should both have the contentment of life in eternal freedom and be able to enjoy the fruits of his desires.

Eventually, through the practice of meditation, the mind is brought back to a single focus that is both serene and clear. When the spiritual light dawns the aspirant gains a new kind of knowledge called *ritambhara*, where only the truth is perceived. Ritambhara prevents the accumulation of further latent impressions. This means that new impressions no longer have the ability to remain latent as seeds, which later manifest as desires in the mind.

Purification, refinement and surrender nourish the state of Samadhi and subsequently weaken the causes of suffering. Ignorance is destroyed when the small self of the individual mind or personality is liberated from its identification with the world as it appears to be, and resumes its status as the large 'Self', which the ancient world called the inner genius.

The *Yoga Sutras* stipulate that non-violence, truth, honesty, sensual abstinence and attachment are the five restraints that one should practice in life. In the Western mind restraint is synonymous with making a great effort. Maharishi says that 'control' is an enemy to progress. It would be more accurate to say that these five restraints naturally develop as the refinement of the central nervous system takes place.

As the nervous system evolves, the behaviour becomes more in line with the highest aspects of Natural Law and the five restraints become embedded in the way of life of the individual. Consequently the five necessities for achieving Samadhi also grow. These are simplicity, contentment, purification, refinement and surrender to the Lord.

When the mind is thoroughly infused with Transcendental Consciousness, the light of the intellect dawns. When this happens the mind becomes steady in Samadhi.

One gains the state of Samadhi through meditation or pranayama. This is achieved when the individual's consciousness becomes one with the object of concentration. Even though this state is not permanent it is then possible to practice *sanyama*. Sanyama is more easily described as the ability to entertain a thought or intention whilst the mind is in the transcendent.

I mention this because sanyama is the process that gives the individual complete mastery over psychic powers or mental concentration. These psychic powers are signs of the growth of evolution and are not a means of inflating the ego of the personality involved. A list of these superpowers is as follows:

Knowledge of the past and future
Knowledge of all speech
Knowledge of previous births
How to know another's mind but not its content
Invisibility
Foreknowledge of death and understanding omens
Friendliness
Compassion
Happiness
Strength

Finding things hidden a long way away
Knowledge of the solar system
Knowledge of the positions of the stars
Knowledge of the movements of the stars
Knowledge of the body
The cessation of hunger and thirst
Steadiness
Spiritual vision – the ability to see the perfected ones
Intuitive knowledge
The awareness of consciousness dawns
Knowledge of Purusha
Entering another person's body
Levitation
Divine hearing
Moving through space
The universal state of mind is discovered
Mastery over fire, air, water, earth and space
Attainment of the eight perfections

This last is the highest Sidhi and actually includes most of the others. It enables one to:-

Make oneself small, light or large
Attain anything one desires
Seemingly defy the laws of nature
Bring others under your control
Have perfection in the body
Have complete mastery over the sense organs
Have complete mastery over nature
Attain anything anywhere

The Sidhis or psychic powers can be gained in any of five ways. They can be inherited at birth because the aspirant gained them in a previous lifetime; they can be induced by taking herbs properly prepared by a specially trained guru; mantras; purification; or from spontaneous Samadhi.

In TM it is the mantra that puts the whole of the show on the road. The mind gently follows the inward movement of the mantra to its source. The inward movement of the mind causes the body to receive a very deep kind of rest. The depth of rest allows the body to throw off stresses and malfunctions naturally. The mind is held up on its inward march whilst a stress

49

unwinds and then it proceeds inwards again.

Strictly it is not the changes or interventions that give rise to the perfected Sidhi but the clearing away of stresses or imperfections in the nervous system that allow them to operate unhindered. All minds are created by the ego. Even though the individual mind is lit by the underlying Self it continues to act as though it is separate and self-sufficient. The unenlightened mind is bound fast by the objects of perception. Only the Self is free from the latent impressions which sprout forth like seeds and generate desire for their fulfilment.

An object is experienced only when it colours the mind, but the mind is always experienced because it is witnessed by the unchanging Self. Not being self-luminous, the mind cannot be aware of both itself and the object of perception at the same time. As the earth depends entirely upon the sun for its existence so too the mind is totally dependent upon the underlying Self for its life, form and existence.

When the mind begins to experience the Self as separate from activity, it is naturally drawn towards enlightenment. All thoughts that arise in the mind and so interrupt this discrimination of the Self and non-self are born of the latent impressions which still exist in the mind. It is rather like the clouds in the sky which restrict the uninterrupted view of the sun. If, on a cloudy day, a fresh wind should spring up, soon the sun would be seen in all its glory. Similarly, a mind freed from the interruptions of latent impressions culminates in the finest kind of Samadhi called Enlightenment, which is the state of Unclouded Truth. This finest kind of Samadhi fulfils the aims and objectives of the force of evolution and the transformations of the *gunas*. The gunas, or the three essential aspects of the workings of Nature, are responsible for everything that happens in the universe.

When the three gunas return to their final balance of harmony Enlightenment is gained. The subject is forever established in his own absolute nature – pure unbounded Bliss Consciousness. The gaining of Unity Consciousness is the aim of the process of evolution which drives the whole process of creation. It is the process of desire which upsets the balance of the gunas in the first place. When Enlightenment is achieved by an individual the gunas revert to their original, primordial state of balance.

It is the point at which the allegorical marriage takes place in the folk tale.

# Chapter 7
# The Tale of Many a Tale

Whilst the range and nature of the tales are many and various there are many conventions or symbols within the stories which appear time and time again, and are obviously part of a convention. I thought it would be interesting to look at some of these before attempting any analysis of the tales. However, before setting out on this journey, it is important to remember not to take them too literally. They are in an encoded form and some may have undergone a great many changes since they were copied down for the first time by folklorists.

We need to approach them in the same cautious but open way that ancient Greeks, such as Heraclitus, approached the Delphic oracle. Heraclitus said, 'They are wise with an uncanny ambiguous wisdom, which neither declares nor conceals, but gives a sign.' It is good to keep this in mind, especially bearing in mind the age of many of the stories and the number of changes taking place whilst part of an oral tradition and those subsequently made during their translation into English.

The original meaning of the word 'religion' was to bind back to one's roots or source. In keeping with this, the tradition of the Mystery Religions was always to help the individual seeker regain his true spiritual status and return to the estate he had originally wandered away from.

In fact, the basic template of the folk story, such as *Cinderella*, *Allerleirau* and *Mother Holle*, is the parallel of the life of every initiate. It begins with the individual securely bound to the Wheel of Necessity. Thus, we find the hero or heroine in a state of wretchedness, engaged in some lowly household chore, put upon by both the circumstances of their birth and other people in their environment.

The first glimpse of the dawn, or of life taking a better turn, is the call from the goddess, which takes their mind to the transcendent. The hollow tree in *Allerleirau*; the deep well in both *Mother Holle* and *Iron Hans*; and the sprig of the first branch that knocks the hat (or blinkers) from the intellect were all ciphers for becoming a mystae, and thus being initiated into the highest level of the Mysteries. This initiation took place in February. The new initiates were called the 'newly sown'. It was obviously a technique that gave the seeker the experience of transcendental consciousness on a regular basis. This allowed him the experience of the unchanging field of existence, underlying the ever changing relative phase of existence, thus enabling him to see the basis of life with his eyes closed.

The Mystery Religions saw the human body as the temple of God, and to become one with God involved a life of purification. Initiates dressed in white and ate a strictly vegetarian diet. The purification and the diet is hinted at in *Cinderella*, when the stepmother throws a bowl of lentils into the ashes and tells her she can go to the ball if she separates the lentils from the ashes in a set time.

The mystae would then be faced with a long interval of time in service before they were ready for the second birth – their initiation into the Greater Mysteries one September. This period of time corresponds to the hero or heroine's period of service, to members of the family in the case of *Cinderella*, the King in *Allerleirau* and the fair maiden who served *Mother Holle*.

Following this period of service came the three trials, tests, or transformations, which characterise most fairy stories. As a consequence of the repeated and regular experience of Transcendental Consciousness the 'temple of God' would be purified and the initiate was ready for his 'second birth'.

The second birth into the Greater Mysteries must have been a momentous affair because it corresponds with the realisation of the state of 'enlightenment' or Cosmic Consciousness. Such events were unlikely to take place every September, because the gaining of Cosmic Consciousness is a huge step forward and a massive landmark in everyone's spiritual evolution. It marks the transition from being an 'ordinary person' to one whose every action is totally life-supporting and fulfils the will of God. In addition, the second birth initiate is always aware of his transcendental reality, as well as the familiar field of change he continues to live in. The first court appearance of both Cinderella and Allerleirau highlights the vast contrast between their change from the gross, filthy nature of ignorance in their previous state of existence to the shining, dazzlingly beautiful paragon of all beauty and grace of their enlightened state.

A further refinement takes place as the five senses of the initiate become so purified that it is possible for them to see all the levels of creation from the gross level of everyday life we all see, right down to the Celestial level, where they can directly perceive the devas, gods or angels depending upon the nomenclature of their tradition. This corresponds with the completion of the second task, or the second entrance to the court ball by Cinderella and

Allerleirau in even more stunningly beautiful attire, which is the envy of everyone.

Finally, comes the third birth. This corresponds to the state of Unity Consciousness and marks the transition of the individual from the physical cosmos. The Vedanta says that all of life is really an illusion. There is, in fact, just one reality. Unity Consciousness is the state when every fibre of the person's being becomes united with that underlying field of reality. In *Cinderella* it was her third and most spectacular court appearance; and corresponds to the transformation of the fair maiden by Mother Holle (Demeter), when gold and diamonds fell out of her mouth every time she spoke. This is called the 'sweet talk' of spiritual circles in India and refers to the stream of pure knowledge spoken by enlightened people. As mentioned earlier in the book, gold is always synonymous with God Consciousness.

## Separation from the Source

It will be remembered, that at the source of creation, the Purusha and *Prakriti*, became separated. Thus, at the beginning of many stories the mother of the young hero or heroine was said to have died. The death in question here is not a physical separation caused by mortality but one of awareness.

In the Preface I spoke about the continuing tradition of personifying all the different aspects of an individual's awareness and mentioned Yogananda's version of the Bhavagad Gita and Swami Satyananda Saraswati's book *The Chandi Path*. However, the clearest and best example of this is found in the Tripura Rahasya. Here, an enlightened princess, Hemalekha, is explaining the symbolism of her life story as told to her husband, Hemachuda.

> My mother is *transcendence* – pure Consciousness; my friend is *intellect* – discerning faculty; *ignorance* is Madam Dark, the undesirable friend of the intellect. Her son is the greatest of illusions – the *mind* – his wife is thought or conception or imagination; her sons are five in number, namely *audition, taste, sight, touch* and *smell*, whose mansions are the five senses.[1]

Although her symbolism is not identical to the one used by the Mystery Religions it is near enough to prove that all the stories are allegorical. However, the loss of the mother of all creation – Pure Consciousness – is the same.

According to the Hermetica, in Hinduism and Buddhism the memory of all that has taken place is normally forgotten once a person reincarnates upon the earth. It would be more accurate to say that all previous experiences have become separated from the conscious mind. The death we are talking about here is really one of forgetfulness.

This whole scenario is better resolved by sorting out the so-called Oedipus complex. Common knowledge rather belongs to Freud's misunderstanding of the myth, which is that the son desires to kill his father in order to mate with his mother. In actual fact the real meaning is entirely different. By mother and father we are not speaking about parents, blood relations or anything of that kind. Father, in the sense of the myth, is the mind, the receptacle of desires which causes any individual to take birth in order to fulfil those desires. Mother, in this sense, is the Cosmic Mother – she who rules the entire field of manifest creation in accordance with the will of God. Thus, killing the father, means putting an end to the ego-driven desires of the smaller self, in order to become one with the large Self – which is synonymous with Cosmic Consciousness described in Chapter 4.

In the cases of *Cinderella* and *Allerleirau* the mother was said to have fallen sick and died. Before their death, however, each made a stipulation which remained in the mind of the hearer. The mother of Cinderella impressed upon her daughter to 'always be good and pious and then God will always look after you'; and the mother of Allerleirau said to her father, the king, that he couldn't remarry unless he found any woman as beautiful and pure as she was.

Do you remember Pilot Baba's old word for kundalini – jagadamba? In a state of ignorance we act as if Mother is lost, but when reunited with her everything ends happily ever after.

In *Brother and Sister* and *Three Little Men* the stories suggest that the wife had died and the man had been left on his own. However, the man or father in question is not a separate being as the story seems to imply but the mind of the hero or heroine. It is interesting to remember that the word 'man' is derived from the Sanskrit root *manas*, meaning mind.

In many cases the father marries again. Here again it doesn't mean an actual physical marriage with another person, but that the mind, now extroverted from its non-changing source, has now become wedded to the perceptions of the ever changing relative universe.

The first picture in many Tarot card decks – the Fool – is a good illustration of this. It depicts a good-looking androgynous young person stepping down towards the plains of relative existence. Behind him are the high, pure, snow-capped peaks of the Absolute. He has a naively blithe expression on his face as if he has no idea what is in store for him.

He carries a black rod over his right shoulder with a bag swinging from the end of it by its handles. Inside the bag is the sum total of all his experience in previous lifetimes. His inner dazzlingly white robe of perfect wisdom is almost completely hidden by the outer black cloak of ignorance.

It is a depiction of absolute pure consciousness just prior to becoming encased by a body in the relative world. It precedes the card of the Magician, whose meanings in Hebrew include the sense of personality and 'house'. Thus, the spirit of pure consciousness is about to be encased or housed in the body of a persona.

## The Youngest Child or Simpleton

The hero or heroine is always the youngest son or daughter. They symbolise the spiritualised intellect or buddhi, and clearly represent the most recent faculty; that is why they are referred to as the youngest son or daughter. I don't think we have a modern term for this in the West but Plato used to refer to it as the 'golden thread' or nous. It contained the spiritual life energy which enabled an initiate to ascend the spheres of creation and behold the One. It began with an observation of Nature and then extended to a communication with Nature, which we would call the will of God.

Plato likens our abstract power of reason which binds ideas in a coherent pattern as merely the products of opinion. We can see that he is right because whatever new discovery is made by experts and scientists in modern times has at least two contrasting shades of opinion. The intellectualism of the materialist, whose ideas are not born from the fruit of spiritual experience, cannot possibly understand this. A spiritual experience is beyond words and cannot be conveyed accurately. The words actually seem to form an opaque screen, which ends up obscuring the true nature of the experience.

The buddhi can be envisaged as the newest or most recent manifestation of the atma, the underlying Self of all beings in creation. Being newly manifested it is still unconditioned and pure, whereas the term intellect as we use it is conditioned by all our previous interactions with the world.

Because the buddhi is so near to the atma, or underlying Self, it can be thought of as being like a ray of light newly emerging from the sun – so near that it is almost still part of it. The Dalai Lama says every individual, however weak, poor or deprived their present situation may be, has the seed or potential for achieving perfection. He calls it the 'Buddha Nature'.

Thus, the youngest son or daughter in folk tales is also unconditioned and uncorrupted by the ways of the world. They are always truthful, honest and charitable and go out of their way to help others. Sometimes they are known as simpletons, mainly because the way they interact with fellow life forms in their environment is completely contrary to the ways of the world, as personified by their brothers and sisters. Cinderella, again, is an excellent example of this, as are the youngest brothers in *Queen Bee* and *The Three Feathers*.

They are completely honest and their actions always help and nourish every species in creation. Their behaviour epitomises that of *ahimsa*, or non-violence, advocated in the *Yoga Sutras*. The outcome of the story is always in their favour because they are rewarded for their kindness and thought-fulness by lower creatures in creation.

The heroine in *Mother Holle* is both courteous and sensitive to the sufferings of all aspects of creation, even down to loaves of bread and apples. In much the same way the ducks, three fishes and the ants come to the rescue of the servant in *The White Snake*.

In contrast to their wily, worldly, self-centred older brothers and sisters – our externalised thoughts and desires – their behaviour shows a total submission to Life itself, and because the laws of *karma* are just, they are generously rewarded by fulfilling their greatest wish in life.

The animal, person or thing which points them the right way on their path of fulfilment is always treated disdainfully by their worldly wise brothers and sisters. A good example of this is the fox who befriends the youngest son in *The Golden Bird*.

The term 'youngest child' may have been given because the call to the spirituality in the shape of the Mysteries was the most recent of all the mental and emotional enthusiasms of an individual. I am reminded of the text in the Bible that says 'the last shall be first and the first shall be last'.


## The Older Brothers and Sisters

The older brothers and sisters are also products of the mind. They symbolise the complex web of attractions and aversions of our conditioned minds. As the most externalised aspects of the individual mind, the senses and the surface mind, they are wise in the ways of the world and have thus turned their backs upon spirituality or have no time to pursue it. We recognise them as those ideas which persuade the mind that it is neither sensible or expedient to follow up newly found enthusiasms to improve and to lead a better life. Hence in *The Three Feathers*, *The Golden Bird* and the *Water of Life* the older brothers set off to much more exotic places for their search, whilst the youngest child acts in accord with the simple law, that everything in Nature follows the line of least resistance and always achieves the best outcome.

In the end the elder siblings always receive their just deserts for their selfish and cruel behaviour, such as the ugly, idle daughter of the widow in *Mother Holle*, who was covered in pitch and had toads hopping out of her mouth every time she spoke; whilst the youngest and most innocent always achieves the desired outcome of their spiritual quest.

In a theoretical contest between a university professor and a simpleton, the former would win hands down in any debate about knowledge of any specific subject but in a quest for enlightenment the result may well be very different, because the simpleton would still have intact his sense of awe or wonder and his mind uncluttered by the abstruse conditioning of worldly expectations, opinions and suppositions.

## The Oracular Call to Spirituality

This was the most essential criterion for a person to be admitted into the Greater Mysteries. It didn't matter if the person filled one of the highest positions in the land or was, in fact, a slave. The Greater Mysteries were open to all. Here was one institution which treated everybody equally in the classical past. However, there was one important stipulation. In order to be initiated into the Greater Mysteries one had to receive the call from the goddess herself.

Since the goddess is personified as the dynamic aspect of the Transcendental God, she produced everything in creation. Thus, the call to the Mysteries could take many and various forms. This was certainly reflected in folk tales. The heroine of both *Mother Holle* and *The True Bride* was helped by the goddess in the form of an old woman – the very same form as that adopted by Demeter.

The next most common form of help came in the shape of a little man. This was in fact an allusion to the inner Self – the atma of everybody. Thus, the merchant in *The King of the Golden Mountain* was helped by a mannikin; the soldier in *The Blue Light* by a little man; and the poor woodcutter by a spirit in a bottle.

Divine help often came in the shape of a helpful animal, such as the goat in *One Eye, Two Eyes and Three Eyes*; or the fox in the story of *The Golden Bird*.

## The Initiation

As in life so was it in the story. After the call to a spiritual way of life comes the initiation. The actual initiation took place in caves so it is natural that their folk-tale counterpart follows the same convention. Numerous story initiations take place in a hollow tree, which is an alchemical symbol for the athanor or stove. A good example of this is *Allerleirau*.

There is also another allusion to the dark cave of initiation in this story. Before donning her spectacularly beautiful ball gowns she has to go into her small, dark, windowless room and put them on before making her stunning appearances in court. She kept them inside a nutshell, probably a walnut, because this is the nut most similar to the physical appearance of the brain. The ball gowns were kept in the nutshell because they were always present in a latent form.

The hearth in *Cinderella*, the forbidden room in *Faithful John*, and the bottom of the well that the heroine of *Mother Holle* fell into are all different ciphers for the initiation cave.

## Wells

A well is perhaps the most common meeting place in a small village in an agrarian society, so it is not surprising that wells often figure in the tales themselves. It is also symbolic of the call to the spiritual path. Earlier we looked at water as a cipher of the mind. We found that the surface of the water stood for the most exterior part of the mind, at its interface with the environment. This was seen to be characterised by turbulent peaks and troughs of conflicting desires, alarms, delights and worries. The deeper the water the less turbulence there was. This culminated in a complete state of stillness at the bed of the ocean.

Wells follow the same pattern in that they are another symbol of the mind. A well can be defined as a man-made depression into the earth at the emergence of an underground spring. Here again the surface of the water at the top of the well stands for the surface of the mind, whilst the spring that feeds it is the transcendental source of the mind. It is significant that the fairy story well is often called the 'Well at the World's End', because that is where it is. All creation, even the most subtle aspects of the mind, end in the transcendental field of creation, because it is beyond the sphere of the three gunas, which are responsible for every level of creation.

Hence, a well is the place of entry into the transcendental world in many folk stories. The heroine in *Mother Holle* falls into one and finds herself in a hidden dimension, where she serves the goddess for a just reward. Wells are also one of the ciphers for the Water of Life, which cures all ills. Once again it is the contact with the underlying field of the transcendent that resolves the stresses and therefore cures all ills.

## The Tree of Life

The tree is one of the chief symbols of the World Axis in all traditions. The Seed of Life, the *axis mundi* or Cosmic Tree, is the most ubiquitous of all the symbols of transformation in folk tales. Similar to the mustard seed in the New Testament, it can start from a small seed and grow into a tree so large that all can shelter under its branches.

It is often taken to be the main means of transformation, and in many stories bears the golden apples of immortality (Unity Consciousness) when fully developed. It is often guarded by a snake or dragon. These guardians of the tree are themselves symbolic of the growth of pure consciousness in the form of the kundalini. Like the tree itself, they rise up slowly awakening the individual from his sleep of forgetfulness. Each advance up the spine, or trunk of the tree, reveals a newer and brighter world of greater possibilities for both the individual initiate and the hero or heroine.

The sprig or small branch that Cinderella's father brought home, which she nurtured three times a day with devotions to her mother, is a good example of this. Other examples are *The Juniper Tree*, the Tree of Life in *The White Snake* and the tree which bears the golden apples of immortality in *The Water of Life*.

## The Three Birds

I have noticed that after the third major task or transformation, or ritual death, three birds often make an appearance. There was a symbolic convention in all the major religions to symbolise birds as angels. Thus when a person had become sufficiently transformed by spiritual practices he or she was blessed with the 'language of the birds'. This takes place when a person has become sufficiently reintegrated with his or her source as to establish contact with higher beings, normally referred to as angels or *devatas*. It is this communication which is called the language of the birds. A quote from the Qur'an reads.

And Solomon was David's heir. And he said, O mankind! Lo we

have been taught the language of the birds and have been given abundance of all things.

This abundance also extends to Cinderella, when the bird on the top of her Tree of Life bestows ball gowns of increasingly higher states of consciousness.

In this case abundance is not necessarily material wealth but the wealth asked for by the worshipper when reciting the Gayatri mantra, namely the wealth of gods. This means not only their love, their knowledge and power but also possessing them as part of his or her being in order to fulfil all desires.

The language of the angels is rhythmic poetry. The best examples of this are the mantras of the Veda. Maharishi tells us that Sanskrit is such a refined language that the sound and the form are inextricably linked. Thus a pandit chanting a hymn to a particular deity temporarily becomes united with the object of his worship for the duration of the hymn. Perhaps the Ancient Egyptian language was similarly so refined that it could not be translated adequately into Greek.

The other thing to remember is that angels are responsible for the efficient administration of the universe in accordance with the will of God, so they never make mistakes.

The three stories I am covering use this convention. They are *Cinderella, Faithful John* and *Snow White*.

In *Cinderella* they are the three pigeons, who point out to the prince that each of the ugly sisters he is leading away is not the true owner of the slipper. One of the sisters has cut off a toe in order to make the shoe fit, and the other has cut part of her heel off. The pigeons point out the trail of blood and encourage the prince to find the real owner of the slipper. It is as if to say that it is not the physical or the astral sheath that you want – it is the causal body.

In *Faithful John* the three birds are ravens. They are oracular birds. As Faithful John is able to understand the language of birds, he is able to act upon their prediction, and so both save the king from making three dreadful mistakes and also help bring about his transformation into the Mystery Religion equivalent of higher states of consciousness culminating in God Consciousness.

In *Snow White* three birds come: an owl, a raven and a dove visit her when she lies in the glass or crystal coffin. This makes the whole thing a lot clearer. Although the owl was sacred to both Athena and Demeter, in general both owls and ravens were widely regarded as birds of ill omen. However, the dove is frequently symbolic of the soul. In Christianity it symbolised the holy spirit and in the old world religions it was universally sacred to the Mother Goddess or Queen of Heaven. The Slavs depicted the soul as flying from the mouth of the dead person, in the shape of a dove, to the 'street of birds' as they called the Milky Way.

## The Quality of the Stories

The form and content of the stories follow the pattern of life for all human beings according to the Hermetica. This says that, although our personalities are dictated by the degree of involvement of the gods at the time of our birth, the whole process is overseen by the goddess, who oversees the entire process of the Wheel of Necessity.

Thus, she, like the Mother Goddess of the Indian philosophy of the Tantra, is both the original facilitator of the state of delusion in which we find ourselves, and also the means of escape from our state of predicament. Consequently the stories have the entrancing and engaging quality of making the hearer or reader suspend the sharpness of their wits in order to be enfolded into the warp and weft of their design and plot, just as the individual is overcome by the delusion of *maya* when he or she incarnates.

Each of the stories incorporates the journey to enlightenment of everyman from the time of birth to the third and final initiation out of the cosmos. Consequently each tale is a mnemonic of the birth by the individual into debilitating circumstances of physical birth; the call to a spiritual life by the goddess or Mother Divine; the path through the progressively higher states of consciousness via the three different initiations, often including some of the tenets of Patanjali's *Yoga Sutras*. They all end with the complete transformation of the hero back to his or her initial divine state. Thus, any of the tales related by one of the storytellers of the time would remind the initiate of his ultimate quest in life and inspire him to pursue it wholeheartedly to its ultimate goal.

## The Marriage

Marriage in the so-called fairy stories is the symbol of completion. It is the end of suffering and strife and the advent to unending happiness, which is the eventual goal of all life. Somewhere locked away in all of us is a secret closet which opens whenever we become identified with the hero or heroine in a book, play or film. We suspend all the difficulties that marriage brings and will everlasting happiness to the couple. However, that superlative state of happiness is only a certainty when the female aspect of the individual – the *Shakti* – has climbed the ladder of the chakras to unite with her male counterpart Shiva.

Christianity itself began life as a Mystery Religion. The Eucharist of modern Christianity follows closely in the footsteps of the rituals of Eleusis where the goddess symbolised bread and the god-man wine.

The early Christians knew the extroverted fallen personality as Sophia and the spiritually regenerated psyche as the Virgin Mary. Mary Magdalene is a clear example of this – she enters the gospels as a prostitute and ends up as the apostle to the apostles. In the Last Supper Mary Magdalene is clearly portrayed in the Gospel of John as Christ's beloved disciple with her head resting in his lap. This isn't the conventional interpretation, but it is a common one for students of the Mysteries. According to Luke, Mary Magdalene wiped Jesus's feet with her hair, which would be a great impropriety according to orthodox Jewish tradition, which only allows a husband to see his wife with her hair unbound.

However, we are talking about the Mystical Marriage between a purified devotee united to Pure Consciousness and not a physical husband and wife relationship.

In the Indian scriptures the story and quest of life of every embodied psyche begins in the muladhara chakra where it goes through a long cycle of purification and finally unites with the *Sahasram* – or put more simply Shakti becomes one with Shiva. The tales of both *Cinderella* and *Allerleirau* echo this tradition.

The Great Work in alchemy follows the same principle as the rise of the kundalini: the substance in a hermetically sealed alembic, it is heated and goes through six levels of transformation before the process is complete. The gold is then refined to living gold which vibrates at the same rate as an individual and completely rejuvenates him and transforms him into a god-man in Unity Consciousness, just as Hermes predicted.

In Vedic alchemy the main ingredients were mercury and sulphur. The mercury was given a female gender and the sulphur was designated male. Unpurified mercury is toxic, of course, but after it had been mixed with sulphur and distilled through the secret processes a number of times it became the ultimate elixir.

The purpose of the alchemical processes was to liberate the subtle life force from the gross substance and then feed it back to it again. Each time it was fed back the gross substance became more and more purified. This process was termed *Ouroboros* – the self-consuming serpent.

The final substance was so potent that one did not need to consume it – just being in its vicinity was enough to transmute a physical body into a state of perfect health and ultimate spiritual attainment. Thus it was called the semen of Shiva.

## The Style of the Stories

I am very much taken with Santillana and Dechend's viewpoint that, 'mythical terminology can be handed down independently of the degree of insight of the actual storytellers'[2]. Also their concept of a 'guiding hand' from a remote, distant past, reaching back at least eight thousand years, gently pushing us in the right direction.

I had something of the same experience when writing a shorter version of the folk tales we are going to study. I found myself trying to ginger up the dialogue because it seemed a little flat. As I continued it struck me more and more that this contrasted with the original style of the stories. I paused to think a little more about the style aspect of the stories. Very soon I was won over, because I became sure they were intended to be that way.

At a first glance the style of the narrative is flat and uninteresting. This is in stark contrast with modern storytelling in the form of plays, books and films. In order to quickly engage the attention of a modern reader or viewer, the plight of the hero or heroine is highly dramatised through the technique of vicarious identification. In other words, the reader/spectator/viewer is manipulated so as to form a very strong sense of identification with the hero and an equally strong aversion to the villain.

The folk-tale template is completely different. There is no promotion of the hero's character and certainly no attempt to get the listener or reader to form a bond of identification. The charm of folk tales lays in their contrast to everyday life.

I suddenly realised that identification would divert the mind of the listener from the main purpose of the story, which was to convey a sequence of events in a uniquely stylised way. The intention of the author was to encode the sequential unfolding of the higher states of consciousness leading from the initial revelation from the inner Self, through the different initiations into the Mysteries to the ultimate initiation into Unity Consciousness.

It would have been anathema to the ancient masters of wisdom to have to resort to identification because it was the antithesis of what they wanted to achieve. Identification is ego-driven. As we learned from Persephone in the Demeter myth, and more recently from the work of Joseph Campbell, it is the ego and its rampant desires that created our sorry position in the first place. It takes a one hundred and eighty degree turn away from the externalised ego in order to begin to substitute the fleeting happiness interspersed with worry, disease and suffering for a permanent state of bliss.

In a sentence, the style of the stories was kept deliberately flat and lacking in identification and drama because the original premise of the Mystery Religions was to inform or remind the initiate of the sequential steps of the teaching. I think Santillana and Dechend were right – I could definitely feel the hand of Thoth/Hermes putting me back on the right track when I began to stray.

---

[1] Saraswati, 2002, 49, verse 26
[2] Santillana & Dechend, 1977

# Chapter 8
# Résumé

This part of the book opens with two simple allegories, called *Lucky Hans* and *The Fisherman and His Wife*. These have no need of a detailed ongoing analysis, just a brief interpretation and summary at the end.

In many fairy stories, such as *Cinderella*, the hero or heroine is cast in a debilitated form performing some lowly chore, such as kitchen maid, goose girl or stable lad. Sometimes it is implied that he or she has forgotten their true estate. The sequence of the story is the regaining of this true estate or birthright.

In the case of *Lucky Hans* it is the story of a man who releases himself by stages from the bondage of his attractions and aversions. According to Bayley, 'Hans' means 'ever existent great light'[1]. This fits the bill nicely. In order to uncover this elevated state the seeker in question has to divest himself of many skins of the onion of ignorance or materiality. Each part of the story stems from his pleasure in attaining the next goal and the unexpected aversion which subsequently arises.

The convention I have adopted throughout this book is to retell the outline of the story briefly in indent and then write a commentary about it.

*Cinderella* is the most well known of all folk tales, and *Allerleirau* is a more complex form of the same story. Following *Cinderella* are *How Six Men Got on in the World* and *The Six Servants*. Both are very interesting examples of the personification of supernormal powers, called Sidhis by Patanjali in his *Yoga Sutras*. Thus, the techniques or sutras which the initiates received were encoded in story form as if they were people.

Finally, I would like to deal with four stories in which some kind of alchemical transformation is involved. The most well-known stories are *Beauty and the Beast* and *The Frog Prince*. The four stories I have chosen to illustrate this are *Iron Hans*, *The Golden Bird*, *Faithful John* and *Snow White*.

---

[1] Bayley, 1996, vol. 1, 329

# Part II
# The Stories

# Chapter 9
# Lucky Hans

Hans had served his master well throughout the seven years of his apprenticeship. When the time was up he asked his master for his wages so that he could take them home to his mother.

His master showed his appreciation for the service the lad had given him and gave Hans a piece of gold as large as his head. Hans was delighted by his master's generosity. He wrapped up the huge nugget of gold in a handkerchief, put it on his shoulder and set off with a good heart towards his mother's house. However, the further he went the more uncomfortable he became. The weight of the gold dug into his shoulder and walking with his head on one side made his neck ache.

Suddenly he saw a man on horseback. He envied the man. How nice it would be to be sitting up high in the saddle, with the horse doing all of the work. He hailed the man and bade him good day. They fell into conversation and before long had struck a deal. Hans would exchange his lump of gold for the horse.

Hans was delighted as he sat upon the horse and rode along bold and free. After a while he thought it would be better to make the horse go a little faster so he clicked his tongue and said, 'Hup! Hup!' The horse adopted a sharp trot and before long Hans was thrown off and found himself lying in a ditch. The horse would have galloped off if a countryman leading a cow hadn't got hold of the reins.

Hans fell into conversation with the countryman. The thought of having a docile cow to lead and a constant supply of fresh milk, cheese and butter every day seemed very agreeable to Hans. Before long he had swapped his horse for the cow.

In the heat of the day when he was making for his mother's village Hans was feeling very thirsty. He fancied a nice long drink of fresh milk. He tried milking the cow but no milk came. Hans was no expert in this matter and set to work in a very clumsy way. When the cow couldn't stand it any longer it gave Hans such a blow on the head with his hoof that he was knocked senseless for a time.

When he came to he saw a butcher wheeling a wheelbarrow along the road with a young pig strapped in it. The butcher helped Hans up and gave him a drink from his flask to revive him and gave the cow the once-over with his eye.

'That cow won't give you any milk,' muttered the butcher. 'She's too old. She's only fit for the plough or the knife.'

'I don't care for beef,' thought Hans. 'It's not juicy enough for me. But pork, that's a different story. And then there are the sausages.' He mused.

'I'll tell you what – I'll do you a favour,' said the butcher. 'I will do you a straight swap – the pig for the cow.'

'Let the heavens repay you for your kindness,' exploded Hans in gratitude. Soon the pig was untied from the barrow and exchanged for the cow and the butcher went on his way.

Hans was feeling very happy with himself. He was walking along the road leading the pig feeling as if everything was alright with the world. Presently, a young boy carrying a large white goose joined him. Hans told the boy about his string of good fortune.

'I'm just taking this goose to a christening feast! You try to lift her,' exclaimed the boy. 'She's been fattened up for the last eight weeks.'

Hans took the goose in his arms. 'She is a good weight but then so is my pig,' replied Hans.

The boy looked knowingly. 'There may be a problem with that pig,' he said. 'The Mayor of the last village I passed through has had one stolen. He's sent out a couple of his men to track the culprit down.'

Hans was terrified by the thought of being locked up in a dark cell.

'Will you swap your goose for my pig?' he pleaded. 'You know this area so much better than I do.'

'Okay!' said the lad. 'I don't want to be the cause of you getting into trouble. We'll swap!' With that he took hold of the cord and drove the pig quickly along another road while Hans, free from care, walked home towards his mother's village with the goose under his arm.

As he was passing through the last village he met a grinder who sharpened scissors and knives. He was working at his barrow. The grinder seemed very happy and sang as he worked.

'You sound happy,' said Hans.

'And so I should be,' answered the scissors grinder. 'A grinder is the best thing to be. I've always got money in my pocket. You don't need much to be one – just a grindstone. I've got a partly worn one here. I'll swap it for your goose.'

'You are so kind,' chuckled Hans, thinking how nice it would be to feel some money jangling in his pocket, and handed him the goose.

Sharp by trade and sharp by nature was the scissors grinder. He spotted a large, heavy stone nearby. He picked it up and gave it to Hans.

'Here's a nice strong stone you can hammer upon and straighten your old nails on. Take it with you and look after it carefully.'

Hans picked up the stone and walked towards his home with a contented heart. He thought he must have been born under a lucky star because everything was going so well for him.

As he walked on the stone felt heavier and heavier. He had been on his legs since daybreak and he had to stop for frequent rests. He couldn't help thinking what a burden the stone was and how nice it would be not to have to carry it.

Suddenly, he spied a well and was looking forward to a long cool drink of water. As he stooped to get some water one of his hands dislodged the stone and it fell headlong down into the well. He watched it sink to the bottom and thanked God for having shown him this favour, without any need to reproach himself.

He had now lost the only thing that troubled him. With a light and carefree heart he ran on until he reached his mother's house.

*Lucky Hans* is an example of the archetypal simpleton. On the face of it Hans is every con-man's dream. This is not a tale like *Cinderella*, in which he would start off with an old worn grindstone and end up with a large nugget of gold. Echoing the Bible story that states that it is more difficult for a rich man to attain the kingdom of heaven than a camel to get through the eye of a needle, Hans divests himself bit-by-bit of the obstacles which bar him from being united with his mother, Unity Consciousness.

It is interesting that the story throws up the unforeseen aversions, which arise from fulfilling his desires. The gold digs into his shoulder and makes his neck ache; the horse throws him; the cow was too old to be milked; the pig may have belonged to someone else; the goose apparently caused him no real problems; and the grindstones were too heavy for him. It is stated in the *Yoga Sutras* that it is the aversions that are most difficult to get rid of.

It could be said that this tale is a tongue-in-cheek account of an idiot but this is not so. At every step of the way we see a picture of a lad with an innocent heart and mind who was filled with the belief that God is present in all aspects of life and will make everything come right. The extent of his joy at each step of the unburdening is ecstatic, real and natural.

The title is significant. Why was Hans lucky? He was lucky because he fully co-operated with the natural, sequential unfolding of everything that came his way in life. What we call 'luck' is being in tune with the hidden hand behind all life – Natural Law. A person attuned to the highest aspects of Natural Law can expect Nature to support all of his actions. By divesting himself of all his attractions and aversions the initiate is rewarded at all his steps by the goddess herself. It is the individual ego that causes the mind and intellect to be wedded to the external world of the senses. As the mind transcends and becomes attuned more and more to its primordial reality, happiness naturally increases. Finally, when all the latent desires in the mind are burned up in seed form by the tapas of spiritual endeavour, the initiate recovers his own eternal sense of well being. From then on he lives in a state of unity with God that Maharishi calls Unity Consciousness and Elizabeth Haitch calls god-man.

The last paragraph sums up a heartfelt surge of joy that we will all experience one day: 'There is no man under the sun so fortunate as I,' he cried out. With a light heart and free from burden he now ran on until he was with his mother at home.

# Chapter 10
# The Fisherman and His Wife

We have heard a lot about how important it is for the mind to be content and innocent and not to crave for flashy spiritual experiences or the material trappings of luxury and power. This story is about a person whose mind was not established in Samadhi and who allowed himself to be dragged down into the mire after a very good start. The allegorical story runs as follows.

> Once upon a time there lived a fisherman and his wife. They lived in a pigsty near to the sea. Every morning the fisherman set off with his rod and sat by the sea and fished.
>
> One day he was sitting and looking at the clear water when suddenly his float went down very deep under the water. It was a struggle to pull it up again. He realised that he had a large bite. After managing to draw it up, he found he had a flounder on the end of his line. No sooner than he had drawn it up out of the water, than the flounder spoke to him.
>
> 'Don't kill me fisherman!' it pleaded. 'I am not good to eat. I'm not really a flounder – I'm really an enchanted prince.'
>
> 'Don't worry, flounder,' answered the fisherman. 'What would I do with a talking fish?'
>
> With that he put the flounder back into the water. The flounder dived straight back to the bottom of the sea and the fisherman went home.

One day an angler of the mind was sitting in meditation. The sea, symbolising the state of his mind, was clear, calm and serene. His mind went deep into the transcendent. He had had a spiritual experience. The deepest part of his intellect, or buddhi, had a glimpse of his true nature at the very source of the mind. In allegorical terms this was in the shape of a flounder – a flat fish living on the very floor of the ocean.

There are other stories in the same vein as this. It recalls the Celtic

73

Salmon of All Knowledge and the first incarnation of the Hindu god, Vishnu. The flounder said that he was really an enchanted prince – or in other words the true nature of the seeker – his inner genius. Incidentally the true self of the hero or heroine in most folk tales is an aspect of royalty, probably to signify an exalted state of mind – a parallel to an exalted person in the relative world.

The mind of the seeker was innocent and contented – he wanted nothing and expected nothing. He had contacted that very deep area of the mind called *ritam* where all desires can be fulfilled.

However, it is possible for the mind to fathom ritam without being permanently established in Samadhi. In such a circumstance it is possible for the seeker to become a truly spiritual person or revert to his normal materialist frame of mind and thus undo all the progress he or she has made.

When the buddhi or intellect is weak and doesn't know the true value of things then one can easily be overwhelmed by the material trappings of power and prestige. It is best to have the mind calm, content and settled like the fisherman at the outset of this tale.

> 'Didn't you catch anything today?' asked his wife, seeing that he carried nothing but his fishing rod.
>
> 'I certainly did,' he replied perkily. 'I caught a flounder in the shape of an enchanted prince. He pleaded with me not to kill him so I let him go.'
>
> 'An enchanted prince, eh,' mused his wife. 'Didn't you think of asking him to grant you a wish?'
>
> 'No!' answered the fisherman. 'What would I want with a wish?'
>
> 'Just open your eyes and look around you,' scolded his wife. 'We live in a disgusting little pigsty. You could at least have asked him for a little hut. Go back and call out to him. You saved his life. He won't begrudge you a wish.'
>
> The fisherman didn't like asking anyone for favours but neither did he want a long-running argument with his wife. So for the sake of a quiet life he went back to the sea.

His wife represents his normal everyday state of consciousness. Although the mind of the seeker was serene and contented in meditation this was not his true state permanently. His mind was not established in pure consciousness. His ego or the acquisitive nature of the more superficial area of the mind, symbolised by his wife, was still fully awake.

When he got there the sea looked green and yellow. It had lost its tranquil clarity. He stood on the shore and called out to the flounder. The flounder heard him and swam up to him.

'What can I do for you?' he asked.

'My wife said I ought to have asked you for a wish,' he replied.

'And what did she say you should wish for?' quizzed the flounder.

'We live in a little pigsty,' complained the fisherman. 'She would like a little hut with a kitchen garden and a separate piece of fenced land for the poultry.'

'Your wish is already granted,' answered the flounder and dived back to the depths of the ocean floor.

When the man got home his wife was sitting on a bench outside the door of the hut waiting for him. She showed him round their new home with a pretty parlour, bedroom, kitchen and pantry.

'Isn't that a lot better?' she asked.

'It certainly is,' he replied. 'We'll be content here.'

'We'll see about that!' exclaimed his wife darkly.

The trouble with greed is that is never satisfied. Once the object of desire has been attained the ego becomes more ambitious and identifies itself with larger and grander acquisitions. In contrast with the clearness and calmness of the water, symbolising the state of the fisherman's mind in meditation, this time it turned green and yellow and was no longer smooth.

They lived contentedly in their little hut for a few weeks. After that the wife started to become discontented.

'This hut is far too small for us,' she complained. 'The flounder should have given us something much more suited to our needs – something larger. A stone castle would have been much more practical.'

'This hut is fine for us,' retorted the fisherman. 'What do we want a castle for?'

But his wife's mind was made up.

'You go back and tell him we want a stone castle.'

The fisherman knew it was not right. He wrestled against the idea but his wife was adamant.

'He'll be happy to do it for you,' she cajoled. 'Just go to him. One good turn deserves another.'

When he reached the shore, the colour of the sea had changed. It was still quiet but it had become a thick, dark mixture of purple, dark blue and grey. As before he called out to the flounder.

'Well what does she want now?' he enquired.

'She says the hut is not good enough,' trembled the fisherman in embarrassment. 'She wants to live in a large stone castle now.'

'Go back home now,' soothed the flounder. 'You wife is waiting at the door for you.'

The fisherman sighed and plodded off in the direction of his hut. Imagine his surprise to see his wife standing, waiting at the foot of a flight of stone stairs leading up to the doorway of a magnificent castle. She took him by the hand and showed him round the spacious castle filled with the most expensive, luxurious furniture. In addition to this they had extensive land and shelter for cows and horses and a most magnificent garden with the most beautiful flowers and fruit trees. In fact, it was a home as good as could possibly be desired by anyone.

Even his wife was satisfied initially. 'Isn't it beautiful?' she crooned.

'It certainly is,' replied the fisherman, still awe-stricken with his change of situation. 'We'll let it rest there. We can be content in this beautiful castle for the rest of our lives.'

'That remains to be seen,' mused his wife thoughtfully.

'We will sleep on it and see how we feel later.' Thereupon they went to bed.

In the morning the wife awoke and got out of bed and surveyed the vast acreage of their estate. The husband was just waking up. She poked him in the ribs with her elbow. 'Just look at all that land!' she whooped ecstatically. 'With an estate as large as this we could be king and queen.'

'What do you mean, king and queen?' he exclaimed in surprise. 'I don't want to be a king.'

'Well I want to be queen!' snapped his wife. 'If you don't want to be king that's your decision. But I certainly do. Just you go back to the flounder and tell him.'

'I can't!' moaned the man. 'It's just not right. The flounder has been good to us. He has set us up for life in this beautiful castle.'

But his wife's mind was made up. She could not be persuaded. Being content, wasn't part of her mental set, so with a heavy heart the fisherman trudged back to the seashore. He didn't want to go but he went all the same.

When he got to the shore, he couldn't help noticing the sea. It had taken on a dark grey hue. The waters heaved up from below and smelled putrid. Full of trepidation, he called out to the flounder once more.

'And what does she want this time?' asked the flounder.

'Unfortunately she wants to be queen,' the fisherman muttered apologetically.

'Go and tell her she is already queen,' he replied brusquely, and quickly dived beneath the heaving grey water of the sea.

When he got home this time the castle was much larger and it was guarded by a number of soldiers. A band of soldiers greeted him with kettle drums and trumpets. Everything inside the castle was made of pure marble and gold. As he walked towards a huge pair of double doors, two guards stood to attention and opened them for him. Once inside the court room he saw his wife, sitting on a large throne, studded with gold and diamonds. She was wearing a great golden crown on her head and was holding a sceptre made out of pure gold and studded with diamonds.

The fisherman looked at her with some amazement. 'So you are finally a queen?'

'I certainly am,' she retorted haughtily.

'Well, just be satisfied with what you've got,' he smiled. 'Now there is nothing else to wish for. We can live in contentment for the rest of our lives.'

'Well, that is where you are wrong!' she upbraided him. 'I find the time passes very slowly. I cannot bear it any longer. I want to be emperor. Go to the flounder and arrange it for me.'

'But the flounder can't arrange that for you,' he spluttered with astonishment. 'We already have an emperor in the land. You are already a queen.'

'And you are only my husband,' snorted his wife. 'Go back and tell the flounder that I want to be the emperor.'

The fisherman went off with his tail between his legs. He was troubled in his mind. 'Where will it all end?' he sighed to himself. 'I feel in my bones that something is going to go hopelessly wrong.'

As he reached the sea he saw it looked very black and thick and seemed to be boiling up from below. The fisherman was afraid as he stood at the water's edge and called out to the flounder.

'What does she want now?' asked the flounder.

'Alas!' stammered the fisherman shamefacedly. 'She wants to be the emperor.'

'Go back to her,' replied the flounder in a business-like tone.

'She is one already.'

When he arrived back the whole castle had been transformed. It was made of polished marble, decorated with alabaster figures and gold ornaments. Not only were there lots of soldiers marching up and down and the like, but also high barons, dukes and earls acting as servants.

They opened the doors to him. They were made of solid gold. As soon as he entered inside he saw his wife sitting on a golden throne two miles high. She was wearing a golden crown, about three yards wide, which was set with diamonds and carbuncles. In one hand she still carried the sceptre and in the other, the imperial orb. On either side of her she had a retinue of yeoman arranged in tiers according to height. The husband stood amongst them.

'Wife, so now you are the emperor.'

'Indeed I am,' she retorted curtly.

He stood and looked at her for some time before saying: 'Now you are the emperor -- be content.'

'How can I be content?' she ranted audaciously. 'I have still some way to go before I get to the top. I not only want to remain as emperor, I also want to be the Pope as well. Go to the flounder immediately.'

The fisherman was shocked. His wife's ambitions were surely out of control. 'But we already have a Pope,' he interrupted. 'There can only be one Pope in Christendom. There must be some limit on what the flounder can grant you.'

'Who do you think you are?' scolded his wife. 'You are only my husband. Now get yourself off and go and see the flounder again. If he can make me an emperor he can certainly make me the Pope.'

The fisherman couldn't stand up to his wife and made his way back to the seashore. He felt faint. He had developed nervous twitches and his legs and knees felt weak and trembling.

A strong wind had blown up and clouds raced across the sky. As the evening darkened, leaves were plucked from the trees by the cruel fingers of the wind. The waves rose up and roared like giants before crashing mercilessly upon the shore. Out at sea he saw ships firing their distress cannons as they pitched and tossed like corks on the boiling sea. Some hope remained. The whole sky had not yet been overcome by the raging storm. There was still a small patch of blue.

Full of despair he called out to the flounder again.

'What does she want now?' he enquired.

'She wants to be the Pope as well,' stuttered the fisherman in embarrassment.

'If that's what she wants to be – that is what she is,' pronounced the flounder. 'Go to her, then.'

When he arrived back this time everything had changed again. There appeared to be a very large church surrounded by palaces. Masses of people were thronging everywhere. He had to push his way through the crowds to get anywhere near the church. Once inside he was astounded by the spectacle of his wife sitting upon a huge throne. She was wearing three great big golden crowns and was completely surrounded by ecclesiastical splendour.

The whole place was lit by thousands of candles of all sizes. They ranged from one that was as tall as the tallest tower down to the smallest kitchen candle. Emperors and kings were on their hands and knees, beseeching her and kissing her feet.

Such was her pomp and splendour, the fisherman stood still and looked at her, as though seeing her for the first time.

'So you are now the Pope?' he asked rhetorically.

'I am indeed,' she replied.

'Now be satisfied,' he said quietly. 'You have come so far – you can't be any greater than this.'

Her face became contorted with anguish and her whole body stiffened. 'That remains to be seen.'

When they went to bed the fisherman slept soundly whilst his wife tossed about from side to side wondering what she could be next. However hard she thought, it was all to no avail. The night passed slowly. Little by little the first light of dawn stole into the room. She sat up in bed and saw how beautiful the sky was as the sun rose.

'That is it!' she declared exuberantly. 'I want to be as God is. I want to be able to command the sun and moon to rise.' With no more ado she poked her husband in the ribs with her elbows. 'Wake up you fool,' she commanded. 'Go to the flounder. Tell him I want to be even as God is.'

The poor fisherman was still half asleep. Although his wits were still drowsy with sleep, the words racked through his body like a spasm of severe pain. So great was the shock, the poor fellow's eyes blinked with amazement and he fell out of bed.

'What on earth are you talking about, woman?' he shouted, hoping to bring the silly woman to her senses. 'The flounder certainly can't do that. He has made you both emperor and Pope. He has thus conferred the highest aspects of earthly power upon you but even he can't make you God.'

She ranted and raged. In a fit of violent temper, she totally lost control of herself. Her hair became wildly dishevelled. She tore open her bodice and kicked her husband and shrieked and screamed for all she was worth.

'Go, at once,' she screamed.

The fisherman needed no other invitation. He was so disorientated by his wife's behaviour that he leaped into his trousers and raced out of the door like a madman.

A storm was raging outside. It was a very violent electrical storm, whipped up into an even greater intensity of violence by a hurricane-force wind. It was so fierce that the only way the fisherman could keep his feet was by holding on to trees and posts and fences. Even large mature trees were uprooted from the ground as huge gusts of wind tore them from their moorings and roughly rolled them over on their sides. As houses collapsed like packs of cards, shafts of lightning streaked across the pitch-black sky, followed by deafening claps of thunder.

As he approached the shore, angry mountainous waves reared up with crests of white foam on the top. They crashed down with great ferocity against the cliffs and the shore. Such was the tumult he could not even hear his own words as he called out plaintively to the flounder.

'Well, what does she want this time?' asked the flounder dispassionately.

'She wants to be like God,' answered the fisherman, his neck and throat taut with the strain of embarrassment.

'Go to her,' motioned the flounder. 'You will find her back where she started – in the pigsty.'

And that is where they still live to this day.

Unfortunately, that is the position of most us today. From time to time, or maybe only once in life, we have an experience of the underlying reality of life. As we move through life, it is only too easy to find oneself ensnared by all the trappings of materialism. Very soon we are engulfed by the fast-moving aspirations and burdens of the tide of life in an economically driven society, stripped of all religious constraints.

Of course, we would not take kindly to anybody likening our behaviour to that of pigs in a pigsty, but if we were honest this is how things are. We may live in comfortable homes and be surrounded by all the trappings of a technological culture, but in our heart of hearts we know there is something fundamentally important missing from our lives. Instead of following the pointed finger of the spiritually uplifting experience, it is all too easy to look around and follow the example of everybody else in our society. Unfortunately, the fisherman's wife is not at all like Lucky Hans. She is never content with what she has. She typifies the questing surface mind of the status-seeker. The goal of the bigger house, the better car or the more influential position is always followed by disenchantment. Disenchantment is then the motivating force that drives the individual on to an even bigger and seemingly better style of living. However, ultimately, this results in the same behaviour – except that the mouse wheel of life in a secular material society spins even faster and we have to be even more ruthless to realise the material goal upon which we have set our sights.

In the eyes of Mystery School initiates, the whole thing is a total waste of time. Not only do we waste our time and energy chasing after an illusion, like the fisherman and his wife, we also lose sight of the true goal of life and load up the Wheel of Necessity with difficulties that will come back to haunt us in our next life.

# Chapter 11
# Cinderella

Firstly the name 'Cinderella' is a paradox. According to Harold Bayley, 'ella' means light whereas cinders are dark[1]. There is another school of thought that reaches a similar conclusion by a very different route. This states that the word Cinderella probably is a derivative from the Assyrian god of light, named Sin. A dictionary of etymology says that cinder should be spelled 'sinter' to correspond with the German word. In Old Norse *sintr* meant the brilliant sparks that fly off the anvil when white-hot iron is beaten and which then fall back to become black scales when cold. From this we can safely deduce that, in the beginning, the light of pure consciousness becomes enshrouded or overlain by a grosser state of consciousness – the waking state. The aim of all life is to evolve to its highest form. Thus the pinnacle of human evolution is to liberate the spirit by gradually purifying the body, mind and senses so that the individual's awareness expands through increasingly higher states of consciousness until it reaches God Consciousness.

Maharishi tells us that one of the characteristics of a higher state of consciousness is the ability to accommodate two behaviours directly opposed to each other in the average waking state. In the fourth state – Transcendental Consciousness through to Unity Consciousness – two seemingly opposite themes co-exist without any conflict – such as restfulness co-existing with alertness in the fourth state of consciousness and above.

The whole point to the meaning of life is to not only reawaken this latent spirituality but to develop it to its highest potential. Both the title and the story is an allegory of this process.

In many mythological stories the One becomes the many in order that the creator can both know and be aware of his creation. In other words, the creator takes many and various forms ranging from the very low state of consciousness in the mineral and plant worlds, through the animal and human worlds right up to the celestial. By intimately knowing all these different manifestations the creator is completely cognisant of his creation.

The wife of a rich man fell sick and felt as though her end was drawing near. She called her only child to her bedside. 'Dear child,' she said, 'be good and pious and then the good God will always protect you, and I will look down on you from heaven and be near you.' Thereupon she closed her eyes and departed. Every day the maiden went out to her mother's grave and wept. She always remained pious and good.

What immediately strikes home at the beginning of this story is that it has been Christianised somewhat, in that it no longer follows to the letter the usual sequence. This is probably due to the popularity of the tale. It has been told more often than most.

The Greek word *lethe*, suggesting a death-type sleep or forgetfulness, comes to mind. Not a death in the ordinary sense but specifically a forgetfulness of her spiritual home. The whole sequence of this plot is the process called *alethea*, which means 'unforgetting'.

First of all, it is good to be clear that each of the characters in the story stand for a specific function of the human being. The rich man in question is the intellect of the individual, which is filled with infinite possibilities. The wife that falls ill and departs is the expanded subjective awareness – Pure Consciousness – which one loses when embarking on the path of evolution back to the state of pure unbounded awareness. Cinderella represents, at different stages, the progressive evolution of the spirit of the individual, the evolving soul and the illumined buddhi.

When winter came the snow spread a white sheet over the grave and after a few months the memory of his first wife grew dim. Before long, the man had taken another wife, who was beautiful. She brought with her two daughters who were fair of face but whose hearts were black and vile. The new wife and her two daughters were very unkind to the girl and reduced her to the role of scullery maid – hence the name Cinderella.

The sheet of snow that covered his first wife's grave is an analogy of the surface phenomena of the mind and senses, which completely overshadow the deeper transcendental aspect of the individual mind, ever cognisant of the meaning of life and its deeper purposes.

When this happens, as it does with us all, the mind becomes married solely to the sphere of sensory perception of relative creation. Thus, the new wife is relative creation – the world of constant flux and change. The two shallow step-daughters are the surface mind and the senses. Cinderella represents the awakened spiritual buddhi, which is largely overshadowed in life because the mind and the senses are too busy fulfilling their surface desires.

Throughout the story Cinderella takes recourse to her mother's grave. If we look up the word 'grave' we find three meanings. The first and most popular meaning today is the place where the body is laid in its final resting place. It also means a mound or monument or a place of remembrance; and, thirdly, it means something indelibly inscribed. In the story of Cinderella all three can be used in an apposite way appertaining to the mind.

Firstly, I would like to use it to signify the loss of the very deep subjective aspect of the mind. Focusing always on the objective world, the mind no longer has recourse to its most simple state of awareness. The most simple state of awareness in the transcendent can be termed as the 'mother' of the mind. Like a child seeking solace from its mother, the mind of every individual longs to rest in its most simple state where it is both pure, expanded and utterly content.

Secondly, even when there is no conscious memory of the transcendent there is still some inner motivating force of the inner genius, guiding the mind towards the happiness it is forever seeking. This would account for the indelibly inscribed aspect. Some part of the individualised mind is always seeking this primordial state of consciousness. That is probably why it entertains harmful substitutes that produce an altered state of consciousness, such as alcohol and drugs. Meditation is a state of deep rest for the mind, like a butterfly it comes to a state of rest on the flower in order to rejuvenate itself by sucking the nectar.

Thirdly, there is a vestigial memory of the transcendent indelibly inscribed on everybody's mind. We are always searching for it. Like a well-loved monument, it is a geographical landmark in our consciousness; we often return to in order to reorientate ourselves to the source of all happiness.

> One day the father was going to a fair. He asked his two step-daughters what they would like him to bring them back.
> 'Beautiful dresses,' said one.
> 'Pearls and jewels,' demanded the other.

Thus, the senses wanted to look sensational, whilst the deeper analytic aspect of the mind wanted something of a more lasting value so she chose pearls and jewels.

> 'What about you, Cinderella?' he asked. 'What would you like me to bring you back?'

'Break off the first branch that knocks against your hat on the way home,' she replied.

So he brought back beautiful dresses, pearls and jewels for his step-daughters but as yet nothing for his dear Cinderella. One the way home, a hazel twig brushed against his hat and knocked it off, so he broke off the twig and took it with him.

It is natural for the senses to want to look *sensational*, whilst the deeper-thinking aspect of the mind wanted something of a greater lasting value in the material world. However, Cinderella, whose name means light enshrouded in matter, wanted something infinitely more useful. She wanted a sprig of the first branch that knocked her father's (the intellect's) hat off. She wanted a reliable technique from a long enduring branch or tradition of fully realised masters.

There are two common sayings that would fit the bill here. The first is 'My hat!', which is often uttered when one is surprised by seeing something unusual or hearing the true meaning of a familiar saying, which turns it on its head, and thus means the opposite of what it is generally accepted to mean. The other is to 'take one's hat off' to someone, in other words to accept another's actions or knowledge as being superior to one's own.

An interesting and amusing case of having one's hat knocked off by a mind-blowing illumination was experienced by the great yogi Shankara. He was apparently the first to proclaim and publicise that everything was maya, or an illusion, and that in reality we are all one with the unmanifest *Brahman.* Thus, he paid little attention to the multitudinous desires that arise of the created universe or of the feminine energy which creates them.

One day he was visiting a Shiva temple when a low-caste woman was blocking his way. She was crying hysterically over the corpse of her dead husband. Shankara found the whole spectacle distasteful.

'Get out of my way and let me pass,' he commanded.

The woman eyed him ruefully. 'Aren't you the teacher who says that everything is Brahman?'

Shankara nodded.

'If everything is God there can be no impurity anywhere,' she continued. 'If I am the one pervading reality it is impossible for me to get out of your way!' she exploded.

The great Shankara was too shocked to answer but the low-caste woman was not done with him yet.

'Your great Brahman is no more than this,' she gestured to the corpse of her dead husband.

This outburst triggered one of the most dramatic icons that India has ever created; it thrust itself to the forefront of the great man's mind. It was that of the goddess Kali dancing upon the inert body of Lord Shiva, and with it came the realisation that without the great power of her Shakti the great god would not be able to stir. His conception of an abstract, unmoving Brahman left out the living, moving, creative intelligence – the feminine aspect of creation. The goddess Kali had brought it to his attention. Thus, from the phenomenal point of view, the world is quite real until true knowledge has been attained.

Imagine the horror of his disciples when they saw their great teacher prostrating himself and clasping the feet of the low-caste woman and thanking her for revealing his error.

From that time, Shankara became an enthusiastic follower of the great goddess and wrote many ecstatic poems in praise of her. He also instituted ten monastic orders of monks, called the *dasnamis*. Each of these monastic traditions draws its branch of knowledge from one of the ten aspects of the divine feminine force called the Shakti. Interestingly, one of these – the *Bharati* – is named after the woman. Two other notable ones are *Saraswati*, the branch to which Maharishi's teacher belonged, and *Giri*, which Yogananda and his master belonged to.

> The father gave to his step-daughters the things they had asked for and to Cinderella he gave the sprig of hazel. Cinderella thanked him and immediately went to her mother's grave and planted it.

In Celtic lore the hazel is the ultimate tree of knowledge and the nuts it bears symbolise the receptacles of wisdom. The tree of knowledge is a constantly recurring theme throughout many religious and mythological texts. We have the Tree of Good and Evil in the Old Testament; there is the *Vanaspati* with its thousand branches in the Vedas, to name but a couple.

Many thousands of people, such as myself, are initiated into the knowledge of the Vedic tradition of masters by being given the TM technique. Cinderella also was given the teaching of one of the branches of learning from the tree with a thousand branches. It established itself in the transcendent.

> She wept so much that her tears watered the sprig and caused it to grow into a handsome tree. Three times a day she went and sat down beneath it and watered it with her tears. A little white bird always came to the tree and if Cinderella expressed a wish the little bird would grant it for her.

The story has probably become distorted from the far-off original. As it is written today it speaks of Cinderella planting the branch on her mother's grave and watering it with her tears. This gives the impression that if you weep and wail then all will be well. However, the transcendent is a state of bliss. Contact with the transcendent makes you feel happy so tears of joy would be better. Also three is still the number of times the holy men in India worship their aspect of the deity.

More importantly, Cinderella was regular in her practice of the technique. Three times a day she went and sat beneath the tree to practice her meditation. Guenon reminds us that birds in myths and folk tales are usually associated with higher states of consciousness. A telling factor is that white stands for purity of intention. In this case, I believe it stands for a very deep part of the mind near the transcendent, called ritam, which automatically fulfils every desire. It is important to note that desires at this level of the mind can only be life enhancing – it would not be possible to wish for something negative.

It is significant that Cinderella did not ask the bird to change her situation in life from scullery maid to something with more prestige and grandeur. One of the precepts of traditional spiritual teaching is to be content with what you have because that is the only way to live out your *dharma* and expiate your karma. Dharma can be defined as the role you have inherited by your birth and your karma is the store of good and bad deeds of your former lives which become active in this lifetime. In his commentary on the Bhagavad Gita, Maharishi states that it is far better to follow your own dharma even though it may seem lesser in status than that of another. Great harm can come from aping somebody else's life because it can take them completely off the path of their own evolution of consciousness, which we are all engaged in, knowingly or unknowingly.

Maharishi states that once the mind is established in Cosmic Consciousness, Natural Law or all the laws of Nature will carry out your wishes. The text shows that all the desires were pure because the little bird was white and white stands for purity.

> The king gave orders for a festival to be held lasting three days, to which all the beautiful young girls in the kingdom were invited so that his son could choose himself a bride.

The king is God and his kingdom is the transcendent. The doors of the transcendent are always open, but only the worthy, who have perfected their mind and nervous system, have permanent access to it. People who rigorously practice the technique they have gained from a realised master gain increasing access to it daily. Even people who practice no technique at all can have several experiences of the transcendent in their lives.

When the two step-sisters heard that they were invited, they were delighted.

'Come and brush our shoes for us, comb our hair, fasten our buckles,' they both said excitedly. Cinderella did as she was told but her heart felt sad because she would have liked the opportunity to go too.

She begged her step-mother to let her go but to no avail. Suddenly the step-mother seemed to half relent.

'I have poured a dish of lentils into the ashes,' she said. 'If you can pick them out again within two hours you can go.'

Cinderella went through the back door to the garden and called for all the pigeons, turtle doves and birds to come and help her, which they did. Within an hour all the lentils were back into the dish.

The same message from the transcendent would be available to all but it would be interpreted differently at different levels of the conscious mind. It depends at what depth in the mind the thought is picked up. The mind and senses are both heavily tuned into relative life and so it was natural for them to turn towards vanity, whereas the buddhi always seeks opportunities for gaining enlightenment and so interprets the invitation from the king on a much deeper level. Thus the step-sisters – the mind and senses – obviously had a different agenda. The level they picked up the message from would be very deeply imbued with the relative, so it is natural for them to want to look attractive.

The step-mother – relative creation – is always trying to keep us from going to the transcendent. Even with the best of intentions, the fast pace of life and the innumerable jobs there are to do every day makes it a question of, 'I must just do this, and then I must just do that', and before long the day has gone and there is no time left. A true seeker of enlightenment always arranges the day so that their period of meditation or spiritual practice is safeguarded. The rest of their relative life is arranged around it.

'Pick the lentils out of the ashes' is an almost impossible task. Most people would have given up and ceded to the inevitable. However, to that deep part of the intellect, the illumined buddhi, an opportunity is still an opportunity. She called on the Absolute to help her go to the festival. 'She went through the back door into the garden': in other words, with the aid of her spiritual technique she was able to direct her attention in the opposite direction inwards from the senses, mind, intellect, ego and so transcend the whole field of relativity. By so doing, all of the laws of Nature were at her disposal. She could do anything and was able to call on all the birds of heaven. In only an hour all of the lentils were back in the bowl. (A similar task was set for Psyche by the goddess Venus in the story of *Cupid and Psyche* by Apuleius. In this case it was a great pile of assorted grains which had to be sorted out by nightfall. The heroine in this story was helped by an army of ants, which worked tirelessly for her.)

> Cinderella was pleased and went to her step-mother with the bowl of lentils believing that she could now go to the festival. However, the step-mother reasoned, 'You have no suitable clothes to wear and cannot dance. You would be the laughing stock and also make us look foolish.' When she saw the maiden's tears she seemed to half relent, but in actual fact set her a near impossible task. She emptied two dishes of lentils into the ashes and set her a challenge, saying 'If you can pick them all up in an hour you can go.'
>
> Once more Cinderella went into the back garden and called upon all the birds to help her. In less than half an hour they were finished and all flew out again.
>
> But the step-mother said, 'All this will not help you. You have no clothes to wear and that is that. You would make us a laughing stock if we allowed you to go with us.' With that she turned her back upon Cinderella and hurried away with her two proud daughters.

Once again Cinderella went deep into herself and, with the aid of a great deal of 'Nature Support', the impossible task was soon accomplished. As I said a little earlier, the surface mind and senses would interpret the invitation at a very different level than the source of the mind. Therefore it wasn't to be that Cinderella would go to the festival in fine material clothes. She would go in the raiment of the soul.

> As nobody was at home now, she went to her mother's grave beneath the hazel tree and cried: 'Shiver and quiver little tree, silver and gold throw over me.' Then the bird threw down a magnificent gold and silver dress and slippers embroidered with silk and silver. She put on the dress at top speed and went to the festival.
>
> Her step-sisters didn't recognise her. Cinderella looked so beautiful they thought she was a foreign princess. The prince was

captivated by her beauty and would not dance with nobody else.

This is the dress signifying that she had reached Cosmic Consciousness, or to put it another way, she had realised her inner genius. She had first-footed the ball of the Absolute. Her regular meditations brought about regular infusions of pure consciousness in her mind and nervous system, so that she could embrace the Absolute, though not on a permanent basis.

She danced throughout the evening. When she wanted to go home the prince wanted to go with her to see where she lived but she sprang into the pigeon house and evaded him. When her step-mother and sisters came home Cinderella lay in the hearth, amongst the ashes, wearing her dirty clothes with a dim oil lamp burning on the mantlepiece.

Apparently, there is some evidence that the name 'pigeon or peacock' is symbolic of the 'Father of the Everlasting One'. Also the Holy Ghost is symbolised by a dove. At the baptism of Christ the heavens are said to have opened and a dove or pigeon descended. However, I am not qualified to state categorically that the Holy Ghost and Cosmic Consciousness are synonymous.

The next day the festival began anew and her parents and step-sisters had already gone.

Cinderella went once more to her hazel tree and repeated the verse: 'Shiver and quiver, my little tree, silver and gold throw down over me.'

The bird threw down a much more beautiful dress than before, and when Cinderella appeared at the festival everybody was aston-ished by her beauty. The king's son waited until she came and instantly took her by the hand and would dance with no other.

As before, when the evening came she wanted to leave but the prince wanted to see her home. As before, she sprang away from him and escaped by climbing a pear tree. When her parents and step-sisters came home she was curled up in her usual place amongst the ashes.

The next time she received the perpetual invitation to the spiritual wedding, she was wearing the gown signifying God Consciousness. In this state of consciousness, her mind and sensory perceptions were so fully developed that she could see all the celestial divinities and hear all the heavenly sounds.

She could perceive the divine even on the surface value of life.

Her evolution was not yet complete but she had achieved the very exalted state of God Consciousness. It is significant that she climbed a pear tree to escape the prince. Bayley tells us that the pear was esteemed as an image or symbol of the human heart[2]. According to Le Plongeon a pear or heart-shaped fruit tree was dedicated to Isis[3]. In sculptures its fruit resembles a human heart. Maharishi says that whilst Cosmic Consciousness fully develops the mind, it is the full development of the heart that stabilises into God Consciousness or the prophet state defined by Elizabeth Haitch.

> On the third day, when her parents and sisters had gone to the festival, she went once more to her mother's grave and entreated the tree. This time the bird threw down a dress and slippers more magnificent than anybody could imagine. She put them on. When she got to the dance the prince was captivated. He only danced with her and if anybody else asked her to dance he said, 'This is my partner.'

When she went to the wish-fulfilling bird in the Tree of Life for a third time she was given the superlatively beautiful dress of Unity Consciousness. The highest and final link in the chain of the evolution of consciousness had been forged. This time it would be permanent. Never again would there exist the pang of separation.

> As before, when the evening came she wanted to leave. The prince was anxious to go with her, but she escaped from him so quickly that he couldn't follow. However, he had got wise to her behaviour and had had the whole staircase covered in pitch. As a result, as she ran down the stairs her left slipper came off and remained stuck.

It is difficult to say why she persisted in running away from the prince. Maybe it means that the mind was so accustomed to the sphere of sense perceptions that at first it automatically gravitates to external activity. But once the mind and senses are used to being linked in Unity Consciousness they will forever be forged in oneness. I am not sure why footwear should be a symbolic link with the divine. As slaves always went barefoot, it stood to reason that a person wearing shoes was a free man and used to making his own decisions. However, it also carried the aspect of control. In wedding lore the bride who has the bridegroom's shoes automatically has the bridegroom too. Taking off one's shoes at a holy place is an act of submissiveness and reverence.

However, one shoe is a different proposition. It would fit the bill to describe people with one foot in the door of divine consciousness. It was a sandal in the story of *Jason and the Golden Fleece* and a slipper in that of *Cinderella*. Footwear may be significant because one foot always reaches the desired destination first and so the same convention was used to describe a significant spiritual signpost.

In India they have a phrase, 'the atma on the move', which means the person's true Self comes to escort the small self back to her true home. In this story, the Absolute, in the form of the prince, comes for his bride – the enlightened buddhi. Part of her clothing was stuck in the pitch. Pitch is unremittingly black, and black in the distant past was a symbol of the divine dark of inscrutability, silence and eternity. Alternatively, it could mean that she had become so used to being stuck in ignorance that the Absolute, in the shape of her prince, would have to come personally to escort her to her real home.

> The king's son picked up the slipper. It was small and dainty and golden. He fingered it affectionately and went to his father and said to him, 'Only the one whose foot fits this slipper perfectly shall be my wife.' With that he set off to search throughout the kingdom for his future wife.

The mind had left the ball of the Absolute for the third time but not for long. This time the prince, or the 'atma' – self-referral consciousness – came back to claim her. He found her clad once more in the dress of relative creation.

He recognised her immediately and took her away to be his bride in Unity Consciousness. From that day on Cinderella would live in Unity Conciousness in a blissful state of heaven on earth.

---

[1] Bayley, 1996, vol. 1, 329
[2] Bayley 1996, vol.1, 249
[3] ibid. 249

# Chapter 12
# Allerleirau

*Allerleirau* is a tale in many respects similar to *Cinderella* but it extends its frame of reference further. Apparently the word 'allerleirau' means 'of many different kinds of fur'. It represents the entire range of the evolution of consciousness from the animal to the highest states of human consciousness. Some versions of the story are called *Mossycoat*, which extends the evolution of consciousness beyond this to the plant or vegetable stage, though the two stories are more or less the same. There is, of course, a previous stage – the mineral kingdom – which is outside the sphere of reference of this story.

> There was once a king who had a wife with golden hair. She was so beautiful that her equal could not be found upon the earth. It came to pass that she lay ill and, as she thought she was going to die, she called the king to her.
> 'If you wish to marry again after my death you must promise me that you will choose one who is as beautiful as I am, and has the same golden hair as I have.' After the king promised her this she closed her eyes and died.

As before, the mother dies. The memory of the expanded subjective awareness dims when the individual *jiva* incarnates upon the earth. Any memory of previous lives is also unavailable. Long golden hair is the symbol of light and wisdom. The king stands for Unity Consciousness. He agrees that he cannot marry again unless he finds her equal – namely the soul of another in Unity Consciousness – and that he cannot become unified with her. It stands to reason that he cannot marry below his station as that would upset the whole of the natural order.

> The king had a daughter who was just as beautiful as her mother and had the same golden hair. The king looked at her one day and felt a violent love for her.

'I will marry my daughter because she is the exact counterpart of my wife; nobody else resembles her,' he announced.

The daughter was very shocked when she became aware of her father's resolution and thought of a strategy to overcome her father's intention.

She said, 'Before I fulfil your wish I must have three dresses, one as bright as the sun, one as silvery as the moon and one as bright as the stars. In addition to these, I want a mantle made out of a piece of skin and pelt of every animal in your kingdom.'

Imagine our state of shock when the king announces his intention of marrying his daughter. This is because we jump to the conclusion that his intentions are incestuous. However, on further thought, it is obvious that unification has got to be the outcome after that individual jiva of divine spirit has progressed right through the entire range of consciousness ranging from the animal to Unity Consciousness. It is the destiny of all living things to achieve a state of Unity Consciousness after many lifetimes. So in that sense the king marries all of his children eventually.

When the dresses and the mantle were finished the king had them brought to her and announced, 'The wedding will be tomorrow.'

Tomorrow, in our time, is incredibly short. There would not be time to arrange a royal wedding in the space of about twelve hours. However, the 'tomorrow' referred to in this story is the celestial tomorrow, which is of a different order altogether. In celestial terms his yet-to-be incarnated daughter could easily complete the whole gamut of evolution by the next morning.

The classical explanation of the time chosen by Veda Vyasa when writing histories covering extraordinarily long periods of time was explained by Maharishi Mahesh Yogi. Maharishi says that Veda Vyasa based his choice on Eternal Being. The greatest life span in the relative universe is that of Mother Divine. If my mathematics are correct, she is reputed to live for 154,586,880,000,000,000,000,000 years.

The breakdown of this aspect of celestial time is as follows:

One life span of Mother Divine = 1,000 life spans of Lord Siva
One life span of Lord Siva = 1,000 life spans of Lord Vishnu
One life span of Lord Vishnu = 1,000 life spans of Lord Brahma
One life span of Lord Brahma = 100 years of Brahma

One year of Lord Brahma = 12 months of Lord Brahma
One month of Lord Brahma = 30 days of Brahma
One day of Lord Brahma = 1 Kalpa
One Kalpa = 14 Manus
One Manu = 1 Manvantara
One Manavantara = 71 Chaturyugis
One Chaturyugis = 4,320,000 years – the total span of
the four yugas: Sat, Treta, Dvapara
and Kali – broken down as follows:

Sat Yuga = 1,728,000 years
Treta Yuga = 1,296,000 years
Dvapara Yuga = 864,000 years
Kali Yuga = 432,000 years

This fascinating aspect of this view of time is that each yuga is arranged like the segments of the spokes of a wheel, and is therefore cyclic like the seasons. During the long period of Sat Yuga life is bliss. Everybody lives in a state of great fulfilment, fully in accord with the highest aspects of Natural Law. The is no deviation from right action. There is no disease, poverty, crime or any other aspect of disorder. Wishes are instantly fulfilled and because there is no violation of Natural Law there is no need for religions.

In Treta Yuga virtue drops by about a quarter so there is need for a code of conduct to minimise the violations of Natural Law. Religions are formed. Life is no longer heaven upon earth but still extremely good.

In Dvapara Yuga only 50 per cent of the full value of Natural Law is displayed. All the signs of illness, disease, poverty and natural disasters, which are so much in evidence today, are beginning to make their mark.

In Kali Yuga – our own time – only 25 per cent of the full value of Natural Law is exhibited upon the earth. Here we have the full-blown catalogue of disasters we read of in the newspapers or see on our television screens every day. The media confronts us with so many instances of fire, famine, drought, flood, pestilence, environmental degradation and genocide, that unless there is an emotive overtone to the presentation it barely makes an impression upon our consciousness.

The truth is that only very great masters like Maharishi know the highest aspects of Natural Law, thus we unconsciously violate it many times a day only to reap the inevitable consequences. There is very little spirituality left. That which remains has largely freed itself from the orthodox religions. Orthodox religions have thus had to resort to large-scale reshuffles to bring their liturgies and rituals up to date.

Kali Yuga was believed to have begun about five thousand years ago with the death of Lord Krishna. Now, going back to our commentary on *Allerleirau* – how long would it be before tomorrow? In the Hindu scriptures Lord Brahma is taken to be the creator so we will judge what half a day in his life is. According to my reckoning one day in the life of Lord Brahma is 492,408,000 years, so half a day of his life would be a little short of 250 million years – more than enough time to gain Unity Consciousness.

> The princess resolved to run away. When everybody was asleep she took three different things from her treasury – a golden ring, a golden spinning wheel and a golden reel. She put the three beautiful dresses into a nutshell, put on her mantle of fur and blackened her face and hands with soot.
> She walked the whole night until she reached a great forest. She was very tired so she got into a hollow tree and fell asleep.

We return to the theme of the one pure consciousness becoming the many. She took with her three ball gowns, which she kept safely locked up in a nutshell, as well as a gold ring, a golden spinning wheel and a reel of golden thread. The nutshell containing the three ball gowns is obviously the brain, especially as it strongly resembles a walnut. It was clear that she hadn't lost her memory prior to incarnating because she took with her everything she would need to evolve back to Unity Consciousness.

She commended herself to God and walked on until she reached a hollow tree. The hollow tree is a motif for a tube as fine as a hair which is supposed to extend the whole length of the spine from the muladhara chakra to the thousand-petalled lotus in the brain. She rested in the hollow tree and fell asleep. The tree motif is similar to the Tree of Life in *Cinderella*. Just as the ascending growth of the tree in *Cinderella* brings forth the successively beautiful ball gowns and the successful outcome with the prince, so the ascent of pure consciousness up the spine brings the illuminated consciousness to *Allerleirau*.

The sleep she experienced was obviously *Yoga Nidra* – a deep meditative sleep. She obviously transcended and forged a link with the king – who always symbolises the state of Unity Consciousness.

> The sun rose but she slept on. She was still sleeping when the king went hunting in the forest. Before long his dogs were sniffing and barking around the tree.
> The king said to his huntsmen, 'Go and see what kind of wild beast has hidden itself in there.'

The huntsmen came back. 'A wondrous beast is lying in the hollow tree,' said one. 'We have never seen anything like it before. It has a skin made up of many different kinds of fur. It is fast asleep.'

'Good!' replied the King. 'See if you can catch it alive. We'll fasten it to the carriage and take it back with us.'

When the huntsmen laid hold of her, Allerleirau was terrified.

'I am a poor child deserted by my father and mother,' she screamed. 'Have pity on me and take me with you.'

'You will be useful in the kitchen,' they said. 'You can sweep the ashes, fetch and carry wood and water, pluck the fowls, pick the vegetables and do all the dirty work.'

When they got back they pointed to a dark closet under the stairs where no light entered and said: 'That is where you can live and sleep, hairy animal.'

Thus Allerleirau was taken into service. In other words she set out on the long road of the evolution of consciousness. She was still wearing her hairy mantle, symbolic of low evolution. Like Cinderella, she is trustworthy and obedient in service and always sees things in their most positive light. Many tales have this element of having to learn a trade, become an apprentice, acquire a skill or go into service.

The same applies to people practising spiritual techniques. Maharishi likens the regular practice of meditation to the ancient method of dying cloth. First dip the cloth into the dye and then leave it out in the sun. At first most of the colour will fade in the light of the sun during the day but some will remain. Keep on doing this and more of the colour will stay fast until one day the dye is completely fast. Similarly, dive into the transcendent with the mind and it will come out suffused with Transcendental Consciousness. Concentrate then on your daily round of activity. The activity of the day will remove most of the benefits but some will remain. This round of deep rest through TM, coupled with daily activity will eventually transform the physiology to be able to continue working at its peak all day. This is called a state of Cosmic Consciousness.

Allerleirau helped the cook with the menial work. She lived in a state of great wretchedness for a long time. One day there was a great feast to be held at the castle.

'May I go upstairs for a while to have a look?' she asked.

'Yes, okay,' replied the cook. 'But be back here in half an hour to sweep the hearth.'

Allerleirau took her little oil lamp and went into her den. She washed the soot off her face and hands so that her true beauty shone through once more. She opened the nut and took out the dress that shone as golden as the sun.

When she went up to the festival everybody made way for her because they thought she was the daughter of a king. The king went over to her and gave her his hand and danced with her. As he danced he thought in his heart, 'I have never seen anyone so beautiful before.'

'Going into her little den' is an allegory of diving down into increasingly more refined states of her own mind until it comes to rest in a state of pure consciousness. However, this time it was a milestone. She had realised Cosmic Consciousness. Her consciousness had been expanding gradually and was now on a different footing. She had attained Cosmic Consciousness. The beautiful golden dress was symbolic of this elevated state of mind. They danced in meditation and then she went back to her round of activity in the relative universe.

As soon as the dance was over she curtsied politely and disappeared. Nobody knew where she had gone. The palace guards were questioned but nobody had seen her. She had run back to her little den and quickly taken off the beautiful golden dress. She blackened her face and hands with soot and put on her mantle of fur.

She was about to set about her work when the cook came over.

'Leave that until the morning,' he said. 'I would like to go upstairs to take a look. I would like you to make some soup for the king but make sure you don't drop any hairs into it.'

Allerleirau made bread soup as best she could and when it was ready she fetched her golden ring from her little den and dropped it into the soup. When the dancing was over the king had his soup brought to him. The cook took it up to the king to drink. When the king tasted the soup he was enraptured by its wonderful taste. He knew that somebody other than the cook had made it because it had a superlative taste, so he questioned him further.

'I know you didn't cook it because it tasted better than usual,' said the king. 'And it was cooked differently.'

'You are right – I did not make it,' answered the cook. 'It was made by that hairy animal in the kitchen.'

The king had Allerleirau summoned to him. She admitted

cooking the delicious soup but denied all knowledge of the ring because she felt that she was not yet fully ready to reveal her true intentions to the king.

In actual fact her denial or admittance would not be necessary because the king is really God and he knows the state of play of everybody's intentions already.

Maharishi tells us that each time the mind transcends subtle changes occur in the physiology so that the body can maintain this new state. In Cosmic Consciousness the digestive processes are supposed to turn the food we eat into *soma* – the ambrosial nectar of the gods. This how the king could tell that someone other than the cook had made the soup.

Whilst on the subject of food, he tells us that the quality and taste of the food depends upon the quality of the mind of the person preparing the food. In addition, if the food is cooked to be offered to God first and then eaten, a person enjoys the blessings of God. Such a mind will be pious, progressive and graceful.

The significance of the ring is similar to its function in a wedding ceremony – namely it joins two people together. In the context of this story it is a symbol binding the relative mind and the Absolute together for all time in a state of Cosmic Consciousness. In terms of the Mystery Religions the ring was symbolic of the zodiac. It represented the round of tasks bequeathed from previous incarnations to be completed before the estranged individual soul was reunited with the All of Everything.

Some time later there was to be another festival at the palace. Once again Allerleirau begged the cook to let her go and have a look.

'Yes,' he replied. 'But make sure that you are back in half an hour to make the king the bread soup he so much enjoys.'

Without ado she ran into her den, washed the soot from her face and hands quickly and went to the nut. She took out the dress as silver as the moon and put it on. She looked a true princess. She was so beautiful that the other guests turned to look at her and made way for her. The king was delighted to see her again and went up to her. As before they danced together, but as before, as soon as the dance was over she disappeared so quickly that the king could not tell where she had gone.

Once more she sprang back to her den, took off the dress and soon became the hairy animal again. Afterwards she went into the kitchen to prepare bread soup for the king. When the cook had gone upstairs she fetched the little gold spinning wheel and put it in the king's bowl. The king relished the soup and, as before, he was perplexed by the golden spinning wheel.

This time the cook confessed that he hadn't cooked the soup. The king questioned Allerleirau again about the little spinning wheel but once more she denied all knowledge of it.

Allerleirau had continued to practice her spiritual technique by diving deep into pure consciousness. This produced a sustained period of spiritual growth when she progressed from Cosmic Consciousness to God Consciousness. Great refinements were made to her physiology as the organs of perception were able to appreciate deeper and deeper levels of the relative universe. The donning of the silver dress is a clear indication that the state of God Consciousness had been achieved. Silver is symbolic of purified emotions and often stands as the feminine complement of the masculine gold. In alchemy it is the union of the two perfected opposites: sulphur and quicksilver; silver and gold; king and queen; or bride and bridegroom.

The spinning wheel symbolises the sutras or Sidhis which join the relative and the Absolute phases of creation together in the state of God Consciousness. The Sanskrit word *sutra* means thread. The *Yoga Sutras*, perfections or Sidhis are the threads which stitch the relative phase of life to the Absolute. The golden spinning wheel is the symbolic means by which the threads are stitched.

There was yet a third festival. This time Allerleirau wore a dress which shone like the stars. This time the king ordered the dance to go on for a long time. During the course of the dance he contrived to place a golden ring upon her finger without her noticing. At the conclusion of the dance he tried to hold on to her but she tore herself free and rushed back to her den. She quickly blackened her face and hands. Time was short; she had no time to take off her dress that shone like the stars in the night sky so she put on her mantle of fur to cover it up. In her haste to prepare the soup she forgot to blacken one of her fingers. She put a reel of golden thread into the bottom of the bowl and then poured the soup, which easily covered it. The cook came and took the soup up to the king.

The king drank the delicious soup and summoned Allerleirau to him once more. He spotted the ring he had slipped onto her finger in the dance and clutched at her wrists. Her mantle fell open slightly revealing her dress which shone as brightly as the stars. He tore off the fur mantle and her long golden hair cascaded and tumbled around her shoulders in all its beauty. She could no longer hide herself.

When she had washed all the soot from her face she was easily the most beautiful person who had ever lived.

'You are my dear bride,' said the king. 'We will never again be parted from each other.'

All taints of lower evolution were removed. She was united with the king and danced with him forever. The process of evolution had reached its climax. She had achieved Unity Consciousness. No longer could the true Self of the spiritual seeker be hidden from view by the outer trappings of carnality. In the story, not only had the King or God conferred upon her a symbol of union but also the dress of Unity Consciousness could no longer be covered up. The final summation of the story is the king saying 'Never again will we part from each other.'

I believe that the reel of golden thread is symbolic of the unity which binds together the relative and Absolute phases of life. Also 'reel' is a kind of dance and is therefore a play upon words, emphasising the eternal dance of the relative and Absolute phases of existence together, which in India is called *lila*.

Summarising, all of creation leaves the Absolute phase of existence to slowly evolve over a period of many lifetimes to its original state of purity. Hidden within her many disguises of the jiva or dweller in the body is the potentiality to rise to the three higher states of consciousness symbolised by the ring, the spinning wheel and the reel of golden thread.

# Chapter 13
# How Six Men Got on in the World

Once upon a time there was a very gifted man who was adept at all
kinds of skills. He had served in the war and had conducted himself
bravely but once the war was over he received his dismissal and three
farthings for his expenses on the way.
'Wait!' he said. 'I shall not be content with this. If only I can meet
the right people on the way the king will have to open the treasury to
me.'

A brave and resourceful 'old soldier', after many lifetimes on the relative
field of life, was given his 'dismissal' and 'three farthings' expenses. The
dismissal he earned was Cosmic Consciousness or, in the terms of the ancient
Mysteries, he had realised his inner genius. One can be sure of this because
in that state the mind is fully developed so there is no need to reincarnate
upon the earth. His expenses were the three relative states of waking,
dreaming and deep sleep. Whilst he still experienced the three relative states
of consciousness, he now experienced them as the master and not the
servant. He no longer lost his awareness during deep sleep; he was no longer
tied to the vicissitudes of the dream state; and nor was he subject to the
attachments and aversions of the waking state, though he remained totally
effective in it. However, he had not achieved the 'full penny' of the fourth
state called *turiya*. His ambition was to evolve to Unity Consciousness in
order to gain enlightenment and so have access to the entire treasury by
being the master of all the laws of Nature.
Firstly, there is the necessity of evolving from Cosmic Consciousness to
God Consciousness. This is done through the agency of some of the Sidhis
from the *Yoga Sutras*, as taught by a fully realised master.

He went into the forest and watched a man pick up six trees as if
they were blades of grass. 'Will you be my servant and accompany
me?' asked the old soldier.

'Yes,' answered the other. 'But first of all I must take this little bundle of sticks home to my mother.' When he returned the two went on their way together.

Today, if we want to learn a skill or profession we would enrol at a college or university or serve an apprenticeship. However, if we wanted to learn something of ultimate value, such as a technique that would help us to evolve to a higher state of consciousness, we would have to look further off the beaten track for a realised master. They do exist, and one may be sufficiently fortunate to become a pupil of one of the great teachers of our time, such as Maharishi, Sai Baba, Muktanada or Sivananda.

Over two thousand years ago one might find such a person living in a forest, living off fruits, berries and roots. The Upanishads were composed by masters living in 'forest academies' in ancient India. Nearer home, we had the druids, with their own bardic laws. Such a master would initiate the seeker into the practice of the Sidhis, especially if he had already realised the state of Cosmic Consciousness. Like the hero in this tale, his next step to God Consciousness involves perfecting the sphere of the senses so as to perceive the finest level of relative existence. This would enable him to climb the ladder of evolution from Cosmic Consciousness to God Consciousness. The seeker in the story obviously found such a master.

Alternatively the Sidhis may have come spontaneously, as Patanjali said they could. The first Sidhi he received was one that gave him enormous strength.

When they had gone a little further they saw a huntsman kneeling. He had shouldered his rifle and was taking aim and about to fire.
'What are you going to shoot?' asked the master.
'Two miles away from here is a fly sitting on the branch of an oak tree,' answered the huntsman. 'I want to shoot its left eye out.'
The man was greatly impressed. 'Will you come along with me?' he asked. As soon as the huntsman was ready he went with him.

The teller of this tale has ventured a long way down the road of exaggeration of normal sight to give a glimpse of what it would be like to develop the Sidhi of supersight. However, this is nothing compared with the ability to see beyond the surface value of creation, right through the molecular, atomic and sub-atomic particles of relative existence, which is conferred through the perfection of this particular Sidhi.

The three went on together. Soon they came to seven windmills whose sails were revolving at great speed, although there was no sign of wind. They were perplexed, since not a leaf stirred on the nearby trees.

'I have no idea what is driving those windmills,' said the man. Further on they saw a man sitting on a tree. He was shutting off one nostril and blowing air out through the other.

'What on earth are you doing?' asked the man.

The nose-blower replied: 'Two miles from here are seven windmills. I'm making them turn – can't you see them?'

'Come with me,' said the master. 'If we four are together we can carry the world before us.' The nose-blower got down from his tree and went with them.

Having acquired supersight, as well as great strength, the master could see the windmills of the heavens turning even though there was not a breath of wind to be felt anywhere. Knowledge of the positions of the stars, planets and constellations can be had by practising sanyama on the relevant Sidhi or from being an adept in pranayama. In this story the ability was obviously earned through the practice of pranayama, for in the story it was a nose-blower that made the seven windmills move. As the story says, pranayama is the process of shutting one nostril and blowing the air out of the other and then inhaling through the empty nostril. Maharishi calls pranayama 'super oil'.

We must remember that the ancients had the basic slogan of 'as above, so below', which means that everything out there in the physical universe is also contained within each individual. The Bible tells us that man is made in the image of God. There is the probability that the seven windmills are a cipher for the seven chakras in the subtle body, which have to be opened before each higher state of consciousness is gained. At the same time, the seven windmills are the windmills of the gods, and probably refer to the positions and influences of the five visible planets of the old world: Mercury, Venus, Mars, Jupiter and Saturn, and the sun and moon. However, they could equally well represent the stars of the Great Bear, which the sages of ancient India called the seven Rishis. In the book *Hamlet's Mill* Giorgio de Santillana and Hertha von Dechend decode the epic Finnish saga *Kalevala*. This describes the two bears, Ursa major and Ursa minor, as being the two sails of Hamlet's mill, which revolve around the pole star Polaris. The flour churned by the mill of the gods is a figurative description of the Milky Way.

The main thrust of their book is the likelihood of a very advanced civilisation prior to the ancient Egyptians passing on in allegoric form the catastrophes that can occur on earth at the end of a precessional age before the rebirth of a golden age. As we have ascertained earlier in this study, we are now nearing the end of the age of Pisces before we enter the new precessional sign of Aquarius.

> After a while they saw a man who was standing on one leg. He had taken off the other and laid it beside him.
> 'You have arranged things very comfortably to have a rest,' observed the master.
> 'I have to,' replied the man. 'I am a runner. To stop myself running I have taken off one of my legs. With two legs I can run faster than the birds can fly.'
> 'Please come with me,' pleaded the master. 'If we five are together we can carry the whole world before us.'

The ability to run faster than the birds can fly is likely to be the fifth of the eight psychic perfections. This is called *prapti* and it gives one the capacity to reach anywhere. The eight psychic perfections are as follows:

1. Anima – the yogi can make the body as small as an atom
2. Laghina – the body can be made light
3. Mahaima – the body can be made large
4. Garima – the body can be made heavy
5. Prapti – the capacity to reach anywhere
6. Prakamya – the unobstructed fulfilment of desire
7. Vashitwa – control over all objects, organic or inorganic
8. Ishitva – capacity to create or destroy at will

These eight Sidhis appear as the result of the complete mastery of the gross and subtle aspects of the elements called the five *Mahabhutas*. In addition to this, the body is also perfected, so as to achieve the maximum beauty, grace, energy and hardness.

> So the runner went with them. It was not long before they met a man who wore a cap entirely over one ear.
> 'Why don't you wear your cap properly?' asked the master. 'It makes you look an idiot.'
> 'There is a good reason for that,' replied the man. 'If I set it straight horrible consequences occur – a terrible frost sets in and the birds are frozen in their flight and drop dead on the ground.'
> 'Oh come with me,' said the master. 'If we six are together we

can carry the world before us.'

'Alright!' said the man with the cap and they all went on their way together.

The fifth Sidhi he acquired was the mastery over the Mahabhutas. These are: Purusha, Prakriti, the three internal organs, the five cognitive organs, the five *tanmatras* and the five natural elements of ether, fire, air, water and earth. The Purusha is the transcendental reality of every individual. It is the basis of all the subjective aspects of life. He is the silent witness of every action and event past, present and future.

Prakriti or Nature is the primal substance from which the whole of creation emerges. Its three aspects, which are responsible for all changes and modifications, are called the gunas. These are respectively *rajas, tamas* and *sattva. Rajoguna* provides the spur of activity; *satoguna* the upward progressive movement of evolution; and *tamoguna* is the agency that checks or retards. Even though the direction of evolution always tends to be upwards, tamoguna is always present both to destroy the previous stage and to give the new stage of creation stability. Satoguna is the force that helps it develop into a new stage.

It can be said that the five elements of ether, fire, air, water and earth are the building blocks of all creation and our physical senses, the tanmatras, are their qualities. Thus, ether, or *akasha*, is space, the medium through which sound travels and gives rise to the faculty of hearing; air gives rise to the essence of touch; form in fire; taste in water; and smell in earth.

The mastery over the mahabhutas was personified by a man who wore a cap entirely over one ear to prevent a great frost that would make the birds fall out of the air. This reminds one of the earth and the position in which it wears its polar cap.

The attainment of yogic powers by an individual is a great responsibility and so warrants these abilities being kept under constant control to render them safe. Imagine what it must be like to have the huge forces of Natural Law seeking to carry out the desires of an individual?

What a safeguard it is that the full attainment of the Sidhis is only possible in a state of God Consciousness, where such attributes can be used only to enhance the life of mankind spiritually. Also it must be remembered that from the state of Cosmic Consciousness onwards all the actions of an individual are in accord with the highest aspects of Natural Law, thus ensuring that only life-enhancing outcomes are possible from people in higher states of consciousness.

The next part of the story serves as an analogy to demonstrate the perfection of the Sidhis.

Soon the six came to a state where the king had made a proclamation concerning his daughter.

He said: 'Any man who can beat my daughter in a race can be her husband. However, if he loses the race then he also loses his head.'

'I would like to enter,' declared the master. 'But I would like this man to run for me.'

'Very well,' said the king. 'But in that case his life must also be staked so that his head and yours both set their sights on the victory.'

Obviously, whether we are aware of it or not, the goal of everybody in the human race is to move to the top of the ladder of the evolution of consciousness. All the individual pieces on the draughtboard of life will one day be made up to kings. Thus, eventually everybody will attain Unity Consciousness or god-man, which is the status of the king in the story we are considering. But first of all the state of God Consciousness must be won after Cosmic Consciousness has been achieved. If the daughter is the first offspring of the king then she must be the state of God Consciousness. However, we must not lose sight of the fact that she also symbolises the evolving consciousness of the master.

> It was a race to bring back a pitcher of water from a far distant well. The king's daughter was given a pitcher and so was the runner. The runner stooped down to buckle on his other leg. Both runners started at the same time. In a very short time, when the king's daughter had only travelled a few steps, the runner swept past her like the wind. In an instant he had filled his pitcher and was turning back. Halfway back to home he suddenly became overcome with fatigue and lay down for a rest. He put his pitcher down and rested his head on a horse's skull and fell asleep.

Bayley reminds us that, 'water, whether in the form of the sea, river, fountain, well, rain or dew has been universally employed as a symbol of the cleansing, refreshing, invigorating qualities of the spirit'[1]. Thus, the pitcher each one of us carries in the race is our own nervous system. The speed of the runner illustrates the superiority and effectiveness of the Sidhis as compared with the intellect. Or, put another way, the Sidhis vastly enhance the spiritual evolution of an individual.

However, the role of the Sidhis is not only to perform so-called superhuman feats when whispered to the transcendent but also to root out hidden stresses, which lay like dark seeds waiting to be awakened. Rest is the best antidote to activity.

In the meantime the king's daughter, who could run as fast as any mortal, reached the well and ran back with her pitcher full of water. She noticed the sleeping runner with a smile, quietly emptied his pitcher and ran on.

All would have been lost if the huntsman with supersight had not been standing at the top of the castle observing everything. He raised his rifle, took aim and cleverly shot the skull of the horse from under the sleeping runner's head. The runner promptly awoke, refilled his pitcher from the well and was back ten minutes before the king's daughter.

A spiritual master gives a devotee a parcel of Sidhis sufficient to accelerate the growth of higher states of consciousness. The sequence of the story tells us that only one Sidhi is employed at a time and it is quickly followed by another within a suitable period of time. After employing the Sidhi that enabled the master to be anywhere, he reverted to his intellect, which is much slower. He then employed the Sidhi which gave him supersight, and allowed him to win the hand of the king's daughter.

The king was very peeved at the thought of giving away his daughter to a common discharged soldier. She was not at all happy with the idea either, so they talked together to discuss the best plan of action.

Suddenly the king thought of an excellent strategy. His plan was to get rid of the six of them in one fell swoop.

'Congratulations,' he beamed. 'Now it is time to celebrate your victory. Come with me.'

He conducted them to a room made of iron, with iron bars on the windows. Inside the room was an enormous table filled with delicious food and drink.

'Go in and enjoy yourselves,' he said. As soon as the six were inside, he ordered all the doors and windows to be bolted and commanded the cook to light a huge fire under the iron floor and make it red hot.

There are a couple of things to be straightened out here. Firstly, the king, who is really God, doesn't set out to make people suffer. Our difficulties in life are just desserts, because they arise as debts from our previous actions.

111

In other words they are the karma carried forward to us. Neither has the king's daughter an evil disposition. She is the goddess in charge of all created things. She drives the dynamically active process of relative creation. As such she can seem ambivalent. As we have seen in the earlier part of the book, the masters of the Mystery Schools considered the unrealised seeker as essentially two people – the surface persona and his latent inner genius. To the ego-driven person, she seems to be the creator of all difficulties, because he is always swimming against the tide of spiritual evolution. However, to the seeker of enlightenment, she is the mother goddess who smoothes out all the difficulties from his path.

The heated iron room is an analogy of the stove or vessel, in which the psyche of the alchemist is perfected through his practice of tapas. Tapas is the process of practising austere penances, such as very protracted meditations or standing on one leg in order to obtain a boon from the gods, but generally it is taken to be any systematic behaviour that hastens or enhances the spiritual evolution of a person.

> Soon the six began to feel quite warm. They were guileless and thought the heat was coming from the food. However, once they found that the doors and windows were bolted they realised they were trapped inside. The king must have had an evil intention.
>
> 'Don't worry,' exclaimed the man with the cap pulled over one ear. I will cause such a frost to come that the fire shall creep away in disgrace.' As soon as he straightened his cap a great frost crept across the room. Even the food on the dishes began to freeze.

The spiritual hero of this tale could have used any one of three Sidhis to achieve this result. He could have used his mastery over Nature; his ability to fulfil all of his desires; or he could have employed his mastery over the five elements of fire, air, water, earth and space.

> The king allowed a couple of hours to pass before he unbolted the doors and windows. He thought they would have perished long ago in the fierce heat. Not a bit of it. The six were so cold that they wanted to warm themselves up.
>
> Thinking that the cook had not carried out his instructions, the king went down to the cook to give him a piece of his mind. The cook directed the king's attention to a huge fire still burning fiercely under the iron room. The master and his six servants had outwitted him, but the king still had a plan up his sleeve.

It is interesting to note the similarity of different aspects of Nature. For some time, scientists have noticed the behaviour of some substances when the temperature drops to near Absolute Zero. At such temperatures liquid helium becomes unbounded and no longer conforms to the classical laws of Nature. It starts to climb up the sides of the container instead of sinking to the bottom as any liquid does at normal room temperature. Also near Absolute Zero, electricity flows without any resistance. If harnessed, the same power could last forever. At normal temperatures it is the resistance in the metal that causes the power to fade and need to be replenished. At super-cooled temperatures a magnetised rail could carry trains and cars indefi-nitely because the north and south poles of all the molecules in the steel rail line up in an orderly and coherent manner, in the same way as all the photons of light line up in the coherent beam of a laser.

Some scientists have noticed the parallel between the human mind near the transcendent and these supercooled substances. It seems that increasing order in Nature naturally occurs when the temperature decreases. A similar increase in order occurs in the thinking of people practising TM and the TM-Sidhi programme.

> The king had one more stratagem up his sleeve. He would bribe the man to renounce his claim to his daughter. The hero was clever. He asked for all the gold he could carry. The king assented. The man summoned all the tailors in the kingdom to make a gigantic sack.

As I said earlier the term 'sutras' really means threads binding together everything into one unity. Thus, the sack the tailors made was the perfection of the individual's body and nervous system. It was big enough to carry an infinite amount of gold. We have mentioned before the allegory of the alchemists, of changing base metal into gold, or in this case the mortal, physical, subtle and causal bodies into an immortal, perfected, spiritual body.

The full use of any Sidhi can only be got by releasing the last stress which prevents it from operating fully. In this story the final stress, or the final trace of negativity, was symbolised by a troop of soldiers, sent by the king to cut down the hero and his five mental servants. These were all laid low by the nose-blower. It is well known that pranayama can bring about a state of complete evenness, or Samadhi, in the body and mind, leading eventually to its full perfection.

Pure consciousness, in the shape of the king, was giving the master the opportunity to demonstrate his mastery of the elements or mahabhutas. The master yogi easily overcame the extreme heat of the fire by producing its opposite – extreme coldness. There may well be another allegory here.

In much the same way as the molecules in a supercooled magnet line up in a very ordered manner as the temperature significantly decreases, so the integration and orderliness of all parts of the brain of a person practising spiritual development techniques, such as TM or the TM-Sidhi programme, continues to increase until a state of pure transcendence is reached. At that point a state of pure integration or synchrony has spread to all parts of the brain. An eminent Russian brain scientist named Liubimov says this is completely new and nothing else produces the same effect. In physics it is known that a change of state occurs after a phase transition. A phase transition takes place when approximately 1 per cent of the molecules of water freeze. This is a sufficient quantity to change the rest of the molecules of water to ice. The same thing happens when water is boiling. Until the magic 1 per cent is reached, only hot water is in the saucepan. However, once 1 per cent of the molecules of hot water are changed to steam a phase transition occurs, which quickly converts the rest of the water to steam.

In the physical world it has been observed that decreases in temperature produce corresponding increases of orderliness. It appears that transcendence in the human mind bears an increasing similarity with supercooling in the physical world. Both display a marked increase in orderliness and thereafter display characteristics which cannot be matched at normal temperatures. For example, liquid helium cooled to near Absolute Zero temperatures will not pour. It wants to go in all directions or, to put it another way it becomes unbounded. It transcends its former limitations. So does the mind. During normal operations, a normal person in the street cannot perform supernormal feats such as the Sidhis, but if he learns how to transcend the source of his mind then all becomes possible. A person who has perfected the mastery of the Mahabhutas could certainly balance extreme heat with extreme coldness.

The king was at his wits end. He summoned the master to him.

'If you renounce your claim on my daughter I will give you as much gold as you can carry.'

'Alright your majesty – it's a deal,' smiled the master, thrusting out his hand to the king to seal the agreement. He nodded in the direction of the strongman. 'As long as my friend over there does the carrying. In fourteen days I will come to collect it.'

Before he left, all the tailors in the kingdom were summoned to sew a sack as big as a house.

The king's jaw dropped when he saw the size of the sack the

strong fellow was carrying. 'What a lot of gold he can carry away,' he thought to himself. The king commanded sixteen of his strongest men to fetch one ton of gold but this barely covered the bottom of the sack. Little by little the king ordered all his treasure to be brought out but it still only half filled the sack. Finally, he had seven thousand carts of gold brought out but there was still room for more.

However, the strongman said: 'I will tie up the sack, even though it is not full.' With that he swung the sack up on to his shoulders and walked away with the master and his friends.

The master had no intention of stopping at God Consciousness. As he said at the beginning of the story, 'The king will have to give me all of his treasure.' In other words, he had set his heart on attaining Unity Consciousness – the grandest prize of all. The seven thousand carts of gold refer to both his perfection of the seven states of consciousness and also the seven kingdoms of creation: mineral, vegetable, animal, the intellect, the inner genius, the prophet and the god-man.

All the tailors in the kingdom sewing a sack as large as a house, symbolises the application of the Sidhis attaching the individual to the infinite with their threads. Hence, even all the gold in the kingdom could not fill the sack. This fits in with the description of the relationship between the manifest universe and the unmanifest universe in the Rig Veda. One of the verses says that only one quarter is manifest – three quarters are not manifested.

When the king saw one man carrying away the wealth of the entire nation upon his back he became angry and sent two regiments of mounted soldiers to pursue him and bring back the sack of gold.

The soldiers quickly overtook them and said, 'Put down that sack of gold and come quietly, or we'll cut you to pieces.'

'Rather than have that happen, I'll blow you all into the air,' smiled the nose-blower and he closed one nostril and blew out of the other. The soldiers shot into the blue sky, over the mountains and became separated one from the other.

Seeing that the six could not be stopped the king gave up his pursuit and the six divided up the wealth and lived in perfect peace and contentment all the days of their lives.

In the allegory there must have been some stresses remaining, which were personified as the soldiers. However, the nose-blower, being a master of the art of pranayama, was soon able to flush these out and so perfect the master's nervous system. Since his nervous system was now fully evolved the master could now fulfil his mastery over the laws of Nature and enjoy a quality of life that must be called heaven upon earth.

---

[1] Bayley, 1996, 243

# Chapter 14
# The Six Servants

A very long time ago there lived an old sorceress. It seemed as if she had no other thought than to lead mankind to destruction. Her daughter was the most beautiful maiden under the sun. She was proclaimed as the supreme prize. In order to wed her, the wooer first had to perform a task. If he failed he would lose his head.

One may sensibly ask the question – why a sorceress? The Mother Goddess, the creatrix of the entire show of relativity, has often been likened to a witch or sorceress, whose creation of the whole field of relativity is no more than a magic show or illusion.

It is the task of each of us to do a one hundred and eighty degree turn of the mind, away from the mechanistic theories of the material world, in order to become united with the high spiritual aspect of life, her daughter, which is both our true selves, the perfected individual soul and the rightful inheritance of all mankind. Apparently, when the individual incarnates he completely loses all memory of his previous existence, which includes all his past lives, but he does carry with him the skills and spiritual development he acquired.

The quest for the daughter of the queen (the sorceress) is really a quest to perfect the soul of the individual seeker after truth. The deeds he has to accomplish are the steps by which his individual consciousness becomes perfected into pure Unity Consciousness.

News of the maiden's beauty had reached the ears of a certain king's son. His mind became entranced by the thought of her.

'Will you give me your permission to demand the hand of the maiden in marriage?' he asked his father.

'Not on your life,' replied the king. 'If I were to let you go I would be sending you to your death.'

At this news the boy became sick at heart. He lay on his bed for seven years. No physician could cure him. His father was at his wits end.

Finally, he gave in and said to his son, 'Alright, you have my blessing. I know of no other way of curing you.'

As soon as he heard this, the son got off his bed and joyfully set out on his way.

When an individual has had the call to pursue the quest for spiritual knowledge and development no amount of seeming common-sense advice from well-intentioned parents and friends can deter him. The bait of succeeding in a brilliant career, making a fortune or having a happy and fulfilling family life is of little consequence. He has to grope on towards the eventual goal.

The fact that the hero is a 'king's son' shows that some considerable progress has been made on the path. The king is often symbolic of Unity Consciousness. A fledgling seeker is cast in the same mould or substance as the perfected but he still has some way to go. There are some imperfections in the material. The ancient alchemists masked their quest for the perfection of mankind by giving the impression that they were in the business of trying to transform base metal into gold. Thus, we begin the tale with our hero already on his way. He has already reached Transcendental Consciousness and could even have got as far as achieving Cosmic Consciousness.

We know this because without some infusion of the Absolute into the relative mind the Sidhis would not have any effect. This is because the surface level of the mind, where we carry out most of our day-to-day thinking and activity is far removed from the very deep level of the mind, which makes it possible to harness the most powerful laws of Nature to carry out feats that would be classed as impossible for the surface level of the mind.

As he was riding across the heath he saw something resembling a huge heap of hay lying on the ground. When he got nearer he could see that this enormous expanse was a man's stomach. It was the size of a small mountain.

'If you are need of any help, take me into your service,' said the Stout One, standing up.

'What use would such a clumsy fellow be to me?' asked the prince with a smile.

'This is nothing,' replied the Stout One, patting his stomach. 'When I want to I can make myself three thousand times fatter.'

'If that is so you will be very useful to me.'
So the Stout One went with him.

When I read about the Stout One I was immediately reminded of the Norse god, Loki. He was depicted as having an enormous capacity for food. Both the Stout One and Loki allegorise the infinite capacity of the Absolute. Everything comes out of it. It exists in material form for a while and then returns to the Absolute. From the point of view of the allegory everything is food. Everything emerges from the vibrating energy of the unified field. The rate of vibration slows down and it becomes solidified into different aspects of matter. It exists in material form for a brief period of time and then returns to the unified field, whilst another wave of energy takes its place and continues the material form. This is the ceaseless pulse of life in the material world.

In terms of the eight perfections, the infinitely large stomach of the Stout One is a personification for the yogic mahaima – the ability of the yogi to make the body very large.

They had not gone very far when they came across a man lying on the ground with his ear pressed into the turf.
'What on earth are you doing?' enquired the king's son.
'I am listening,' the man replied.
'What are you listening to so attentively?' added the king's son.
'I am listening to what is going on in the world,' answered the man. 'Nothing escapes my ears. I can even hear the grass growing.'
'Can you tell me what is going on in the court of the old queen with the beautiful daughter?' asked the king's son quizzically.
'Yes!' answered the other.' I can hear the swishing of a sword striking off another would-be wooer's head.'
'I can certainly make use of you!' exclaimed the king's son. 'Come along with me.'

The allegory continues. After practising the ability to make himself infinitely large the seeker then introduces the sutra for divine hearing into his mind. Apparently, sound travels through the finest of the five elements, called akasha. By practising samyama on the organ of hearing and its relationship to the akasha it is possible to gain access to the so-called super-physical sounds. There are four aspects of sound: the physical, audible, mental and transcendental. We are used to the notion of our hearing being restricted to a certain range, even though cats and dogs far exceed our capabilities, whereas in yoga sound is a continuum.

The ability to hear sound beyond our normal restricted range of hearing can be developed bit by bit. When a sound goes out of the range of normal hearing the sound does not stop. It continues in a more subtle or attenuated form. Divine hearing is the process of becoming sensitive to sounds just out of normal hearing and thus extending our ability to hear them.

> As they went on their way they saw a pair of feet and the beginning of a pair of legs but not the rest of the body. After they had walked on a long way they came to the body and after walking on a greater distance they came to the head.
> 'What a tall person you are,' said the prince with a smile.
> 'That's nothing at all,' replied the Tall One. 'If I want to I can stretch out my limbs and make myself three thousands times taller than this. I can make myself taller than the highest mountain. I would be pleased to enter your service, if you would find me helpful.'
> 'I certainly would!' exclaimed the prince. 'Come along with me.'

This is another of the eight perfections called prapti. It is the ability to reach anywhere. As an allegory, the Tall One in the story talks about stretching his limbs three thousand times. In actual fact this ability is gained by the yogi from the comfort of his lotus posture or seated position. It harnesses the ability of the mind to travel great distances mentally rather than physically, although the latter is also possible.

Recent research by Dr Tony Nader has revealed that the human body is really cosmic. He has located the parts of the human body which have a direct correspondence with the sun, moon and the planets. By becoming one with the cosmos an individual would naturally have access to all that exists both far and near. It is interesting to recall that Robert Cox defines this form of enhanced perception as 'non-localised awareness'.

> A little further along the way they saw a man sitting by the side of the road, whose eyes had been bandaged up.
> 'What's the matter with your eyes?' asked the prince. 'Are they sensitive to the light?'
> 'No! Nothing like that,' replied the man. 'I keep it on as a precaution so that I don't injure my fellow man or the environment.'
> 'That sounds interesting,' said the prince. 'Tell me more.'
> 'I keep the bandage on because my eyes are so powerful,' continued the man. 'Whenever I take it off, whatever I am looking

at splits to pieces.'

'That's fantastic!' exclaimed the prince in surprise. 'I could certainly use a person like you.'

'I would be glad to be of service,' replied the other.

This is the eighth perfection known as ishitva – the ability to create or destroy at will. The ability to create or destroy at will presupposes the control over all objects organic and inorganic, which is called vashita – the seventh perfection. Also the ability to create anything would automatically grant him the fulfilment of all desires, which is the sixth perfection.

> Further along the road they came across a man lying down in the hot sunshine. He was shivering so much that not a single limb of his body was still.
>
> 'I can't understand how you can be shivering so much on a hot sunny day such as this,' stated the king's son.
>
> 'That's easily explained!' retorted the man. 'You see, I have a quite different nature to you. The hotter it is outside, the colder I feel. But when it is very cold outside I feel hot. I am the kind of person who would swelter with the heat if I were to be surrounded by ice at the North Pole, and yet shiver with cold in the middle of a fire.'
>
> 'You are a strange fellow,' said the prince. 'But if you would like to enter into my service, I would be pleased to have you.'

The ability to balance an excess of any one element by another would confer upon a seeker the ability to have full control over all the elements. This is called the mastery of the *bhutas*, which are the five possible forms of the elements – namely their gross and subtle forms, their real form, their universal form and their purpose.

> As they travelled onwards they saw a man who was able to extend his neck so far that he could see whatever took his fancy. He delighted in looking all about him. He was even able to see over the mountains.
>
> 'What are you looking at so eagerly?' enquired the king's son.
>
> 'I have such sharp eyes,' answered the man, 'I can see every forest, field, hill and valley in the world.'
>
> 'I would be delighted if you would come with me,' said the prince, 'for I am in need of such an ability.'

On the path to Unity the hero meets and becomes acquainted with six Sidhis or perfections, which are personified as servants. Each of the Sidhis enable him to carry out an extraordinary feat. It is through the application of these feats that the princess is won.

The first servant who entered the service of the king's son was an exceedingly fat man who could consume any amount of food or water. In allegorical terms this means that the young man first became acquainted with the Absolute, infinite aspect of creation. He was much bigger than anything that can be conceived in relative creation.

Next he comes across a man with his ear pressed down into the turf, who is busy listening to the grass grow. Thus, the hero gains the facility of being able to hear anything in the universe.

After this he encounters a tall man who has the ability to make himself taller than anything else that can be perceived. Thus, the hero now has the ability to change his size whenever the need arises.

A little further along the road (to Unity) he meets a person whose eyes are so sharp that he can strip relativity down to its finest aspect in God Consciousness. Thus, he has to keep this power hidden from the light of day in normal circumstances or he could destroy any aspect of the relative universe his eyes alighted upon – so he keeps his eyes bandaged up. In actual fact, the mind also has the ability to see in the sense of understanding so it could have the alternative meaning of his mind being so discriminative that he could take apart any aspect of creation if he chose to.

The next Sidhi the hero gains along the path to Unity is the ability to endure extremes in temperature. He meets a man who was of 'quite a different nature'. He shivers when the sun is hot and is hot when the temperature is icy. This particular Sidhi was often applied by seekers following a spiritual master. I have heard stories about Maharishi, when he was a disciple of Guru Dev, displaying his mastery of this particular Sidhi by dipping a robe or blanket into the icy water of the River Ganges, high up in the Himalayas, and drying it purely by the heat of his body in sub-zero conditions.

Lastly the hero meets a servant who could see everything. His sight could scale the very heights of mountains or the skies or plumb the very depths of the seas. Thus, he gains the sixth perfection of being able to see anything in the universe. He had the Sidhi of super sight.

Thus, in this story alone we have come across six of the eight perfections we encountered in the *Yoga Sutras*.

> By and by the king's son and the six servants came to the place where the aged queen lived. He didn't reveal his true identity but set her a challenge.

'If you will give me your beautiful daughter I will perform anything you ask of me.'

The sorceress was delighted to have such a handsome specimen, who was so eager to fall into her net.

'I have three tasks for you,' she smiled knowingly. 'If you perform all three to my satisfaction, you will be the husband and master of my daughter.'

The young man and his retinue came to the place where the queen, or sorceress, lived. That is a way of saying that his mind and perceptions were now able to operate on the very deep level. It is significant that the aged queen says, 'you will be husband and master of my daughter'. In order to be her husband he must gain the status of perpetual unity with the Absolute sphere that exists beyond the source of waking consciousness. Once he has gained this unity, he becomes master of all creation too because all the laws of Nature automatically come under his command.

'That's very kind of you,' he replied. 'What is my first task to be?'

'Now you are talking,' she smiled wryly. 'The first task is no easy one. I dropped my ring into the Red Sea. I would like you to go and fetch it for me.'

The king's son went home to confer with his servants.

'Our first task is to recover the queen's ring from the Red Sea. It is no easy task.'

The recovery of the queen's ring is really a cipher for stilling or escaping from the Wheel of Necessity. Every person upon the earth is really in the grip of working out the seeds of past karma, accruing from good and bad past actions, which will bear fruit in this lifetime. The reason why an initiate may be able to escape from the wheel in one lifetime is because he his able to roast so many of his latent impressions, or past karma, in the tapas of the transcendent. Each time he transcends, his mind is infused with Transcendental Consciousness. The desires sprout in the normal way but because he is constantly yoking his mind to the transcendent they are burned up by the ardent heat of his tapas and do not become externalised to produce the seeds of future karma.

The aged queen is not an ordinary sorceress. She is also the queen of the manifest universe and all that pertains to it. The hero has to prove himself fit for initiation to a higher phase of action. She has hidden a ring in the very depths of the Red Sea. Normally, we would think of the Red Sea as being in the Middle East, but in ancient times the geography of the home territory reflected its counterpart in the sky. For the Ancient Egyptians the Nile was the earthly reflection of the Nile in the sky – namely the Milky Way galaxy. The beginning of creation in the book of Genesis, also speaks of God separating the waters of the sky from the waters of the earth. Whilst the story seems to give the impression that we are talking of the earthly Red Sea, I am quite sure that the one in the sky is the one intended, especially as it is in connection with the ring of the Great Goddess.

Neither is the ring he has to retrieve as straightforward as it seems. The ring in question is the Ring of Necessity. In a sense it is not the ring he has to retrieve. It would be more accurate to say that he has to retrieve himself from it. In other words, he has to transcend the binding force of the fates that keeps him chained to the wheel of birth and rebirth. A ring is also symbolic of the binding together of two people for all eternity. In this case, the marriage of his fully developed personality with the celestial sphere of life, symbolised by the sorceress's daughter. The acquisition of the ring marks his permanent establishment in the state of Cosmic Consciousness.

Maharishi often uses the analogy of the mind being likened to the ocean. At the surface level of the mind there is the turbulence of waves forming, climbing higher and then crashing upon the shore as thoughts. As the mind entertains the mantra the attention passes through quieter and quieter levels of the mind until the realm of eternal stillness is reached and transcended. Thus, his task, figuratively, is to transcend the waters of the mind and retrieve the ring of Unity.

The six servants began to discuss the matter.

'I will find out where it is,' said the sharp-sighted person, and he looked down into the depths of the water. 'There it is!' he exclaimed. It is down there, hanging on a pointed stone.

'It would be easy for me to get it out if I could only see it,' said the Tall One.

'That is no trouble at all,' chimed in Stout One. Thereupon, he lay down at the water's edge and began to drink all the waves that fell into his mouth. Soon he had drunk up the whole of the sea until it was as dry as a meadow. The Tall One stooped down, extended his arm and hand and picked up the ring.

In a figurative sense, three of the Sidhis were used. The sixth servant, or the Sidhi of supersight, enabled the young man to locate the ring. The Stout One, with the infinite stomach, was able to suck up all the water until it was as dry as a meadow and the tall man was able to retrieve the ring.

Put into normal terms, the mind of the king's son was so permeated with

Transcendental Consciousness that very little remained in the sphere of relativity, so it became very easy for the two Sidhis to carry out his desire and still the Ring of Necessity. The stilling of the Wheel of Necessity is the accomplishment of Cosmic Consciousness, which the Mystery Schools called the inner genius. The mind of the king's son would now always act in accord with the will of his father – namely God. Just as the Lord's Prayer says 'Thy will be done on earth just as it is in heaven'.

The king's son was very happy and with great delight he handed over the ring to the old sorceress. She was clearly astonished.

'Yes, this is my ring,' she said with some surprise. You have safely performed the first task – now I will give you the second. She pointed to a meadow in front of her palace. 'Down there are three hundred fat oxen feeding. You must eat all of them, even every piece of bone, skin and hair. Down below in my cellar lie three hundred casks of wine. You must drink up all of these as well. If there is so much as one piece of the oxen left or one drop of the wine not drunk, your life will be forfeited to me.'

'It would be a sin to sit down at such a feast with nobody to share it with,' exclaimed the king's son.

'Okay!' laughed the old woman maliciously. 'You can have one guest to keep you company.'

Naturally the king's son chose the Stout One to be his guest. In no time, all three hundred oxen were rapidly consumed and, not long after, he drank all three hundred casks of wine. When the Stout One had finished, not so much as a single hair of the oxen or drop of the wine remained.

I take the three hundred to be a cipher for the three relative worlds in the form of the physical, the subtle and the causal. As the Stout One is really symbolic of the transcendental Absolute phase of existence, it is an easy task for him to consume the three relative worlds because it is infinitely large. The Rig Veda speaks of manifest creation as being less than a quarter of the unmanifest.

In a sense the Stout One is very much like the kundalini serpent we have met whilst analysing other stories. Usually, this is thought of as a spiritualising regenerative force ascending the very fine tube of the shushumna to the top of the head. Whilst this is true, we must remember that it is always depicted as a snake. Whilst snakes certainly rise up, they actually swallow their prey whole just as the Stout One is doing to the Red Sea in the heavens; just as the transcendental aspect of the mind swallows the relative.

Whilst on the subject of three hundred, it is interesting that kabbalists ascribe it to the Hebrew letter *shin*, pronounced 'sheen'. This numerical value is identical with the Hebrew words *Ruach Elohim*, which mean the life breath of the Divine Ones or the Holy Spirit. The literal meaning of *shin* is 'tooth', whilst it is symbolic of a 'serpent's fang'. Just as a tooth breaks up the form of food ready for digestion, so the serpent's fang represents the power which kills the false personality and its sense of separateness.

Thus, *shin* is also a limitless extension to the mode of consciousness common to most human beings, and implies conscious immortality.

When the meal was over, the prince went to the old queen and told her that he had successfully performed the second task also.

She smiled in surprise but added, 'Nobody has ever done so much before but one task still remains.' Smiling to herself she thought, 'You won't be able to escape me. I'll soon have your head.'

'Tonight I will come to your chamber and bring my daughter to you,' she resumed, turning her attention back to the prince. 'You shall encircle your arms around her but when you are sitting there together, beware of falling asleep. When the clock strikes twelve I will come to your chamber. If my daughter is no longer there you will be lost.'

'It couldn't be easier,' thought the prince. 'I'll have no difficulty in keeping my eyes open.'

However, just to be on the safe side, he consulted with his servants, who told him that foresight is a good guard when there is treachery afoot.

When night fell the old queen brought her daughter to the chamber and delivered her into the arms of the prince. As soon as the old queen had gone, the Tall One wound himself round the two in a circle and the Stout One stood on guard by the door so that no living creature could enter.

There the maiden sat in the arms of the prince. She did not say a word. The moon shone through the window and illuminated her face. The prince was entranced at her wondrous beauty. He was in the heights of happiness just to sit there and gaze upon her lovely face.

All went very well until eleven o'clock, when the old woman cast a spell upon them all. Suddenly they all fell asleep and the young maiden was carried away. They all slept soundly until a quarter to twelve, when the spell wore off.

The prince was beside himself with grief. 'All is lost,' he wailed. 'Be quiet!' interrupted the Listener. 'I want to listen to the universe to see what is going on.'

All went quiet whilst he listened.

'She is on a rock, three hundred leagues away,' announced the Listener. 'This is a job for you, Tall One, only you can save her. You can be there in a couple of steps.'

'Okay,' replied the Tall One. 'But I need Sharp Eyes to come with me so that we can destroy the rock.'

Sharp Eyes climbed upon the Tall One's back. They were there in the twinkling of an eye. The Tall One took the bandage from the eyes of his friend without looking round. One glance from his sharp-sighted friend was sufficient to shatter the rock to pieces. With no more ado, the Tall One picked up the maiden in his arms and carried her back to the prince in less than a second. By that time, his friend had put the bandage back over his eyes ready for the Tall One to take him back too.

Before the clock struck twelve they were all sitting as merrily as before. On the hour the old sorceress had a malicious look upon her face. She believed that the maiden was three hundred leagues away and that the young man was about to lose his head.

When she entered the chamber, she was astonished to see the maiden still in the arms of the prince. She had clearly been outsmarted.

'Here is somebody who knows more than I do,' she said to herself and was forced to keep her part of the bargain and hand her daughter over to the prince.

The time is obviously related to the third initiation into the Mysteries. This one always took place at midnight, when the initiate emerged from the solar sphere to the polar. It always took place in darkness because it was seen as the culmination of the spiritual sun.

In God Consciousness the initiate could perceive the celestial realm of life with his five perfected senses. It is clear that he could see, hear, smell, taste and touch in this refined sphere of life. This must relate to what is known in Indian philosophy as *Saguna*. The god with form. Unity Consciousness is the state of becoming one with the formless God. This is called *Nirguna*.

The daughter of the sorceress is a cipher for the perfection of his own being – his complete realisation in Unity Consciousness. In the story she is chained to a rock. As we have found earlier, a rock unpolluted by the chisels and tools of men was a well-known symbol of God without form in many areas of the world.

When the prince was holding the maiden in his arms enjoying the rapture of looking into her lovely face, that was Saguna, God Consciousness where the sight and sounds of all the gods, goddesses, angels, devas etc. can be enjoyed. However, at one remove from this sphere is Nirguna – the God without form.

The allegory of this final initiation was to depict the near-perfected self or soul in the form of a maiden and chain her to a rock three hundred leagues away. We have already established that three hundred refers to the Hebrew letter *shin* as symbolic of the power that breaks down the limitations of form. This is further emphasised by the supersight of the enlightened intellect that disintegrates the shadow of all forms so as to be united with the formless.

Once she saw her daughter in the arms of the prince, the sorceress gave up all claim to her daughter and was willing to cede to one who knew more than she did. At the achievement of God Consciousness the knower is able to see the finest aspect of the relative creation in everything he sees. In Unity Consciousness the myth of a separate relative universe is shattered because he sees everything as a part of himself. So when unity dawns the last semblance of the rock of relativity is shattered.

From the point of view of the folk tale as a carrier of hidden meaning, this ought to be the end of the story. However, there is also the question of the consistency of the story to be borne in mind. The Frosty One has not yet appeared, and the tale would seem incomplete and would therefore fail in its job to entertain.

> 'It's a disgrace that you have to obey the commands of common people and that you are not even allowed to choose a husband of your own liking,' whispered the old sorceress on her way out of the chamber.
>
> These words incensed the proud heart of the young maiden. She was filled with anger and was seething for revenge. Next morning she ordered three hundred bundles of wood to be assembled and summoned the prince.

In an ordinary story this would be fine. However, in this one the maiden is definitely a cipher for the perfection of the prince's soul. At no other point in this story does she actually emerge as a personality, because the role of a persona is out of keeping with her place in the celestial realms and above. Nothing whispered by the relative ego would have any effect on a perfected soul. She would be both beyond and incapable of pride. However, from the point of the storyteller it would be a good move. I am sure the audience would enjoy hearing some more of the super-powers. It would also both serve to lengthen the story and increase the enjoyment of the listeners, and also make it sequentially consistent.

'Although you performed the three tasks my mother set, I will not be your wife unless you or one of your servants is willing to brave the rigours of the flames for me,' she demanded.

She thought that the prince himself would volunteer because of his great love for her; also because nobody else would love her enough to subject himself to her ordeal by fire. This would free her of him.

'Everyone else has done something except the Frosty One,' said the other servants. 'He must be set to work.'

They put him into the centre of the pile of wood and set fire to it. The fire burned fiercely for three days until all the wood was consumed. The Frosty One sat amid the ashes trembling like an aspen leaf.

'I've never felt so cold in all my life,' he shivered. 'If it had gone on very much longer I would have been numb with cold.'

Now that the king's son had fulfilled the task, the beautiful maiden had no alternative but to accept him as her husband. When the young couple drove away to the church, the sorceress could not endure the ignominy of her daughter having to marry a commoner, or so she thought. She sent out a band of warriors with orders to bring back her daughter and cut down all those that opposed them.

However, the sharp ears of the Listener heard everything. He conferred with the Stout One and devised a plan. The Stout One, who had swallowed some sea water, spat twice and a huge lake appeared. It quickly swamped the warriors and they were drowned.

When the sorceress knew what had happened, she sent an army of mailed knights to finish the job. However, the rattling of their armour soon alerted the Listener to their intentions. He quickly undid the bandage in front of the eyes of Sharp Eyes. No sooner had he fixed his attention on them than the knights splintered into fragments like broken glass.

The king's son and the maiden rode on undisturbed to the church. When they had been blessed, the servants took leave of their master. 'All your desires have been fulfilled,' they said. 'You need us no longer. We will go our own way.'

Even if there was any dispute about the last piece being tagged on the end of the original, there is no doubt about this last section. The prince had definitely won his heart's desire, achieving Unity Consciousness in the shape of the sorceress's daughter, hence he had no further need of the five Sidhis, personalised as servants. This further lengthening of the story sounds very reminiscent of another tale. When I first read it I thought I had slipped back to another tale called *King Thrushbeard*, which is a tale about a king who tames his haughty wife by making her believe she was married to a beggar instead of a king. As in this story, the king was wholly successful.

Half a league from the palace, where the prince lived with his father, was a swineherd out tending his swine. As they were approaching the land of the swineherd the prince rounded on his wife. 'Do you know who I really am?' She was taken by surprise. Before she could answer, he continued. 'I am really a swineherd. That man over there is my father. We shall both have to set to and help him now we are home.'

They dismounted at the inn. The prince arranged that the owners of the inn should take away the maiden's royal clothes during the night. In the morning the maiden woke up with nothing to wear. By this time, the prince had already gone. It was only after a great deal of imploring by the maiden, that the innkeeper's wife reluctantly gave her an old gown and a pair of worsted stockings.

'Think yourself lucky,' snorted the innkeeper's wife. 'If it hadn't been for your husband's kindness, you wouldn't even have had these.'

The maiden had not seen through her husband's ruse and now really thought she was a swineherd and began to tend the swine with him. She realised too late that she deserved this fate to pay her back for her haughtiness and pride. After a week had gone by she felt at the end of her tether. She was not used to working long hours at a menial task. She felt tired out and had sores all over her feet.

Suddenly, two well-dressed people stopped to speak to her. 'Do you know who your husband is?' they asked.

'Yes, he is a swineherd,' she replied. 'He is out on business at the moment.'

'Well he wants you to go to him,' they added. 'We'll take you to him.'

To her surprise, they took her to the royal palace, which was not far away. Looking rather overawed she entered the great hall. There, on a raised dais stood her husband dressed in a splendid regal costume with a crown upon his head. Naturally, she didn't recognise him.

Suddenly he came over to her and took her in his arms and kissed her. 'You made me suffer so much for you that I thought you needed paying back in kind,' he smiled.

The wedding was celebrated with much style, pomp and circumstance; I wish I had been invited too.

As we have said much earlier in the book, more often than not the storyteller would have no idea of the original meaning of the tale, therefore they would not think twice about the need to alter it to please their audience. Also, once the addition had been made, it would make a far more fitting conclusion for the maiden to become loyal and penitent towards her husband.

# Chapter 15
# Iron Hans

A large hairy man lived at the bottom of a deep pool. He was discovered and captured and locked in an iron cage.

There are any number of versions of this story. You may be more familiar with *The Frog Prince*, where the the main character is a princess. In this version the iron cage is the unpurified physical human body in which the inner genius, or the true Self finds himself imprisoned. Like the serpent in Genesis, Iron Hans has the key to all the knowledge of good and evil in the world. In terms of Indian philosophy he is the kundalini, which ascends the whole length of the shushumna – a sheath running the whole length of the spine. Kundalini is usually symbolised as a serpent, which lies coiled up, fast asleep, in the lowest of the chakras called the muladhara chakra.

It is the awakening of this power that causes it to ascend and to arouse the five other chakras, before it culminates into full realisation or enlightenment when it reaches the seventh chakra, called the thousand-petalled lotus, in the brain. Thus, to complete the symbolism in this particular story, the iron cage in which Iron Hans was imprisoned is the muladhara chakra. It is made of iron because this symbolised the base metal of the average man, which the alchemist would transmute into gold. The deep pool he lived in was the very depths of the individual mind, very close to the transcendent.

The fact that Hans is large and hairy conveys a Neanderthal, gross or unpurified appearance. It is well known that the quest of the alchemist was to turn base metal into gold. Whilst this more material consideration may have been the motivation for some, most people now accept that this was a mainly a smokescreen that saved the alchemist from getting into trouble with the intolerant religious authorities of his time. The real task for the true hermeticist was to work on the base metal of his own nervous system and to perfect it so as to become divine, or at one with God. Iron was considered as the starting point of the process, which transformed man as an animal into an enlightened divine being.

> One day the king's son was playing with a golden ball. As he was playing, the ball fell into the cage. Iron Hans would not give the boy back his ball unless he opened the cage.

The motif of the golden ball and the well is also found in *The Frog Prince* and the ancient Indian epic, the Mahabharat – which brings us back to the question of antiquity! That epic is at least five thousand years old and may well have borrowed the motif from an earlier tale. 'The king's son was playing with a golden ball.' At face value, 'playing catch' immediately comes to mind; but this knowledge hidden in ciphers – so let us look again. A ball is also a sphere. A sphere is made up of an infinite number of circles. A circle in picture writing was a serpent swallowing its own tail – the small self turning back to its inner self.

A sphere, especially a golden sphere, symbolises perfection, the home of all possibilities in both the manifest and unseen world. The king's son was playing with the idea of attaining eternal perfection. His aim or lifelong task falls at the feet of his inner genius – the Self. Thus this piece of text is not about a little boy playing ball but an entreaty to his inner self to guide him through all the unseen difficulties he will have to face. In terms of the individual, the king's son is the buddhi or awakened intellect. The golden ball he was playing with is an authentic technique which gives him access to the pure field of Transcendental Consciousness. As previously stated, the king's son represents the individual man or woman who is already acquainted with the pure consciousness of the Absolute, because the king or prince in these tales always symbolises Unity Consciousness.

The cage he had to open was the key to all knowledge, which in the past has always been closed to anybody who wasn't initiated into the knowledge of a particular tradition of masters. When one learns a spiritual technique the individual is initiated into the knowledge of a long line of realised spiritual masters, which can be many thousands of years old. India is the only country where this long tradition is still intact, though it may well exist in some of the Sufi traditions. The ceremony which precedes the giving of the technique is not a part of the modern Hindu religion. It is to focus the mind of the teacher on the long and venerable line of masters from which the knowledge came.

> He would not give the young prince his ball back unless the cage was opened and he was let free. The boy, for his part, said that he couldn't because his father forbade it and even if he wanted to he couldn't because he didn't know where the key was. Iron Hans told

him that the key was under his mother's pillow. The young prince threw caution to the winds and opened the cage. Iron Hans was free.

In actual fact, if the golden ball is a metaphor for an initiation technique, which I am quite sure it is, there is no way the cage would not open towards the transcendent once the young prince started to entertain the mantra. As previously mentioned, the iron cage is not only the physical human body where the inner genius is imprisoned, it is also the muladhara chakra, where the kundalini is figuratively sleeping.

Iron Hans took the boy deep into the forest and sat him down by a golden well. The boy had to see that nothing fell into it.

At this point Iron Hans, as the ascending kundalini, becomes the mentor of the young prince and the boy his apprentice. The newly awakened mind of the prince was taken deep into the forest of knowledge of an old and established tradition of masters. The freeing of Iron Hans obviously parallels the awakening of the kundalini in tantric texts. Like God in the Genesis story of Adam and Eve, Iron Hans forbade knowledge of the Tree of Good and Evil. Similarly the boy was not allowed to let anything in relative creation have any contact with its source in the form of the golden pool. Strangely enough, the boy seems to have been given the task of guardian, rather like the dragon who guards the tree of golden apples.

However, just as the quest of the alchemist was to turn base metal into gold, the power of pure Transcendental Consciousness is able to purify and transform the individual nervous system so that it can reflect the truth of the Absolute at all times. Thus, when the boy put his sore finger into the pool it turned to gold, for nothing can withstand the power of Transcendental Consciousness to transform the individual. Next a hair falls in. This also turns to gold. Finally, whilst looking into the pool, his shoulder-length hair fell in and turned to gold also.

The boy tried to hide his golden hair by tying it up in his handkerchief. The giant already knew what had happened.

'You have not stood the trial and can stay here no longer,' he said. 'Go forth into the world. There you will learn what poverty is. But as you have not got a bad heart, and as I mean well by you, if you fall into any difficulty, come to the forest and cry Iron Hans and then I will come to you. My power is greater than you think.'

As in *Cinderella* and many other stories, a period of apprenticeship is necessary. I have mentioned before the role of work to make fast the dye of the Absolute. The initiate has had a spell with his master in the seclusion of the forest, where he has had a lot of exposure to Transcendental Consciousness. The need now is twofold – he has to temper the new flexibility given to him by the Absolute and to share his newly found prowess with the relative world.

> The king's son left the forest and walked along beaten and unbeaten paths until he reached a great city. He looked for work but couldn't find any. Finally, he went to the palace and asked if he could be taken in. Eventually, the cook took him into service to fetch and carry wood and water and to rake the cinders.

It is significant that he could not find a place in relative creation. He had already transcended so the only place he could find was at the palace – the palace being the citadel of Unity Consciousness. As a new initiate he could only command a very menial place in the pecking order. In keeping with the tradition in many other stories this was symbolised by beginning as a scullery lad.

> Once, when no one else was at hand, he was asked to take food to the royal table, but as he didn't want anybody to see his golden hair he kept his cap on. The king was outraged. As he had never seen the boy before, he chastised him.
> 'When you come to the royal table you must take your hat off,' he said.
> The boy said he had a sore head. That was the reason he kept his cap on. The king called for the cook and scolded him for letting anybody so rude and disrespectful serve his table and told him to get rid of the boy. But the cook had a kind heart. He exchanged the lad for the gardener's boy.

This passage only reinforces the position of the novice initiate and how far he had to go before he became one with the king himself. The king would, in fact, have known the boy because he had transcended and was on the spiritual path. His verbal attack on the boy to remove his cap would have been a test of his resolve to keep the oath he had promised to his mentor Iron Hans.

> One day he was working in the garden. It was very hot so he took

off his cap so that the air could cool him. As the sun shone on his golden hair it glittered and flashed and reflected onto the walls of the princess's bedroom. She wondered what it was. Then she saw him and commanded him to bring her a garland of flowers. Hastily, he put his cap on and gathered a garland of wild flowers. As he was going up the stairs to her room he met the gardener.

'How can you give a princess such common flowers? Go quickly and pick only the rarest and prettiest and give them to her.'

'No!' said the lad. 'The wild ones have more scent and will please her more.' With that he respectfully gave them to her.

'Take you hat off, it is not polite to wear it in my presence,' she scolded.

He once more pretended to have a sore head so she tore his cap from his head and his splendid gold hair tumbled around his shoulders. He wanted to run out but she held him fast by the arm and gave him a couple of ducats. He cared nothing for the gold pieces and gave them to the gardener for his children to play with.

The path to Unity Consciousness should be an innocent one. Any good experience one has on the way should be a sign that you are travelling in the right direction. The innocent way he conducted himself was noticed by the princess and the simplicity and heartfelt truthfulness to the gardener is a sign of his complete lack of guile. Another sign of progress on the spiritual path is a gradual increase in Nature support – things start going well for you.

However, that does not mean giving way to the acquisitive side of your nature – to acquire wealth and success for its own sake. The boy gave his gold pieces to the gardener's children to play with.

The princess summoned him on two further occasions to bring her a wreath of wild flowers. Each time she tried to snatch his cap from his head and gave him a handful of gold pieces. On both occasions he resisted the attempt to reveal his golden hair and gave the gold pieces to the gardener's children to play with.

These were two further tests to make him break the terms of his apprenticeship. The initiate was gaining spiritual credibility quickly. The princess symbolised pure consciousness every bit as much as the king and is part of the same lineage. The gift of money she gave on each occasion shows that he is succeeding on the spiritual path. The gift of money probably refers to the Gayatri mantra or something similar. It is not actual physical wealth in the form of money but spiritual wealth especially as they are golden ducats. The money is either a cipher or one of the many changes that can take place in a story in an oral tradition over a long period of time. The Gayatri mantra is invoked in all pujas. It is a gift to mankind from the goddess in her three aspects to the sage Vishwamitra. In the part that is most recited the worshipper entreats: 'we meditate upon that Light of Wisdom which is the supreme wealth of the Gods. May it grant us increase in our meditations'. The fact that he didn't hoard it but gave it away is further testimony to his progress.

> Soon afterwards the country was overrun by war. The king gathered an army but he did not know whether he could offer any opposition because the enemy had superior military strength. The gardener's boy said, 'I am grown up now. I want to go to war, only give me a horse.' The only one left in the stable was lame. It only had three good legs.

'The country was overrun by war' means that the mind of the seeker was beset by problems or doubts. It was, no doubt, that his increase of esteem in the relative world was causing him problems. Deep stresses were unwinding in his physiology, culminating in conflicting desires, which were affecting his spiritual development. He wanted to overcome these problems. The lame horse symbolised his spiritual progress. Transcendental Consciousness had not stabilised in his physiology to become Cosmic Consciousness. The all-important fourth leg had not yet fully recovered its full range of powers. Only the waking, dreaming and deep sleep states of consciousness were strong and could be depended upon.

> He mounted his lame horse and rode it, hobblety jig, towards the deep, dark forest. When he came to the outskirts he called out Iron Hans three times so loudly that his voice echoed through the trees. Thereupon the wild man appeared instantly and asked him what he desired.
>
> The lad said, 'I need a strong, sturdy horse, for I am going to war.'
>
> 'I will give you this and more,' said Iron Hans. A stable boy appeared leading a spirited steed, followed by a great troop of warriors equipped with iron armour. The gardener's boy mounted the spirited courser and led his troop into war. When the lad got near the battlefield many of the king's troops had already fallen and those that were left were ready to give in.
>
> Suddenly the boy with his army of iron soldiers broke down the

enemy and beat down all who opposed him until there was not a single opposing soldier left. Instead of returning home in triumph with the king, the boy called out to Iron Hans. He exchanged the spirited steed and troop of soldiers for his lame horse again.

The novice initiate began to use the technique he had been taught. It took him to deeper and deeper levels of his individual mind. However, when it reached near the transcendent, called ritam, he experienced a fundamental change in his meditation. He had entered the realm of Bliss Consciousness. Any doubts or unresolved stresses he had fell away. After his triumphant sojourn on the transcendental field of consciousness his awareness went back to the waking state. His original lame horse, or the three-legged one, refers to the waking, dreaming and deep sleep states of relative consciousness, whilst the magnificent chargers Iron Hans gives him have their basis in the Absolute, fourth state of consciousness – Transcendental Consciousness.

The princess went to meet her father when he returned to the palace. News had travelled fast. She congratulated him on his victory. 'I am not the one who secured the victory,' said the king. 'It was a strange knight who came to my assistance with his soldiers. I will proclaim a great feast that will last for three days to celebrate the victory. You will throw a golden apple. Perhaps we will be lucky. The unknown knight might well catch it himself.'

Once again the lad called out to Iron Hans.

'I want to catch the golden apple that the princess is going to throw,' he said.

'It is as if you have caught it already,' replied Iron Hans. 'You shall also have a suit of red armour and a spirited chestnut horse to ride upon.'

When the king's daughter threw the golden apple the hands of all the knights went up to catch it but it landed safely in the lad's hands and he rode swiftly away.

On the second day Iron Hans equipped him as a white knight and gave him a white horse to ride upon. He caught the second apple the princess had thrown and rode quickly away. The king grew angry. 'He must appear before me and tell me his name. If the same thing happens tomorrow pursue him and bring him back.'

On the third day the lad was dressed as a black knight and rode a black steed. Once again the king's daughter threw the apple. The lad caught it and rode quickly away. The king summoned his men to pursue him with their swords drawn. One of the king's men injured the lad's leg with the point of his sword. The boy's horse leapt so violently that his helmet fell from his head, revealing his beautiful shoulder-length hair. The lad escaped but the king's men rode back to tell their sovereign what they had seen.

This part of the story, from now on, is very much reminiscent of *Cinderella* and *Allerleirau*. Iron Hans has become the equivalent of the wish-fulfilling tree, equipping the boy in increasingly splendid knights' costumes, each one representing the higher states of development. His first visit to the feast was symbolic of Cosmic Consciousness, or the inner genius. His suit of red armour and the chestnut horse is meant to depict God Consciousness, and finally his black armour and steed Unity Consciousness. According to Bayley, red symbolised love and black, in ancient times, didn't have the sinister meanings it has since acquired[1]. In those times it symbolised the 'divine dark' of inscrutability, silence and eternity.

The golden apple thrown by the princess on each occasion is his prize for gaining the next highest state of consciousness. Gold symbolises wisdom and the highest state of development, according to the alchemists. No other knight at the feast could have caught the golden apple because no other could match the evolution of consciousness of the boy.

Bayley tells us that the Irish, Gaelic and Russian words for apple all resolve into 'the orb of God'[2]. He also reminds us that there is a tradition in mystic folklore that golden apples were said to restore a person's youth. Maharishi tells us that a fully developed person is also in perfect health with his mind and faculties working perfectly together. Thus, each time the golden apple is thrown it is both a gift and a testimony from the divine that one has evolved into the next higher state of consciousness.

The following day the princess asked the gardener about the boy.

'He has been to the festival too and has shown my children the three golden apples he has won,' said the gardener.

The king summoned him into his presence. The princess took the little red cap from his head and his lustrous golden hair fell about all around his shoulders. They were amazed to see how handsome he was.

'Are you the knight who came to the feast each day dressed in different colours, who caught the golden apples each time?' asked the king.

'I am,' replied the boy and took the golden apples from his

pocket and gave them to the king. 'I am also the knight who helped you win your victories over the enemies. Not only that, I am the son of as great a king as yourself.'

'I see,' said the king. 'Is there anything I can do to please you?'

'Yes,' he retorted. 'Give me your daughter to be my wife.'

The maiden laughed. 'I have already seen by his golden hair that he was no ordinary gardener's boy.' She went up and kissed him.

His mother and father were invited to the wedding. As the guests were sitting at the tables at wedding feast the music suddenly stopped. The doors opened and a great king with his retinue entered the hall. He went up to the lad and embraced him.

'I am Iron Hans,' he announced. 'I was enchanted into thinking I was a wild man but you have set me free. All the treasure that I possess shall be yours.'

And no doubt they all lived happily ever after. The true identity of the lad was established and all his marvellous feats were out in the open. The divine spark, which has always been there right from the most unevolved state, has now grown to envelop the entire mind and nervous system of the individual. True to the terms of his apprenticeship, the lad did not go around proclaiming his new-found spiritual development but waited until it became apparent to all.

The princess took off his little cap and his golden hair, signifying light and wisdom, fell down on to his shoulders. He was no longer the gardener's boy. It was recognised by both the king and the princess that the lad before them was now, like themselves, divinity incarnate. It is fitting that the princess completed the job. This is another example of 'atma on the move', and the transition from God Consciousness is automatic.

Finally, to seal the story, Iron Hans enters the frame as a great king. He is, in fact, the lad transformed from iron to gold. As the hairy giant he possessed within himself the potential to become king. Once his illumined buddhi, symbolised by the lad, awakened the kundalini from its sleep state in the muladhara chakra, things began to move. From that low initial state of waking consciousness he climbed out of the well of ignorance into the divine golden sunlight of Unity Consciousness.

---

[1] Bayley, 1996, 355
[2] ibid. 302-303

# Chapter 16
# The Golden Bird

A great many years ago there lived a king. He had a beautiful pleasure garden behind his palace. The pride of place was given to a splendid tree, which bore golden apples. It was the king's custom to have them counted when they were nearly ripe. One particular morning it was reported to him that one of the apples was missing.

As soon as he heard this he immediately ordered that a watch should take place every night beneath the tree. The king had three sons. He asked his eldest son to take the first watch as soon as night fell. Unfortunately, the eldest son fell asleep on the stroke of midnight. When they awoke next day another apple had gone.

On the following night the second son volunteered to be on watch. Like his brother, he too fell asleep on the stroke of midnight. In the morning yet another apple was missing.

It was the turn of the youngest son on the third night. The king had little trust in him because he did not have the worldly wisdom of his brothers but he grudgingly agreed to let him have a turn.

When darkness fell, the youth lay down beneath the tree but kept awake. He did not let sleep master him. He heard the clock strike midnight and was surprised to hear a strange rustling in the air. In the moonlight he saw a bird whose feathers shone like pure gold. The bird alighted upon the tree. It had just plucked off one of the golden apples, when the youth shot an arrow at him.

The bird managed to escape with the apple in its beak but it had been hit. One of its tail feathers floated down to the earth. The youth picked it up. In the morning he took it to the king. He related the whole incident to his father. After a meeting with his most learned ministers, the king declared that the feather was worth more than his whole kingdom. That being so, he avowed that he wanted the whole bird.

We have spoken of the Tree of Life being an ubiquitous, world-wide symbol. Before going on to analyse this story I would like to quote a piece from Bayley on how the native population of Papua New Guinea conceived of the future state awaiting all mankind, as it is pertinent to the understanding of this story.

> Up on the Astrolabe Range there blooms, invisible to the human eye, a great and gracious tree. In and around about it dwell all those who lived good lives before they died. Those fortunate souls dwell there forever without care and in great happiness.
>
> There, lovers and loved relations will be reunited, while those who are already dwelling beneath its shade may and do come back to watch over the living, so that each soul on the earth has an unseen but ever present guide and helper.
>
> The wicked have to pass through sickness, pain and trouble before they reach the tree, but eventually they too will be gathered beneath its branches.[1]

The pleasure garden at the back of the king's castle is the transcendental plane of existence underlying the entire relative field of life. His tree is the Tree of Life, whose trunk is the axis of all spheres of creation. Golden apples usually signify immortality. We all hang on it, and after many lives achieve immortality. I am not sure about the term 'ripe'. The three sons could easily be the causal, astral and physical bodies, which characterise all three aspects of mankind. It could mean ripe for manifestation or it could mean nearing enlightenment. From what follows it must be the latter because of the midnight hour.

Normally, this was the time of initiation into the Greater Mysteries but because of its place in the story and what is yet to come, it is more likely an initiation into the Lesser Mysteries. The storyteller or one of his predecessors may have changed the time from midday to midnight to heighten the background suspense and add another layer of drama to his craft.

The king is the inner genius or large Self incarcerated in a body. He naturally feels that his all-knowing mind and his fully developed, life-supporting aims and aspirations are cramped, and lack most of their normal effectiveness within the confines of the gross and astral vehicles of relative existence. His aim is to spiritualise these vehicles of expression by gaining possession of the golden bird. This golden bird was almost certain to be the phoenix – a universal symbol of resurrection and immortality. This viewpoint is given further weight by the fact that the Slav version of the story is called *Ohnivak, the Bird of Fire.*

The younger, simpleton son is the illumined buddhi because he was the only one of the three sons to stay awake and perceive the truth. He had a glimpse of the cosmic reality underlying all creation. The arrow was not a real arrow. It was an arrow of thought which came into contact with one of the tail feathers of the golden bird of the transcendent. This is a very nice way of describing the initial spiritual experience of a person. A solitary tail feather from the rear end is often as good as it gets in the way of experiences of spiritual illumination. The king or individual had a heightened experience of reality. In counsel with the deepest aspects of his being, he declared that the experience was worth more than the whole relative kingdom. He vowed that one day he would achieve the permanent state of Cosmic Consciousness.

The Slav version is much more full than the Grimms' recording of the tale. In this, the simpleton prince acquired the feather from the wing of the bird of fire. The radiance of this solitary feather was so beautiful and bright that it 'illumined all the galleries of the palace and they needed no other light'. Could there be a better description of a human mind lit by divine revelation?

Consequently the king could think of nothing else than how this magnificent bird could be acquired. One day he could bear it no longer. He summoned his three sons to his royal chamber.

'You see the state I am in, my children. If I could hear the bird Ohnivak sing just once, I would be cured of this sickness of the heart.'

Moved by his father's cry from the heart, the eldest son volunteered to try to track it down.

Never mind the long passage of time – look at the dramatic effect a simple change in punctuation can make! If we were just to add a full-stop after 'state'. It would read:

'You see the state. I am in my children. If I could hear the bird Ohnivak sing just once, I would be cured of this sickness of the heart.'

He certainly would because all of his children would be blessed with the language of the birds – namely the rhythmic speech of Veda – would become embedded into their conciousness and so grant them the wealth of the gods that makes life free from fear.

The eldest son trusted in his own worldly cleverness. He thought he'd soon discover the golden bird. He had not gone far when he saw a fox sitting at the edge of a wood. He cocked his rifle and took aim.

'Don't shoot me!' exclaimed the fox in alarm. 'I'll give you some good advice. You're going in the right direction to the golden bird.

In the evening you will come to a village where two inns stand opposite each other. One of them is lit up brightly and full of merriment. It seems enticing – but do not go in. Go into the other one. It's not much to look at – but it's the one that will suit you best.'

'As if I'd take any notice of you,' the king's son mused and he pulled the trigger. Luckily the fox stretched out his tail and ran making a quick getaway. Consequently the bullet whistled harmlessly over his head. The fox quickly slid into the woods and out of sight.

In the evening the eldest son came to the village of the two inns, just as the fox had said. People were singing and dancing in the brightly lit inn. They were having a good time. The other inn looked very dull by comparison. So the eldest brother opted for a life of riotous living and consequently forgot about the golden bird, his father and all the good advice he had been given in life.

The ancient Egyptians revered jackals as the best maker of tracks in the desert. They followed the tracks of a jackal so as to not get lost and also avoid the worst valleys and precipices. They called the jackal Up-uat – the opener of the ways. In folklore, the fox was the European equivalent of the opener of the ways because they made paths through the dense woods and forests. The ancient Egyptians saw Osiris as the 'opener of ways to the gods' and Anubis as the pathfinder. That is why the latter is given a jackal's head in the Egyptians' pantheon.

It is interesting to see the easy blending of the ancient and modern in this tale. We have, on one hand, European folklore in the shape of the fox blending easily, on the other hand, with the modern form of armament, the rifle.

Back to the analysis of the story. The village is the human mind. On the surface there are the bright lights of the senses saying, 'Go out! Have a good time! Have sex! Get drunk!' On the other there is the small voice of the spirit saying 'Meditate – follow a spiritual life.' Needless to say the eldest brother chose the former and completely forgot the reason why he had come into the world.

Several months went by. The eldest son did not return, so the second son set out to find the golden bird. He too saw the fox, received good advice and took the same path as his brother, ending up in the brightly lit inn. Needless to say, after several more months had passed the younger son pleaded with his father to let him go in search of the golden bird.

For a while the king would not hear of it. He thought his youngest son was not as bright as his two elder brothers and was even less likely to find the bird. However, the son kept on pressing until at last the king weakened. He let the youngest son go on his travels for the sake of a quiet life.

Once again the fox was sitting at the edge of the wood waiting. 'Don't kill me, prince,' he begged.

'Don't you worry, little fox,' answered the lad good-naturedly. 'I'll not harm you.'

'You won't regret it,' the fox replied, and proceeded to tell him about the village and the two inns. 'What is more, I'll help you get there more quickly. Hop on behind me – on my tail.'

The lad hopped on. No sooner than he had sat down than the fox was off like a rocket. He ran up hill and down dale with the wind fairly whistling through their hair. In no time at all they had arrived at the village. The lad got off the fox's back and went into the more sober of the two inns and spent a quiet night there.

The illumined buddhi of the youngest son was wide awake. It was natural for him to be non-violent. Consequently he had the full support of Nature in all his actions. Neither was he so foolhardy as to cock a deaf ear to good advice. The wise person sifts through the whole welter of thoughts and experiences that come his way and treats them with equal distinction. He knows that his next cue for spiritual advancement may come from the most unlikely source. When it does his awareness is wide awake and ready to execute an adept hundred and eighty degrees away from the external world of the senses to the transcendental field of life.

Whilst the fox is the opener of the ways in this story, the true spiritual guide lies within. In fact, it must be synonymous with the unseen from the Papuan story of the Tree of Life. The young prince obviously had something of a divine revelation and followed it.

In the story of Ohnivak, the fox as the opener of ways is more pronounced. This version has the youngest prince on horseback. The fox sets off in front of him and clears the road with his bushy tail. By this means mountains were cut down, ravines were levelled and rivers bridged.

Next morning the prince was up early and on his way. He hadn't gone far when he saw the fox sitting in front of him.

'I'll give you a bit more help if you would like me to,' proclaimed the fox. The prince nodded. 'Carry straight on. Don't deviate an inch and you'll come to a castle. Outside the castle you will find a whole regiment of soldiers fast asleep. Go straight through the middle of them. They will not awaken. Go straight into the castle and go through all the rooms until you come to the one with the golden bird. You will find it hanging in a wooden cage. Nearby it is a showy, golden one. Don't be tempted to take the bird out of the common wooden cage and put it into the golden one or you may run out of luck.'

Once again the fox stretched out his tail for the prince to sit on. As soon as he had sat down they were away, with the air whistling through their hair. Soon they came to the castle. Everything was just as the fox had said. The regiment of soldiers was fast asleep. He went inside and found the golden bird. It was shut up in a wooden cage. Nearby was the golden cage. He could also see the three golden apples lying on a shelf.

He was enraptured by the sight of the golden bird.

'It would be such a pity to take him back in this shabby old cage,' he mused. 'Such a splendid-looking creature deserves to be in that golden one.'

So he opened the cage door and put the bird into the golden cage. The bird uttered a shrill cry. The soldiers awoke and rushed in to arrest the Prince. The next morning he was taken into court and sentenced to death.

The sleeping soldiers in front of the castle bring to mind an analogy that Maharishi sometime uses. It is clear that not every meditation ends up in the transcendent, because of the legion of latent desires lying dormant, waiting to be awakened. When the body gains the deep rest, it has the tendency to normalise itself and some of the latent desires, which he calls stresses, begin to unwind as thoughts. On other occasions, however, the mind goes straight to the transcendent. Maharishi describes this as 'tiptoeing through a herd of sleeping elephants'[2]. Tiptoeing through the regiment of soldiers seems to be exactly the same kind of expression.

When approaching the castle or fortress of the transcendent it is important to be single-minded. If a person allows his mind to become engaged with some interesting or significant aspect, such as the golden cage, before the goal is reached, his attention will be both diverted and extroverted. The mind will then be taken prisoner by the realm of relative existence, just like Persephone, when she was captivated by the narcissus, and subsequently taken prisoner by Hades.

The prince was also urged to put the golden bird into the plain wooden cage. But why a wooden cage? As wood is one of the most basic building materials used by man, it was often equated, symbolically, with the fundamental aspects of life itself, such as 'life force', 'motherliness' and either 'carrying' or 'containing'. In a similar vein, Swedenborg considered that it symbolised celestial goodness in its lower corporeal plane. This sounds like a grandiose way of saying that it symbolised Transcendental Consciousness.

This initial foray into the sphere of the transcendent is experienced by all fairy story heroes and heroines. It is synonymous with the initiation into the Lesser Mysteries. Whilst the prince had entered the castle of the transcendent, it was as a novice. He had made a very good start but had by no means gained full realisation. The legions of desires and attractions of the outside world soon awoke and 'arrested' his progress. He had come face to face with the prize but he was not sufficiently advanced to carry it off and he was thrown back into the prison of his physical body, where he would become once more a prey to the fates.

It was significant that he was sentenced to death by the court of justice next morning. Morning, or rather midday, was the time set for the initiation into the Greater Mysteries. The death in question is the death of being restricted to the alternating states of consciousness of waking, dreaming and deep sleep. Having achieved a glimpse of Cosmic Consciousness, the prince would be forever aware of two aspects of reality – his true unbounded Self and the ever changing world of relative universe. The king that tried him was obviously an aspect of the Absolute.

However, as an afterthought the king set him a challenge.

'Bring me back the golden horse, which can run much faster than the wind,' he bargained, 'and you can go free with the golden bird as your reward.'

The king's son set off in a sorrowful mood. He had little chance of finding such a magnificent creature. As luck would have it, who should he see but his old friend the fox sitting on the road ahead of him.

'You know you should have listened to me don't you?' chastised the fox. 'If you had followed my advice, this would never have happened. Still, never mind – what's done is done. Keep your chin up. I can help you find the golden horse,' he continued enthusiastically. 'As before, keep straight on until you come to a castle. The golden horse is kept in the castle stable. Don't worry, the grooms will be fast asleep. You can slip in quietly and lead out the golden horse. There is one proviso, however; be sure to put on the common saddle made of wood and leather and not the gold one that hangs by its side.'

As before, the fox stretched out his tail. No sooner had the king's son jumped on his back than the fox was away like the wind, travelling over stock and stone. Once again everything was just as the fox had said. The grooms were snoring outside and it wasn't difficult for the king's son to tiptoe into the stable. He saw the two saddles hanging up side by side. As he reached over for the common saddle he couldn't help noticing how much better the gold one looked, and thought it more befitting for such a magnificent animal to have a golden saddle than one made of wood and leather.

He impetuously began to buckle on the golden saddle. Before he had even fastened the first strap the horse neighed loudly. The grooms awoke and threw the king's son into prison. The next morning he was sentenced to death by the court but the king spared him if he could bring back the princess from the golden castle. If he did, he could keep the golden horse as well.

It should not be overlooked that the king's son was able to ride away on the golden horse in order to bring back the beautiful princess from the golden castle. Gold is the alchemist's symbol of perfection. The white or golden horse was often seen as a heavenly animal and a steed of the gods. It was also a symbol of strength harnessed by reason.

This steed of the gods, harnessed by the reins of reason was none other than the permanent state of Cosmic Consciousness – the full development of the mind.

His heart was heavy as he set out but he brightened up when he saw the trusty figure of the fox sitting on the path in front of him.

'I ought to leave you to your own fate,' sighed the fox. 'But something inside of me tells me to take pity on you. I will help you out of your trouble once more. This road leads straight to the golden castle. You should reach it by this evening. At night, when everything is quiet, the beautiful princess goes to the bathing house to bathe. When she goes inside give her a kiss and take her away with you. There is one proviso – don't let her say goodbye to her parents or it will all go wrong for you.'

As before the fox stretched out his tail and the king's son seated himself upon it. Soon they were away over stock and stone. His hair whistled in the wind.

They reached the golden castle. Everything was just as the fox had said it would be. The king's son waited until midnight. Sure enough, when everything else was fast asleep, he saw the princess on her way to the bathing house. When she drew level with his hiding place he sprang out and kissed her.

'Come away with me?' he pleaded.

'I would like to,' replied the beautiful princess. 'But first I want to say goodbye to my parents. They will only worry if I disappear without so much as a word.'

The king's son remembered what the fox had said and stood his ground. But the princess fell at his feet. She sobbed and pleaded with him. His heart went out to her and his resolution evaporated. As soon as the maiden approached the royal bedside, not only her father, but the whole castle awoke. Soon the young man was seized and thrown into prison once more.

The next morning, after he had heard all the evidence, the king pronounced sentence upon him.

'I find you guilty and sentence you to death,' he said. 'However, if you can remove the hill in front of my window in eight days, I'll both spare your life and give you my daughter as a reward.'

The act of performing ablutions is always a symbolic act of purification before an initiation. The midnight hour was always the time of initiation, especially an alchemical initiation. The *magnum opus* referred to in many alchemical works states that the soul is purified by washing. The beautiful maiden was symbolic of the full development of the heart in God Consciousness. This represents the total fruition of the psyche and the culmination of all man's psychic potentialities, in other words, the ability to carry out all the Sidhis and to see and hear the entire range of beings in the celestial sphere of life.

According to experts on symbolism, the number eight is the final goal of the initiate. It is the regaining of the paradise of the primordial state before the fall – the end of man's spiritual quest. It is one step beyond the seven planets of the Ring of Necessity and therefore corresponds to leaving behind the solar cosmos and consequently the entry into the polar.

Bayley believes the number eight is the number of regeneration because it is composed of the two twin circles of Love and Knowledge[3]. Significant to our study, it was also regarded as the magic number of Thoth/Hermes. It is interesting to add that the number eight drawn on its side, horizontally, is the cipher for eternity or infinity.

The number eight has similar symbolic connotations spanning and traversing many cultures. It is the Pa Kua of Feng Shui; the mandala pattern that Hindu temples are based upon; and also the full octave of musical notes, plus one – signifying a new beginning. Many of these symbolic meanings are also enshrined in the baptismal font of a church. The font is octagonal in shape and the act of baptism is both a rite of purification and regeneration. There are also eight beatitudes.

It is also interesting to note that Krishna was the eighth child born to Devaki. According to a prophecy, her eighth child born was destined to kill the demon king, Kansa. That is why the demon king had Devaki locked up in prison. However, no amount of human machination can thwart the Absolute.

In most cultures, hills and mountains represented a symbolic ladder connecting the earth and the sky and, by extension heaven and earth. The removal of the hill or mountain is the last step. Once the summit is reached, the initiate has no longer any need for its support. He has gone beyond the eight compass points of the Cosmos and is seeking entry into the polar field of Unity Consciousness.

There is yet another important level of meaning regarding karma. Through our many reincarnations we have built up a mountain of karma. Maharishi calls this *Sanchitta* karma – the total karma we have built up. However, it is impossible to take all this with us for a single incarnation. Instead, we bring with us a smaller amount called *Prarabdha* karma, which by means of an illustration, he calls a full suitcase. This is the amount that has to be worked through in this lifetime.

> The king's son worked for all he was worth. He dug and shovelled earth for seven whole days without stopping. When he looked up to survey his work he saw that he had achieved very little. He was on the point of giving up all hope when the fox suddenly appeared on the evening of the seventh day.
>
> 'Although you don't deserve my help, I can't leave you in this state,' he said with a wry smile. 'You go away and have a good sleep. I will do the work for you.'
>
> As soon as the youth awoke next morning he went straight to his window and looked out. The hill was gone. It had completely disappeared. Full of joy he ran to the king and pointed excitedly towards the window.
>
> 'Look!' he exclaimed, fairly hopping with excitement. 'My task is fulfilled. You promised me the hand of your daughter.'
>
> Being a man of his word, the king ruefully gave the youth his daughter

Thus, the fox had cleared away all his outstanding karma. The youth was now totally free.

The number seven is significant at this point. Firstly, there are seven basic metals in alchemy involved the completion of the Great Work of making the human individual divine. The number seven is also the number of ascent and of ascending to the highest point and attaining the centre. The Mithraic cave in the Mysteries of Mithras had seven doors and altars and a ladder of seven rungs depicting the seven grades of initiation into the mysteries. Finally, the seventh day was always held to be a day of rest because any work carried out that day was thought to be in opposition to the sun and therefore both dangerous and unlucky.

Most important of all was to let the immortals of the transcendent come to clear away the obstacles whilst the individual rests with his mind deep in the state of Yoga Nidra – the sleep of union or yoga.

Full of joy the two young people set off together. It wasn't long before the fox met up with them.

'You have certainly come away with the best result possible,' mused the fox thoughtfully. 'But don't forget that the golden horse also belongs to the maiden of the golden castle.'

'How can I get it then?' asked the youth.

'I am coming to that,' continued the fox. The first thing to do is to take the beautiful maiden back to the king who sent you to the golden castle. There will be great rejoicing and delight at her return. They will gladly give you the golden horse. As soon as they bring it out to you, mount and act as though you are in a hurry to leave. Shake hands with everybody before you go but leave the beautiful maiden until last. Make it look like you are about to say a fond farewell. Rein the golden horse round and go over to where she'll be standing. Hold your hand out to her. As soon as your hands clasp together, swing her up on to the horse and gallop away. They will be taken by surprise. They won't be able to do anything about it because the golden horse runs quicker than the wind.

The youth carried out the instructions perfectly and the king's son carried off the beautiful princess on the back of the golden horse.

When the states of Cosmic Consciousness and God Consciousness are integrated, it is a much shorter step to achieve the final goal of Unity Consciousness in the symbolic form of the golden bird.

Although the golden horse ran faster than the wind, the fox was soon alongside them.

'Now I will tell you how to get the golden bird,' he said. 'When you get near the castle where they keep the golden bird, let the princess dismount. I will take care of her. When you ride the golden horse into the castle yard there will be a tumultuous cheer and great rejoicing. They will immediately bring out the golden bird for you. As soon as you have the cage in your hand, gallop back to us. The maiden will be ready to ride off home with you.'

Once again everything went according to plan.

It is not surprising that the phoenix, or the bird of fire, was the only cure for the sickness of heart of the king in the Slav version, called *Ohnivak*. In a dictionary of symbols[4] the phoenix is described as having all the attributes of the Cosmos. Its head was seen as a cock (symbolic of the sun); the concave, curving sweep of its back to where its tail begins, and then the returning convex curve of its breast, symbolised the crescent moon; its wings were synonymous with the source of the winds; the tail plumage was likened to the burgeoning world of plants and symbolised the trees and flowers; and, finally, its feet symbolise the earth.

The holistic aspect of a thing is always held to be more than the sum of its parts. A very good dictionary of traditional symbols reads as follows:

Its colour delights the eye; its comb expresses righteousness; its tongue utters sincerity; its voice chants melody; its ear enjoys music; its heart conforms to all the laws of Nature; and its breast contains all the treasures of literature; and its spurs make it invincible to all would be transgressors.

From the point of view of gaining the highest level of spiritual evolution – Unity Consciousness – the story could easily end here. However, a story is a literary device and has its own set of rules and its needs a nice balanced feel about it and a fitting conclusion. So, as the saying goes, there are still a few eggs to fry!

This is a model we have not yet encountered. In this one there is a symbolic ritual death and transformation to make it complete.

The king's son was about to ride off with his treasures when he was suddenly taken by surprise.

'Now what about my reward?' mooted the fox. 'I have given you a great deal of help – now what are you going to do for me?'

154

'Anything you like,' replied the king's son confidently.

'Good! I was hoping you would say that,' interrupted the fox. 'When we reach that wood over there, I want you to shoot me and chop off my head and feet,' he demanded.

But the king's son thought he must be joking.

'That would be a fine way to show my gratitude.' he answered sarcastically. 'I couldn't possibly do that to you – especially after everything you have done for me.'

'Oh well, if that's the way it's got to be!' sighed the fox. 'Well, I must be off now but before I go – here's one more piece of advice. Don't buy any gallows flesh and don't sit at the edge of any well.'

The King's son stood perplexed as he watched the fox disappear into the wood. He mused on the three unusual utterances of the fox. 'Shoot me and then cut off my head and paws; don't buy gallows flesh; and don't sit at the edge of any well. I certainly don't know what to make of any of that.'

Like the prophecies of the oracles in ancient cultures, such as the prophecies of Nostradamus, these employ universal symbols to convey prophetic predictions. They never resorted to the linear form of language we have become used to in modern times. This shows us again that folk tales were not intended to be taken at their face value, even if the meaning does seem intelligible to the linear intellect. We tend to attend only to the here and now in a cause and effect way of trying to sum up what is going to happen in the future. The language of the folk tale is more cryptic and open to many different shades of meaning. The same can also be said of the language of astrologers, and the aphorisms of Patanjali, for that matter.

The king's son set off towards home, with the beautiful maiden seated behind, clinging on to him, with her arms around his waist. The road took him back to the village with the two inns, where his brothers had tarried. The village was bustling with activity.

'What's going on?' enquired the king's son.

'We are about to execute a couple of real villains,' answered the villager.

'What have they done?' replied the king's son.

'Don't you mean "what haven't they done?"' he joked ruefully. 'They are about as nasty as they come.'

The king's son recognised them as his brothers.

'Do they have to die or can they be set free?' he asked.

'Only if you pay for them,' replied the villager. 'But I can't think of anyone who would want to do that.'

Being a straightforward and generous young man, the king's son didn't think twice. He handed over more than enough money. The villager shrugged his shoulders and nodded to the executioner to cut the two villains down. He opened his fist to show how much money the youth had given. The executioner grinned and cut the two men free. Very soon they all set off together.

Soon they came to the wood where the fox had first greeted them. It was a hot day and the journey was tiring. By contrast it felt cool and pleasant in the wood.

'Can we rest awhile and have something to eat and drink?' asked one of the brothers craftily.

'Good idea!' replied the king's son guilelessly, getting down from his horse.

He sat by the edge of a well and chatted cheerfully with his brothers and shared his fare with them. It was good to see his brothers again. He was taken completely off guard when they suddenly turned on him and threw him backwards into a well.

Believing him to be dead, they took the golden horse, the maiden from the golden castle, and the golden bird and set off for home, as the conquering heroes, to their father.

'Here we are, Father,' the two brothers shouted triumphantly. 'Not only have we brought you the golden bird, but also the golden horse and the beautiful maiden from the golden castle.'

Naturally, the king was pleased to see his two eldest sons home safely and was delighted with their success. But it didn't cure his sickness of heart because the golden bird did not sing; the golden horse was obviously pining and would not eat; and the beautiful maiden did nothing but sob all day.

The Bhagavad Gita says that it is impossible to tell an enlightened person from outward appearances. He or she does not necessarily look or act any differently from most other people as they go about their daily activity. However, there is an enormous gulf subjectively, between the motives of the enlightened and those of the unenlightened people, such as you or I. They only act in ways that nourish every level of creation. We tend to act in ways that seem to directly benefit ourselves or our family.

The same distinction can be made between the surface of the mind and its much deeper aspects. Once the mind comes out of meditation the ego takes over again and we continue to assume the ownership of all our actions. The same thing is happening in the story. The king's youngest son became separated from his two more worldly wise brothers at a certain village of the senses, when the mind was traversing its vertical path to the transcendent. Free from the dragging influence of his lower nature, the buddhi aspect, symbolised by the king's son, went on to realise the inner treasures at its source.

On the outward stroke of meditation – at the same village of the senses – the king's son is reunited with his two worldly brothers. Consequently the ego took over and his higher mind was pushed to the bottom of a deep well and left for dead. With the mind no longer in contact with its own transcendental source it is not at all surprising that the higher states of consciousness, symbolised by the golden bird, the golden horse and the beautiful maiden, were masked by the individual ego and no longer functioned.

> However, the youngest brother was not dead. The well was dry and he had fallen onto some moss and was unhurt. Nevertheless he was unable to climb out on his own. Once again his friend, the fox, came to his rescue.
>
> He leaped down the well and told off the king's son for not heeding his advice.
>
> 'We can't give up now,' he said. 'Grab hold of my tail and I'll pull you up.'
>
> No sooner was it said than it was done.
>
> 'You are not out of danger yet,' warned the fox. 'Your brothers have filled the wood with spies who have been told to shoot on sight.'
>
> Luckily there was a tramp sitting on a stile at the side of the road. He was more than ready to change clothes with the king's son. Greatly changed in appearance, the youth strode boldly up the road that led to the palace. He did not look suspicious in any way and was not challenged by the guards at the gate.

The swapping of clothes is reminiscent of the homecoming of Odysseus to Ithaca in Homer's great poem *The Odyssey*.

> Nobody in the castle recognised him but as soon as they sensed his presence, the golden bird began to sing sweetly; the golden horse began to eat; and the beautiful maiden from the golden castle stopped crying.
>
> 'What caused everything to change so suddenly?' Asked the king, with a look of astonishment on his face.
>
> 'I don't know,' answered the beautiful maiden. 'But I feel so

happy now. I feel that my true bridegroom has come home.'

Thereupon she related the full story of how she had been won by the king's youngest son; how he had saved his brothers from the gallows; and of their despicable behaviour by the well.

At once the king commanded everybody in the castle to be brought before him. Amongst them was the youth in ragged clothes. The beautiful maiden recognised him at once and showered him with kisses.

When they saw their younger brother dressed in the clothes of the tramp, the two elder brothers went taut with guilt and made a run for it. They were easily overcome by the palace guards and put to death. The king's youngest son was married to the beautiful maiden of the golden castle and was declared to be heir to the throne by the king.

When mind has realised the status of Unity Consciousness the whole of life is filled with bliss. It is a state of heaven upon earth. Its qualities always transcend external appearances. Once the illumined buddhi or nous of the king was unified with the three highest states of consciousness, his state of bliss would know no bounds. It is not surprising that the golden horse (Cosmic Consciousness) began to eat (or function); the beautiful maiden from the golden castle stopped crying and could feel the presence of her beloved; and finally the golden bird (Unity Consciousness) began to sing.

The two wicked brothers put to death were the ego-driven mind and senses of the waking state.

Sometime afterwards the king's son was out walking in the woods when he bumped into his old friend the fox.

'You have everything a man could ever wish for', mused the fox ruefully. 'Unluckily for me there is no end to my round of suffering. Yet strangely enough it is in your power to free me. I asked you once before to shoot me and cut off my head and feet, but you thought I was joking.'

The king's son was so moved by the entreaty of the fox that he overcame his reservations and did the deed. Imagine his surprise when, the moment after he had completed the task, the fox was transformed into a live human being. He turned out to be none other than the brother of the beautiful princess. At last he was released from the magic spell which had been laid upon him. From that time on they all lived in a state of complete happiness.

Santillana and Dechend have noticed how members of the dog family, in the shape of wolves, jackals and foxes, turn up often in myths about the precession of the equinoxes[5]. The golden bird is not a precession myth, but the fox in question may well be a variant of Sirius the dog star, who stands at the heels of Orion. Orion was known as Osiris by the ancient Egyptians. Osiris was the god of death and resurrection.

In an account of the struggle between Horus and Seth from the Chester Beatty Papyrus, Osiris, who was thoroughly tired of the long drawn-out feud, sent a message to the two contestants which said, 'There are a great many dog-headed messengers in my land in the West. These messengers of mine are not frightened of any god, and if you do not settle your dispute immediately, I will send them out to kill both of you.' After that Horus was crowned with the white crown and Seth was imprisoned. I do not want to stretch a point into something that doesn't fit but there are some strands common to both stories. No doubt the fox in this story was one of the dog-headed messengers of Osiris, and was both the guide and guru of the nous of the king's son. The punishment of the two evil brothers and the imprisonment of Set has a certain ring of similarity about it; and the marriage of the king's son to the beautiful princess, and being declared heir to the throne, is not very different to the crowning of Horus.

Finally, what about the apparently horrific death of the fox? Fortunately, in achemical terms, the red fox was one of the many symbols used for the philosopher's stone. This was achieved only by very secret methods. Its job was to speed the process of casting out the dross or base substances, leaving only the transformed liquids in the crucible.

In a tract written by an adept called Zosimos of Panopolis in the third century, the process involved 'cutting off the head and sacrificing his meat and muscles part by part, so that the flesh may be boiled according to the method and that he might then suffer the mortification'. This, of course, refers to a symbolic and not a literal beheading. A more humane description would make it plain that losing his head would refer to the part of the mind still wedded to ignorance. In many stories the fox is symbolic of a clever but devious rational mind. The loss of this results in the gain of the higher mind of the in-dwelling inner genius.

The spiritual being that arose from the mutilation of the fox was the brother of the princess of the golden castle – in other words the androgynous being that emerges from the process called the Great Work. These are often described as the Heavenly Twins, when the male and the female aspects of the individual are merged in a single unity.

1 Bayley, 1996, vol.2, 266
2 Quoted from a private TM course video
3 Bayley, 1996, vol.1, 84
4 Cooper, 1999, 129-130
5 Santillana & Dechend, 1969

# Chapter 17
# Faithful John

There was once an old king. He realised he was dying and the reins
of command needed to be passed on to his son.

'Send for Faithful John to come and see me,' he called out
weakly from his death bed.

Faithful John was his favourite and most trustworthy servant who
had served him all his life. When his trustworthy servant knelt by
his bedside the old king began to speak to him.

'My dear friend and faithful servant. My life is almost over. My
son is due to succeed me but I still feel some anxiety about his
ability to rule wisely and justly. He is still very young and needs
some guidance. As you know, young men are often headstrong and
cannot always be relied upon to make the right and just decision.
I want you to be his foster father and teach him all he needs to
know.'

Faithful John nodded his head understandingly. He put his
master's mind at rest. 'I will not let him down. I will serve him with
all my loyalty, even though it may cost me my life.'

The old king smiled: 'Now I can die in comfort.' Then he added,
'When I have gone show him all aspects of the castle: all the halls,
chambers and vaults with all the treasure I have amassed. However,
in the last chamber there is a picture of the princess of the golden
dwelling. You must not let him see it. If he sees that picture he will
fall violently in love with it and will drop down into a swoon and
risk his life needlessly. You must protect him from that.'

'I will do my best,' promised Faithful John.

The old king gave a smile of relief and sank back onto his pillow
and died.

The outset of this story reminds me of the birth of Lord Buddha inasmuch
as the inner reality of life must be hidden from the king's young son at all

costs. Lord Buddha's father went to an astrologer to ascertain the destiny of his son. The astrologer told him that his son would be distinguished in whichever of the two fields he chose. He could either be a great military emperor and leader or a great religious teacher. His father wanted his baby son to follow in his footsteps and be a great military emperor and leader. He was horrified by the idea that his son could be a religious teacher and set out to surround his son with the pleasures of life and to give him no grounds to go outside the precincts of the castle. To go outside the walls of the castle and see all the familiar signs of worldly suffering in the shapes of sickness, old age and death could cause the young man to start questioning the very basic tenets of life and lead him into a monkish way of life.

In the same way the old king did not want his son to see inside the last door of the long gallery. This would cause him to see the picture of the princess of the golden dwelling – which is actually a picture of what his own soul will eventually become. If his son saw this he would lose his interest in worldly kingdoms and the pleasures of the senses and would follow the spiritual path to the transcendent.

It is significant that the picture of the princess of the golden dwelling is in the last chamber in the Long Gallery. The last 'chamber' in the gallery of human consciousness is the transcendent. Working inwards from the most exterior aspect of human consciousness we have the environment, senses, mind, intellect, ego and then beyond these five relative aspects of consciousness is the innermost aspect and source – Transcendental Consciousness.

After the old king's body had been carried to his grave and laid peacefully at rest, Faithful John told the young king everything about the castle and the kingdom that he needed to know. After a suitable period of mourning had passed the faithful servant approached the young king.

'It is now time you should see your inheritance,' he said. 'I will show you every aspect of your father's palace.'

He conducted him to all the rooms and vaults of the castle and let him see all the magnificent apartments and all the riches the old king had amassed. However, the young king was observant. He noticed that there was one door that had not been opened.

'Why do you always walk past this one?' he enquired. 'Why don't you open it for me?'

'There is something inside it that your late father didn't want you to see,' frowned the old man worriedly.

But the petulance of youth prevailed.

'Open it for me or I shall break it down,' demanded the young king.

Faithful John held him back and said: 'I promised your father before he died that I would shield you from what is in this chamber. It could easily be the worst for both of us.'

However, the young king's mind was made up.

'If you don't let me see inside this room it will certainly be my downfall. I shan't be able to rest day or night until I have seen what is inside with my own eyes.'

Faithful John knew that he was in a corner. He was now the faithful servant of the young king and hadn't any choice. Amidst a mixture of great misgivings and a sorrowful heart, Faithful John selected the particular key from the great bunch he was holding and opened the door. He knew that the picture was positioned in such a way as to command your complete attention, once the door was opened. The old man went in. He hoped that by standing in front of the picture he would hide it from the king and so spare him the consequences.

However, the young man would not be thwarted. He stood on tip-toe and stared over the old man's shoulder. When he saw the magnificent portrait of the princess which shone with gold and precious stones, he was so captivated by its beauty that he fell to the ground in a faint.

Faithful John carried the young man up to his bed, laid him down and revived him with a glass of wine.

This piece reminds me of one of the teachings of Jesus, when he said 'my house has many mansions'. In folk tales the city or the palace often stands for the human body. An example of this is the City with the Nine Gates – the nine gates being the orifices of the human body.

As soon as he saw the portrait of the princess of the golden dwelling, the young king went through a one hundred and eighty degree turn in his awareness, which is the fairy story equivalent of receiving the call from the goddess. In actual fact, the picture he fell in love with was the picture of his own soul in Unity Consciousness. This is easily ascertained because of her golden dwelling and the precious stones which surround her picture.

'Who is she?' stammered the young king.

'That is the princess of the golden dwelling,' answered Faithful John.

'My love for her is so great that if all the leaves of the trees could speak there would not be enough of them to say how much I love her,' continued the young king. 'I would gladly give my life to win her – you must help me Faithful John.'

The old man thought about the matter for a long time. It was difficult to even catch sight of the princess.

To have an experience of the transcendent is indeed difficult because the mind is usually in an extroverted phase and is solidly locked into the material world. However, there are some occasions when one is in the mountains, walking in the countryside or by the sea or when the mind is not so preoccupied with the world that one is able to slip into the transcendent.

At last the old man thought of a way and said to the king:
'Everything she has about her is made of gold – tables, chairs, dishes, glasses, bowls and furniture. Amongst your treasures are five tons of gold. Let one of your goldsmiths fashion these into all kinds of vessels, utensils, wild animals and birds.

Faithful John was right. In Unity Consciousness everything takes on a golden hue. Even the sky looks golden.

It is significant that the young king had five tons of treasure. We know these to be the five senses. If they are refined as to perceive the world in the state of God Consciousness, there is no doubt he would come face to face with the princess of the golden dwelling – or to put it another way, the perfection of his own soul.

The young king ordered the goldsmiths to be brought to him. They had to work night and day until at last the most splendid things were prepared for the voyage. When everything was stowed on board ship, Faithful John put on the dress of a merchant. The king also dressed as a merchant in order to make himself unrecognisable. They sailed across the sea until they came to the place where the princess of the golden dwelling dwelt.

The regular practice of subjecting the human physiology to Transcendental Consciousness and activity in the relative world cultivates the mind and nervous system of an individual to be sufficiently flexible to live the two opposing aspects of life simultaneously. This is the work of the 'goldsmiths': to systematically transform his waking state of consciousness into Transcendental Consciousness; to transform Transcendental Consciousness into Cosmic Consciousness; to transform Cosmic Consciousness into God

Consciousness; and, finally, to transform God Consciousness into Unity Consciousness.

Unity Consciousness is actually our homeland – the place where we set out from, for the purpose of evolving our own consciousness. Like Odysseus, who returned to his homeland of Ithaca in disguise after many years of wandering, we may first return to Unity Consciousness disguised in the unrecognisable garb of the relative life. Thus, the king and Faithful John were both dressed as merchants. Like Odysseus, the young king represents a man proceeding through successive stages of spiritual evolution in order to regain his place amongst those who are beyond the material world.

The craft upon which the king travels is his mind. It is significant that the Greek word for ship is *nous*, which we have established as the illumined buddhi, or the fourth and deepest level of Plato's four levels of knowledge. In some stories the craft of the hero is a ship that can travel through both air and water. In the final analysis the mind is the ultimate piece of craftsmanship because when the full development of the mind and nervous system has taken place it can fully perceive the total cosmic reality. It can travel anywhere and perceive any aspect of reality.

The analogy of water to describe human consciousness was used by both Homer and Plato. Maharishi takes this even further. He describes it as an allegory of the extremes of the human mind; with the waves of the surface of the water being synonymous with the roller-coaster ride of the individual through the ups and downs of relative life. A dive within this takes the mind to quieter and quieter areas of thought with corresponding decreases in turbulence until the mind comes to rest where the water is completely still in the very depths of the mind. With the aid of the right technique or mantra the individual mind can travel from the outermost limits of relative life to the most inward and unifying aspects of Absolute pure consciousness.

'You stay on board,' Faithful John advised the king. 'Perhaps I will be able to bring back the princess with me,' he said. 'So make sure that everything is in order; have the golden vessels all set out and the ship decorated.'

It is now necessary to point out that Faithful John represents the deepest and most discriminative aspect of the mind – the buddhi. Hence the name – Faithful John. The deepest and most illumined aspect of the human consciousness. It is our most faithful servant and incapable of lying or deceitfulness. Being the deepest and most illumined aspect of the human mind, it has to be him that sets foot on the illustrious shore of the Absolute. The young king represents the outer aspects of the mind not yet transformed into pure consciousness and is therefore not sufficiently refined to step 'ashore' from the material world.

In fact, it is now time to refer back to the beginning of the story. The old king and the new king are not necessarily different people. They can easily be the same person at different times or phases of emphasis in his life, especially as Faithful John represents the same buddhi of both. The old king could represent the individual whose interests lay in the external world whilst the new king is the same person except that he has developed inner aspirations to gain the ultimate truth of life. In this respect the young king is the same as the youngest son and the simpleton in other stories.

Faithful John gathered together some suitable exhibits in his apron and made his way to the royal palace. When he entered the courtyard of the royal palace he saw a beautiful girl drawing water from the well with two golden buckets. She was just about to turn around and carry the two sparkling buckets away when she saw the stranger and asked him who he was.

The beautiful girl at the well represents the fount of all knowledge. She stands at the nexus of the relative and absolute aspects of the mind. The golden buckets she has filled are the left and right sides of the human cortex. The sparkling water they contain is the divine wisdom of the Absolute phase of life, which the less refined aspects of the mind distort or even disregard as being out of touch with the real world, the 'real' world being the transitory, ever changing phase of life in relative creation.

'I am a merchant,' answered Faithful John and opened his apron to let her look at the artefacts he had brought.

'Oh, what beautiful things!' she exclaimed and put down her two pails to look at the craftsmanship. 'The princess must see these. She will want to buy all of those.'

She took him by the hand and led him upstairs for she was the waiting maid of the princess. When the king's daughter saw the refined craftsmanship of the samples he had brought with him, she was quite delighted.

It is significant that this is the first time the princess had been called the king's daughter, for the true king is the king of the Absolute, the innermost phase of life. The daughter, though very evolved and refined, is not the finished article. Other transformations have still to take place.

'What beautiful craftsmanship,' she exclaimed. 'I will buy them all from you.'

But Faithful John said: 'I am only the servant of a rich king. Although these things are very good they cannot be compared with some of the things he has on his ship.'

'You must bring them all here to show me,' enthused the princess.

'That would take many days and we would need many rooms to exhibit them properly,' replied Faithful John.

This aroused her curiosity even further.

'Then conduct me to your ship,' she urged excitedly. 'I will go and look at the treasures of your master with my own eyes.'

Maharishi tells us that meditation is not all one-way traffic. It is not only a matter of the mind settling down and transcending its own finest level and coming to rest on the Absolute. The Absolute moves too to refine the innermost phases of the relative mind. He calls it 'the atma on the move'. We have also seen from the myth of Demeter that most of the work comes from the side of the gods or angels. All we have to do is have the desire to evolve spiritually and allow the mind to transcend the finest aspects of relative life.

Faithful John was delighted with this outcome and led her to his master's ship. When the king saw her he perceived that she was even more beautiful than he could dare imagine. The portrait, though very beautiful, did not do her justice, for her beauty far exceeded the likeness. The king's heart was so expanded with love that he thought it would burst. She came aboard the ship and the king led her within to look at the treasures.

Faithful John remained with the helmsman. 'Set all the sails,' he ordered. 'This ship must fly like a bird in the air.'

His master's ship or craft is the mind of the king. It is inferred that Faithful John or the intellect was able to induce the atma – the Self – of everything in the universe to come aboard onto the individual mind of the king and by so doing to refine it further. Meanwhile, the intellect or illumined buddhi stayed in control of both the direction and focus of the mind.

The ancients venerated craft and craftsmanship because they were regarded as useful in the external world and also to discipline the individual mind of the craftsman from the inside, to fulfil the inspirations of the god or goddess of his muse. This was probably why the seven liberal arts were such an important part of the education of the sons of wealthy Greeks in the old world.

The artefacts and usefulness of an external craft were considered as nothing to the discipline of shaping the innermost regions of the individual mind by the presiding deity or source of inspiration. The most used analogy of the ancient world was that of the sculptor who could see a particular deity imprisoned within the stone. It was the art of the sculptor to remove all the unwanted stone that surrounded his inner vision and then the beautiful likeness would be revealed to the world. The potentiality of higher states of consciousness already exist in the minds of everyone. It is just a question of finding the correct teacher, in order to bring about the refinement of the mind, and so make the potentiality of higher states of consciousness a living reality.

In the external world the smith used to be responsible for making every metal implement, from tools and weapons to very intricate and lovely jewellery. Whilst we seldom think of smiths as holy men today, in the past they were often synonymous with the creator. In ancient Greece, Hephasteus was venerated as the great artificer. The Romans had the equivalent in Vulcan. In Great Britain there are stories of Wayland the Smith.

The Vedic and Hindu cultures venerated Vishvakarma as both the architect and maker of the universe. He is seen as an all-seeing, all-knowing god who knows all worlds and has given them all names as well as forms. He forged all the divine weapons used by the other gods and revealed to mankind Sthapatya Veda, the science of building engineering and carpentry. He both built the city of Lanka on Sri Lanka and created the monkey craftsman Nala, who built the bridge across the sea from India to Sri Lanka, which Rama, Hanuman and Sugriva and his monkey army crossed to rescue the abducted Sita.

> The princess of the golden dwelling was so engrossed in seeing all the golden vessels, birds and animals that she didn't notice that the ship was sailing far away from her own country. When she had finished looking at everything, she thanked the young king and turned to go home. She could not see her native shore. She rushed to the side of the ship in alarm. She realised she was out on the high seas heading in a direction that was very far from the land of the golden dwelling.
>
> 'You have betrayed me,' she gasped with horror. 'I have been kidnapped by a merchant. Although you seem to have me within your power – I would rather die than...'
>
> 'I'm no merchant,' the young king interrupted. 'My origins are

no meaner than yours. I only tricked you on board because of my great love for you. The moment I clapped my eyes upon a portrait of you hanging in my castle, my heart could belong to no other.'

The princess of the golden dwelling perceived the sincerity of his words and the truthful expression on his face. She knew it was true and felt drawn towards him. In a short time she consented to be his wife.

When one is in the state of Samadhi one's mind is so engrossed in the blissful nature of the transcendent that it is easy to be oblivious of what is happening in the outside world. This part of the story may well have corresponded to the milestone in an initiate's life when he was initiated into the Lesser Mysteries, when he would have received a technique that enabled him to transcend.

At such a time, it would be true to say that the Absolute, in the form of the princess of the golden dwelling, accepted him as a suitable partner.

While they were sailing over the deep sea, Faithful John sat in the fore of the vessel making music. Suddenly he saw three ravens circling around in the air before coming near to the ship. He stopped playing, for he not only understood the ways of the ravens, he could also understand what they were saying.

Faithful John had obviously been blessed with the language of the birds and was aware of the recitation of the hymns of the Veda within the stillness of his mind.

The fore part of the ship in this case is the buddhi because the mind is in contact with the transcendent. In activity it is usually the other way round, with the senses locked into the ever changing environment. When the mind is at this deep level, it is quite possible to listen to the rhythm of the Veda unfolding the most subtle aspects of creation, which is the basis of the material; or watch the subtlest aspects of creation merge back into the unified field of the transcendent.

The world of folklore is ambivalent about ravens. They are widely known for the power of prophecy but they can be equally the harbingers of darkness and evil as well as wisdom. In alchemy a black raven is symbolic of the Nigredo, the first stage of the Lesser Work, and represents dying to the old ways of the world. Similarly, the raven was depicted as the servant of the sun in the first grade of the Mithraic mysteries.

The ravens talked to each other about the young king, oblivious of the keen interest shown by Faithful John.

'He is carrying home the princess of the golden dwelling,' observed one.

'He may have!' retorted a second. 'But she is not his yet.'

'But he is not far off,' said a third. 'She is already sitting beside him in the ship.'

'A lot of good that will do him!' interrupted the first raven. 'When they land a chestnut horse will leap forward to meet him. The prince will want to mount it. If he does that, it will run away with him and rise up into the air and he will never see his princess again.'

The second raven seemed concerned about the young king's future. 'But is there no escape?' it asked.

'Yes, but only if somebody else mounts it first, takes his pistol out of its holster and shoots the chestnut horse dead, will the young king be saved. But who knows that? Whoever does know it will be turned to stone from the toe to the knee.'

'I know even more than that!' interjected the second. Even if the horse is killed, he still won't be able to keep his bride. When they go into the castle they will find a bridal gown that appears to be woven of gold and silver but in reality it is nothing but sulphur and pitch. If he puts it on it will burn him up right to the very bone and marrow.'

This time the third raven expresses its concern. 'Isn't there any way he could escape such a fate?'

'Oh yes!' put in the second. If anyone wearing gloves comes forward and throws the garment into the fire the young king will be saved. 'But what good will that do? For whoever knows this will become stone from the knee to the heart.'

'I know something too!' put in the third. 'Even if the garment is burned, the young king may still not keep his bride. After the wedding the dancing will begin. As the young queen is dancing, she will suddenly turn pale and drop down as though dead. If somebody does not lift her up and draw three drops of blood from her right breast and spit them out again, she will surely die. But if anyone does this, he would become stone from the crown of his head to the soles of his feet.'

These three prophecies by the ravens are the milestones that map out the next part of the story. Their predictions signify the three major initiations into the Greater Mysteries. The first raven is speaking about Cosmic Consciousness. The chestnut horse that the king will want to mount is the unrestrained ego of the waking state.

The second raven is speaking about the realisation of God Consciousness. The garment it speaks of is not an established state of devotion but only one that comes and goes. True devotion, or God Consciousness, only becomes established after a further alchemical transformation has taken place. The initiate has to be purified further by subjecting his entire being to the fire of the spirit. In alchemy, sulphur is regarded as the spirit, whilst pitch is the burning and purifying agent. By pitch we do not mean the dark, resinous substance distilled from tar or turpentine, but a specific purifying agent used by alchemists.

The third raven speaks of the difficulty of attaining Unity Consciousness after God Consciousness has been achieved. The marriage between the young king and the beautiful princess has already taken place. The mind and senses of the young king are now completely purified. He has now attained a complete and permanent state of devotion. This can be seen because they are dancing together as one. Suddenly, the princess of the golden dwelling grows pale and falls unconscious to the ground. This is symbolic of the ritual death of the initiate prior to his emergence from the solar sphere of life and his entrance into the polar – the state beyond all manifest creation.

> As soon as they reached the shore, a magnificent chestnut horse sprang forward, just as the ravens had foretold.
>
> 'Good!' exclaimed the king 'Just the thing to carry me back to my palace.'
>
> The young king was just about to mount it when Faithful John leaped onto its back, drew the pistol out of the holster and shot the horse. There was an outcry from a group of the king's attendants who were jealous of Faithful John.
>
> 'What a shameful thing to do,' they cried. 'Fancy killing a beautiful animal like that. It was going to take the king back to his palace.'
>
> 'Hold your tongues,' shouted the king. 'He is my most faithful servant. I expect he has a very good reason for acting in this way. Who knows what good may come of this.'

The shore they had reached was the boundary of the conscious mind of the waking state and the transcendent. The chestnut horse that sprang forward was the ego-driven mind on the outward stroke of meditation. This was a great threat to the spiritual evolution of the young king. Anybody used to meditating regularly will tell you how quickly the ego with its sense of 'me' and 'mine' re-establishes itself in the driving seat, once the mind comes out of its inward dive of mediation.

In order for Cosmic Consciousness to be a permanent reality the sphere of the separate ego has to be vanquished. Hence, the trusty servant, the intellect, shot it. Apparently, a yogin treading the path of Rajah Yoga does this all the time. He analyses with his intellect every aspect of life, so as to weigh up if an object or action will help him attain the ultimate state of reality. If he considers it useful in achieving his goal he keeps it. If it does not have its basis in ultimate reality he discards it. After reading one of the Dalai Lama's most recent books, it is evident that intellectual analysis also plays a very large role in Tibetan Buddhism (see Dalai Lama and Cutler, 1998).

They went into the palace. In the hall, draped across a dish, was the bridal garment, looking as though it was woven from gold and silver. The king reached out with the intention of putting it on, but Faithful John quickly pushed him away, seized it in his gloves and threw it on the fire. Once again the other attendants began to murmur amongst themselves about Faithful John's seemingly bizarre behaviour.

'Now look what he is doing,' said one of the most forthright. 'He's even thrown the king's bridal garment into the fire to be burned. Whatever will he do next?'

'Enough of that,' admonished the king. 'I am sure that he had a good reason to do it. He is my most trustworthy servant.'

Maharishi often reminds us that knowledge is different in a different state of consciousness. What the other attendants saw as pure madness would have had a perfectly logical reason if they had known about the prophecy that gave rise to it. Just as the theories of a quantum physicist may seem ridiculous to the common-sense observer, who lacks the sophisticated equipment needed to map the behaviour of sub-atomic particles, so may the observations of an enlightened person seem ridiculous to the crass materialist, who has yet to develop the perceptive machinery necessary to delve more deeply into the truth underlying the surface values of life. Both are right in their own sphere but they relate to different levels of reality.

As I have already indicated when considering the prophecy of the second raven, the burning of the garment is related to the final act of purification before achieving God Consciousness.

After the bride and groom had exchanged rings and repeated their vows of matrimony, the dancing and the festivities began.

Faithful John was ever vigilant as he watched the young king hold his beautiful bride in his arms and whirl her joyously around the dance floor.

Suddenly, she turned pale and fell to the ground as if dead. The faithful servant reacted immediately. He rushed on to the dance floor, scooped her up into his arms and took her into the privacy of a chamber. He proceeded to suck three drops of blood from her right breast and spat them out. Immediately she began to breathe again and made a swift recovery.

The prophecy of the third raven completes initiation into God Consciousness. At face value it looks as though there are some strange things to explain away but, in actual fact, it all remains very close to the original ideas of the Mysteries. It also shows what pains they took to conceal the true meaning, by embedding it in a story-line to sound like something completely different.

First of all, the colour of blood is synonymous with love. This still holds good today in the world of romance. Think of all the bleeding hearts carved on trees, cameos on the bottom of love letters and poems and also, in some cases, tattoos. We must also remember that the state of Cosmic Consciousness evolves to God Consciousness through the path of devotion. The culmination of this process is the full development of the senses so as to perceive the finest or most subtle aspects of creation.

In the world of symbolism blood was regarded as the essence of life and the source of all human activity. As such it represented the generative power of the creator, or creatrix, and was linked to wheat as the staff of life. One of the Gnostic titles for Christ was the 'Great Wheat Ear'. Similarly Horus, was known as the 'Green Ear of Wheat'. Also the great goddesses of the Mysteries, Ceres and Isis, were often represented by an ear of wheat.

According to Bayley, there is a sculpture in the British Museum of Mithras slaying the sacrificial bull[1]. It is significant that the blood flowing from its wounds is shaped into three ears of wheat. Bread has long been part of the sacraments of Sumerian, Semitic, Mithraic and Christian rites. Bread is also the manifestation of the spirit which dies and rises again, like Persephone and Osiris. Although there are obvious differences, this is not a million miles away from the modern Holy Communion service. The sacramental bread and wine represents the body and blood of Christ. When the communicant receives them, he believes that by assimilating them, his body will eventually be transformed into the body of Christ.

However, in the Mystery Schools it symbolised the completely developed human being in its most perfect form. This equates with what

Maharishi terms as God Consciousness.

The young king was incensed by Faithful John's apparently bizarre behaviour. He thought he had taken leave of his senses. 'Throw him into the dungeon,' he commanded angrily.

The next morning Faithful John was tried and condemned to death. He was led up to the high platform and stood before the noose.

'Everyone who faces execution is allowed to have his say.' stated Faithful John. 'May I too be accorded that right?'

'Certainly!' answered the king. 'I will grant you this last request.'

'You have condemned me unjustly,' began the faithful servant. 'I have always been true to you.' With that, Faithful John when on to recount the prophecies of the ravens and how he had no choice if he was going to save his master.

The young king was visibly moved by his servant's statement. 'Oh, my most Faithful John!' he choked. 'I grant him a pardon. Bring him down – bring him down.' But as soon as Faithful John had finished speaking his own testimony, he had collapsed, lifeless, and became a stone.

Naturally the king and queen were very upset and suffered great anguish.

'How badly I repaid him for his loyal service,' bewailed the king.

He ordered the stone figure to be taken up to his bedroom. It stood beside the king's bed. Often he looked at it and wept. 'If only I could bring you back to life my most faithful servant.'

There is a dissonance between the role of the storyteller and the hidden meaning from the mystery teachings. We have been brought up on people being turned to stone by wicked witches and have been conditioned to accept it as a natural consequence within a folktale genre. It appears to be a tragedy that a man so dedicated to serving his king and master has been turned to stone. In actual fact, within the hidden traditions of symbolism being turned to stone has an altogether different connotation.

In the story Faithful John was turned to stone in three phases. Our history of being conditioned by the literal as opposed to the symbolic truth naturally interprets this as a tragic reward for Faithful John, after years of trustworthy and single-minded service to both of his masters.

However, the world of symbolism paints a very different picture. In this context stone symbolises the stability and indestructibility of the primordial state of the Absolute; especially as it was gained by progressive degrees. For example, Guenon believes that the Megalithic builders of Stonehenge and the like were much nearer the godhead than the people of the more recent past because they purposefully built their monuments with undressed stone.

Many ancient societies regarded the use of a metal tool on an altar as a pollution or defilement of the deity to whom the altar was raised. The Tao speaks of the mind attaining the transcendent, as 'going back to the uncarved block', the uncarved block being the primordial state of existence before the separation of Prakriti and Purusha, and after their blissful state of union when the spiritual quest for enlightenment is over.

In the story, Faithful John was first turned to stone from the toe to the knees after shooting the chestnut colt of the ego – this equated with Cosmic Consciousness. It spread upwards to his chest after throwing the impure bridal garment into the fire.

Returning briefly to the myths of both Demeter and Osiris, the goddess, acting as a nursemaid, was interrupted in the act of purging the mortality of the royal child by fire, in order to make him immortal. We normally associate the term 'ablution' with the act of cleansing or purification by water. To alchemists it had another meaning. They regarded 'ablution' as the act of purification by fire. They understood the term to mean igneous water, which was mercury vivified by the action of fire. Without fully understanding the hermetic processes, they were obviously carrying out symbolic rites of self-purification by trying to turn base metals, such as lead, to gold.

The ritual death of the initiate in the Mysteries is associated with the apparent demise of the newly married queen in the story, and marks the transition from Cosmic Consciousness to God Consciousness. At this level of spiritual evolution the complete psychic regeneration of the individual has taken place – his perceptual apparatus has been totally enhanced and he can now see, hear and generally understand fully the nature of life and the universe as perceived by the gods.

There is another layer of symbolism here also. The stone could also be a reference to the philosopher's stone, which appeared near the completion of the Great Work. On the level of minerals, this stone could transmute all base metals into gold. On the level of the individual, it was a stone that could cure all ills and restore a person back to the blissful, primordial state. In actual fact, the act of trying to transmute baser metals into gold could often be a cover to protect the initiate from religious persecution by the authorities of his time, when the only thing he wished to do in reality was to perform the symbolic rites that would eventually change himself into an enlightened person.

Time passed. The queen bore twins who grew fast and were a

175

delight to both parents. One day, when the queen was at church, the king was sitting looking at the stone figure, whilst his two children were playing happily beside him. To have his trusted servant restored to life again would give the king everything he could possibly want to make him happy.

'If only I could bring you back to life!' he sighed.

'Ah! But you can,' uttered the stone figure. 'You can only bring me to life if you are prepared to sacrifice that which is most dear to you.'

'I will give up anything in the world for you,' answered the king enthusiastically.

'Alright,' continued the stone figure. 'You must cut the heads off your two children and sprinkle me with their blood, then I shall be restored to life.'

The king was horrified. The thought of cutting off the heads of his two children filled him with terror. However, the thought of his faithful servant laying down his life for him steeled the mettle of the king. He took out his sword and cut off the heads of both his children. He smeared their blood over the stone figure, and his faithful servant was restored to full health and vigour.

'Your actions shall not go unrewarded,' he stated boldly. With that he put the two heads back on the children and rubbed the wounds with their blood. Immediately they were made whole again and continued jumping around and playing as before as if nothing had happened.

The king was full of joy. When he saw the queen returning home from church, he told Faithful John and the two children to hide in the cupboard. As soon as she came into the room, she told him how she had thought of Faithful John during the service, and the misfortunes that he had been through on their behalf.

'There is a way of giving him his life back again,' said the king. 'But it will cost us the lives of our two sons.'

The queen went pale with horror. The fear of losing her two delightful children cut her to the bone. Then she thought of their beloved servant's fidelity.

'It is the biggest sacrifice a mother could possibly make,' she answered, with tears in her eyes. 'We owe it to him.'

The king was delighted that her sentiments were the same as his. He opened the cupboard and Faithful John and the two children came out.

'God be praised,' she exclaimed. 'He is restored to life and we

have our two little sons as well.'
They lived together in great happiness all the days of their lives.

At this point it is necessary to disentangle our minds from the story, otherwise it is hard to see the wood for the trees in relation to the symbolism used. The young king and queen were joined in God Consciousness after the three drops of blood had been taken out of the queen's right breast. In parallel with this, Faithful John had now been turned to stone in three phases.

In a state of God Consciousness the fully developed mind of Cosmic Consciousness and the fully developed level of feeling, ascribed to the heart, become as one. In this context the king represents the mind and the queen the heart.

The third and last initiation in the Mysteries takes the initiate out of the Cosmos. In other words, he dies to the Cosmos and is reborn in the unified state of Unity Consciousness. Now, firstly, it was necessary to test the initiate to see if the mind and heart were as one. In the story the king, being the fully developed mind, concurs with the fully developed feeling level of the heart. Hence the queen is able to see eye to eye with the husband in the need to go through with the ritual death. Whilst the mind can often cope with such an enormity because it is used to distancing itself from the sphere of feeling, the heart often baulks before doing the right thing.

Thus, there is a kind of test encapsulated in this act. Is the initiate ready for the third birth? Is he ready to renounce all earthly ties in order to become unified with God? This question was put to Abraham in the book of Genesis, as a test of his allegiance to God. He was prepared to offer up his beloved son Isaac as a burned offering, in order to show his unswerving allegiance to his Lord. As it transpired, it was just a test, and Isaac's life was spared. They went through with the sacrificial rite, however; an angel told them there was a ram caught in the thicket by its horns, so they sacrificed that instead.

The same kind of sacrifice is called for in this story. Both the king and the queen, the two complementary sides of a human being, were in complete accord to put aside their earthly natures. In hermeticism, this was known as the hermaphrodite – the perfect human being. It was represented as a hybrid symbol of the perfect balance of the male and female parts of a human being.

In alchemy, a similar but not identical, idea was known as the androgyne. This was conceived of as a person who combines the characteristics and sensibilities of the opposite sex. It was also known as the *materia prima* and the philosopher's stone. As already mentioned, Faithful John is a symbol of this stone. The creation of the philosopher's stone represents the ultimate reward at the end of the alchemical process.

The cutting off of the heads of the twins is actually a rebirth of the individual from a state of God Consciousness to Unity Consciousness. Their faithful servant is also reborn as the intellect in union with God. It is also necessary to clear up the gory business of the blood sprinkled upon Faithful John. Blood itself was regarded as a mysterious substance and was identified with both the life force and the soul. A ritual act of sacrifice, involving either himself or a sacrificial animal, was supposed to free both the life force and the soul.

The initiates of the Mystery Schools of Mithras and Cybele were said to be baptised with blood from the sacrificial steer in order to purify themselves and be transported into a state of ecstasy. In the light of the doctrine of ahimsa or non-violence, written about in the chapter on the *Yoga Sutras*, this makes no sense at all. Any sacrifice that involves the death of a human or an animal is a violation of Natural Law, or the higher aspects of the laws of Nature. In the myth of Demeter, Metaneira offered the goddess a glass of wine. Demeter, disguised as an old lady, instead asked for kykeon, a ceremonial drink in the Eleusinian Mysteries consisting of barley, penny-royal and perhaps some intoxicating or hallucogenic substance.

The blood in question is more likely to be kykeon or a type of wine, since wine is frequently used as a symbol of blood. In Sufism, wine is symbolic of spiritual knowledge. Before the act of creation, when the Purusha and Prakriti were separated, the soul was described as swimming in the wine of immortality. I am sure the blood that anointed Faithful John in this story is actually the wine of immortality.

In alchemical terms, the blood would be part of the philosopher's stone, whose colour is red, mixed with the elements of baser metals being turned into gold. The same is true of the *Rebis*, another word for hermaphrodite in the Great Work, in which the masculine and feminine natures were recombined. This refers us back again to the state of Unity Consciousness; or, to put it another way, the recombining of Purusha and Prakriti, the return to the primordial state when the soul will blissfully swim in the wine of immortality.

---

[1] Bayley, 1996, vol.2, 356

# Chapter 18
## Snow White

Once upon a time, in the middle of winter, a queen sat sewing. She was sitting by an ebony window frame, watching the snow fall like white feathers from the sky. Whilst she was sewing she pricked her finger. Three drops of blood fell on to the white snow.

'I wish I had a child as white as snow, as red as blood and as black as the ebony window frame.'

Soon after, she had a daughter whose skin was as white as snow; whose lips were as red as blood; and whose hair was as black as ebony. Very soon after the child was born the queen died.

Firstly, this is no ordinary mortal queen. She is the Mother Goddess revered by all the initiates into the Mysteries. Nor is she doing some normal sewing. She is the queen of the entire universe. What she is sewing is the entire fabric of creation. The clue to her real identity comes from the colours described. White, red and black are the colours of the three gunas of Nature (Prakriti). They are the finest aspects of creation from which all things are made. Sattva is white and is the building block of everything pure, representing new growth. Rajas is red and is seen as the spur of all activity or growth. The nature of tamas is to check or retard or decay. All three work together in every stage of development. Incidentally red, white and black are also the colours of the three stages of initiation into the Mysteries.

In many mystical teachings it is said that the mind of the individual creates their own body and their own world and then lives in it in very much the same way as a spider spins its web and then inhabits it. Soon after the individual is born the memory of her transcendental mother dies. In common with many of the stories we have covered, this means that all knowledge of her celestial mother is lost or forgotten once the child has been born and the mind is clamouring to satisfy the myriad desires of the ego-driven sense mind.

Thus, *Snow White* is the story of the transformation of the ego-driven sense mind of the individual personality into its ultimate reality of the higher self or inner genius, which, in the case of the average person, is overlaid by many skins of differing states of consciousness.

After about a year had passed the king took another wife. She too was beautiful but she was also proud and haughty. She thought that she was the most beautiful and important person in the world. She had a wonderful looking glass, which could speak but was incapable of telling a lie. From time to time she would stand in front of it and admire herself and say; 'Looking glass, looking glass, on the wall, who in this land is the fairest of all?'

Imagine her self-satisfied smile when the looking glass replied: 'Thou, O Queen, art the fairest of all!'

The new queen is the soul of the individual. Like all individuals who have not progressed to higher states of consciousness, her ego was very swollen and extroverted. Thus, she thought she was separate from the rest of creation. And even superior to it. Consequently, she was very conceited about her looks and her own abilities.

The use of a looking glass was a great idea because it not only added vitality to the story, it also carried its entertainment value forward, and ensnared the reader or hearer into a state of being fascinated by its intricate detail. However, it also gives a clue of what is hidden from the undiscerning reader.

It is said that the mirror cannot lie, or can it? It certainly can't tell the truth either. Its reflective character can never let us see ourselves as we really are. When we look into a mirror the reflection that we see is totally reversed.

The magic mirror through which we view all our interactions with the world is through the human mind. Consequently, our view of the world is always biased in favour of our ego-driven perspective. Thus, many of our interpretations must be equally deluded when we see ourselves through the eyes of our small, individualised ego rather than through the eyes of the large Self, which is our true nature.

The scenario of the magic mirror and the wicked queen represents the entire continuum of the mind from its most gross to its most refined aspect. The dialogue between the wicked queen and the magic mirror clearly depicts this duality, and contrasts the purity of the higher self with the lower machinations and perceptions of the lower sense mind.

As the years passed Snow White was growing more beautiful daily. By the time she was seven she was as beautiful as the day and even

more beautiful than the queen herself. One day the queen went to
the looking glass to admire herself. As usual she said to her looking
glass:
    'Looking glass looking glass on the wall
    Who in this land is fairest of all?'
The looking glass replied:
    'Thou art fairer than all who are here, Lady Queen
    But more beautiful still is Snow White, as I ween.'

In common with all the other stories we have covered, the heroine, Snow
White, is the illumined intellect or buddhi. This is called the 'Buddha
nature' by the Dalai Lama. He affirms that everybody possesses this potential
for the growth of full consciousness, no matter how weak or poor a person's
present situation may be.

Being newly manifested from the atma, the underlying Self of all beings,
it remains unconditioned and pure. This is reinforced by the colour of snow,
which is the colour of sattva. The illumined buddhi exists in every person but
it is usually the darker, coarser thoughts and feelings, represented by the
step-mother, which prevail. As in all other fields, the predominance of
interest in pursuing the spiritual path depends upon how far the individual
has evolved in previous lives.

The queen was shocked and turned alternately yellow and green
with envy. Whenever she looked at Snow White she felt the hatred
in her heart rising. One day, when she could stand it no more, she
summoned a huntsman.
    'I can no longer stand the sight of this child,' she raged. 'Take
her into the forest and put an end to her. Bring me back her lungs
and liver as a token.'
    The huntsman did as he was told and led her away. In the depth
of the forest he took out his knife to pierce her heart. She began
to cry.
    'Dear huntsman,' she implored. 'Don't take my life. Let me run
away into the wild deep forest and I'll never come back again.'
    The huntsman took pity on her and watched her until she disap-
peared into the undergrowth. He was certain a wild creature would
come along and devour her, but he was pleased that the task
wouldn't be on his conscience. It seemed as though a great weight
had fallen from him for he certainly didn't want to kill her. At that
moment a young boar came running by. He took out his knife and
stabbed it and took the lungs and liver back to the queen as proof.

Everything we have seen about the queen is concerned with her vanity – or the preservation of her small self, the ego. There is inevitably a conflict in the mind of every person who desires to develop their spiritual side. After all the entire personality and self-esteem has been built around the material aspects of life. Every new spiritual aspirant proceeds cautiously without an open declaration of their newly found desire for spiritual growth.

There are some allusions to alchemy here. The Great Work of the alchemist began when he lit the fire in the stove. As we are dealing with the transformation of the gross human body into a divine being, this is the wave of initial energy and enthusiasm that keeps the initiate on track from beginning to end. As soon as the fire is lit different phenomena take place, such as the release of vapours, which crystallise.

During this process the gross matter takes on various 'colours of the work'. These are divided into the principal colours of white, red and black, which were the initial colours which brought Snow White into being, followed by the intermediary colours, which included yellow and green (the colours the wicked queen turned), as well as all the other colours in the rainbow.

The huntsman she summons is the intellect. That is the discriminating part of the mind which does the paring and dismembering. At this point in time the queen wants to screen out any desire for spiritual growth from her mind. Apparently, the liver was regarded as the seat of vitality, desires and rage by various peoples of the world but I am not sure of the significance of the lungs.

Obviously, it is not entirely possible to eliminate the finer spiritual feelings altogether so the intellect allowed them to take their chance amongst the tangled growth of thoughts that rise in the mind. In such a situation an individual has to have a very strong will if he or she is to foster the more life-supporting urges of the spirit.

The boar is also a bit of a teaser. It was one of the incarnations of the Hindu god Vishnu. It was also sacred in Babylonia and other Semitic nations. The boar occupied an honoured place in all Celtic legends and was the mount of the sun god Frey, in northern mythology, who ruled over peace and plenty. In addition, the souls of the heroes in Valhalla feasted upon an inexhaustible supply of boar's meat, which probably means that the boar was a personification of god and its meat was a northern form of ambrosia.

In some versions of the story it was the boar's heart that was taken back to the wicked queen. This actually fits our interpretation much better. In India the heart is thought of as the place where the individual stays in contact with the Absolute field of existence. To the ancient Greeks, it was the seat of man's thinking, feeling and wanting. In later times people thought it was intimately linked with spiritual development.

Snow White was all alone in the great forest. When she saw the mass of trees she didn't know what to do, so she ran as fast and as far as her feet would carry her. Finally, she espied a little cottage that was so small and neat and clean that words cannot describe it. Inside was a table covered with a white cover with seven little places set out. Next to the wall were seven little beds side by side, covered with snow-white counterpanes. It was the home of the seven dwarfs.

The forest that Snow White was alone in was all the different branches of thought belonging to the main trunks or disciplines in the world. Without an underlying basis or unified field they are confusing and often seem at odds with each other. The thing to do is to run for cover. Go to the place of singularity – Transcendental Consciousness, the source and goal of all the various disciplines in creation.

The cottage of the seven dwarfs is also the initiate's cave. It is here that he learns to transcend and so discover the safe haven from the ever moving, ever changing nature of relative life. It is easy to equate the dwarf's cottage with the transcendent because its neatness and orderliness is beyond what words can tell. Another clue is the whiteness of the tablecloth and the counterpanes, which reminds us that everything in that sphere of life is pure sattva. We also know that the field of the transcendent is also the unified field of all the laws of Nature.

It is on the borders of the transcendent that we first encounter the seven dwarfs. We are so conditioned by Disney animations and children's story books that it is hard to think of the seven dwarfs before they were characterised into Happy, Sleepy, Dopey, etc. However, that is how we must think of them.

The seven dwarfs are actually the pre-scientific classifications of the primary forces of creation. Four of the dwarfs are the four elements of the ancient Greeks; fire, air, water and earth. It must be remembered that these terms in no way represented the concrete realities whose names they bear. They stood for the states of matter as they arose and coarsened from their very abstract value in the transcendent to the solid material state they manifested as upon the earth.

Fire was held to be the most subtle of the elements and corresponded to the idea of both the ethereal fluid of light, heat and electricity and with the initial movement of atoms. Air symbolised the support and volatility of matter in its gaseous state. Water stood for all possible liquid states. And, finally, earth symbolised matter in its solid state.

The other three dwarfs are Mercury, Sulphur and Salt, the three elements of transformation of the alchemists. These latter three are the Western equivalent of the three gunas. Mercury represents primordial matter or the philsopher's stone. Sulphur is similar to rajas – it represents that which burns or energises. When applied to human beings it is associated with rage, greed and anger. Salt, like tamas, is symbolic of a destructive power that tears things down.

However, these forces cannot be thought of as good or bad. In order to put up a new building we must first tear down an old one. As was mentioned earlier, all three of the gunas are present at all times in every undertaking.

> Snow White was a little frightened when she first saw the seven dwarfs but they were friendly and asked her name and were interested in everything about her. They agreed that if she looked after their house then she could stay for nothing.
>
> From that time on she kept house for them. Every morning the dwarfs went to the mountains to look for copper and gold. They did not come back again until it was time for their supper in the evenings. The girl was left alone all day so the dwarfs warned her to be on her guard.
>
> 'Beware of your step-mother – she will be sure to know you are here; so don't let anyone in.'

After her first sortie into the transcendental sphere of life it is only natural that her awareness would always be open to it. By opening her mind to that unbounded awareness every aspect of her mind and physiology would be opened up to the gods and devas to rebuild and purify. As the stresses or the impediments to evolution were removed, the devas and their minions (the dwarfs) would begin to rebuild her body so that it would reflect the total knowledge of the Absolute. In alchemical terms, the gold they were apparently seeking was the full spiritual development of the individual.

However, the old desires, tastes and instincts laid down when she was still the wicked queen were only dormant and could sprout into new self-perpetuating low desires at any moment. The neophyte, spiritual aspirant has always to be on the alert.

> One day in a moment of idle curiosity, the queen turned to her magic looking glass. Assuming she had put an end to Snow White, she couldn't but think that she would get the right answer when she asked:

'Looking glass, looking glass on the wall
Who in this land is fairest of all?'
The looking glass replied:
'Oh, Queen, thou art fairest of all I see
But over the hills where the seven dwarfs dwell
Snow White is still alive and well
And none is so fair as she.'
From that moment she knew that the huntsman had deceived
her. She was overwhelmed with envy. Once more she set her mind
to the task of killing Snow White. At last she thought of a plan. She
would disguise herself as an old pedlar woman and go over the
seven mountains to the cottage of the seven dwarfs.

Whilst the egocentric aspect of every individual thinks they are the most
wonderful, attractive and talented person upon the earth, a deeper part of
the mind knows this is not so. As we have mentioned previously, the desires
of the gross human body are at their strongest and it is easy for a wave of
anger or envy from the more superficial level of the mind to blot out a
person's objectivity and their higher nature.

Many cultures have the idea of heaven or the transcendent as being the
pinnacle of the last of a line of mountains, each one rising higher than the
one before, so as to make a stairway or ladder up to heaven. It is significant
that Snow White should be fairer, especially as regular infusions of the
transcendent were now a part of her life.

In this disguise she went over the seven mountains to the little
cottage of the seven dwarfs. She knocked at the door and cried,
'Pretty things to sell, very cheap, very cheap.'
Snow White opened one of the little windows and looked out.
'Hello, my good woman! What have you to sell?' she called out.
'Some very pretty things,' answered the old woman. 'I have got
some stay laces of all colours,' she added, pulling out one that was
woven in bright silk.
Snow White unbolted the door and bought the pretty laces.
'Come to me,' beckoned the old woman. 'You do look a sight. I
will lace you up properly for a change.'
With that Snow White, without a trace of suspicion, allowed
herself to be laced up by the old woman. However, the old woman
laced her up so tightly that she could not breathe and fell down as
if dead.
Not long afterwards the seven dwarfs came home. They were

shocked to see her lying so still on the ground. As they lifted her up they saw that the laces were tied too tight so they cut them. Immediately after that Snow White began to breathe again and in a little while came to life again.

The dwarfs told her that the old woman was no other than the wicked queen, and said that under no circumstances was she to open the door of the cottage again.

One is instantly reminded of the plight of Persephone. As soon as she allowed her attention to become extroverted by the narcissus, she was carried off into the underworld by Hades. The same can be said here of Snow White. No sooner was her attention diverted away from the Self than disaster struck.

But what of the stay laces? Strings, like a chain, often symbolise the connection between heaven and earth. According to Hindu, Buddhist and Platonist ideas a person's body or individual soul is attached to his spirit or persona by an astral golden string.

In *Advancement to Learning,* Bacon refers to the fable of the golden chain, namely that 'whilst men were not able to draw Jupiter down to earth, Jupiter was able to draw them up to Heaven'[1].

Blake puts it this way:

> I give you the end of a golden string,
> Only wind it in a ball;
> It will lead you in at Heaven's gate,
> Built in Jerusalem's wall.[2]

However, I think we are dealing with another animal altogether. I think this part of the story originally referred to the first of the three initiations of the initiate. The wicked queen is no other than Demeter in disguise. As we have mentioned before the cottage is another version of the initiate's cave. This is where the initiate first has the experience of transcending the relative field of Nature and first experiences Transcendental Consciousness.

When the mind goes in towards the transcendent the need to breathe becomes less and less until it reaches the transcendent. Anybody who has had this experience will know that once the mind goes out of the transcendent to prepare for normal life in the relative field of existence, it is accompanied by a deep intake of breath.

In the story it seems that the golden string has pulled the mind and body of the individual so as to yoke it tightly to the Absolute. On the outward stroke of meditation it is as if the dwarfs, or the forces of Nature, loosen it again so that one is able to cope with the demands of relative life.

Once again the wicked queen was labouring under the illusion that she was the most beautiful and went to her magic looking glass to have this confirmed. But, as before, she learned that Snow White was still much more beautiful, and was still alive and well.

Once again her mind was consumed with envy. This time she made a poisonous comb and once again set off, over the seven mountains, to the cottage, in the guise of another old lady.

She knocked at the door and cried, 'I've got some good things to sell – very cheap.'

Snow White looked out of the window, full of curiosity.

'Go away,' she exclaimed. 'I'm not allowed to open the door.'

'You don't have to,' wheedled the old woman craftily. 'You can see just as well by looking out of the window. Look at this!' With that she held up the poisonous comb.

Snow White liked the look of it and so let herself become so beguiled that she opened the door. When they had struck a bargain, the old woman said that she would comb the girl's hair properly before she went. Snow White innocently turned to let her give her ebony hair a good comb. No sooner had the comb entered her hair when the poison took effect and she fell senseless to the ground.

'You paragon of beauty,' sneered the old woman. 'You're finished now.'

With that she hurriedly picked up her basket and left.

Fortunately, it wasn't too long before the seven dwarfs came home. They found Snow White lying on the ground. They quickly found the comb and took it out. Soon after that she revived and told them about her encounter with the old woman. Once again they warned her to be on her guard and not to open the door to anyone again.

I believe we encounter here one of those artful pieces of literary embroidery that both make the story plausible and mask the real significance of what is being conveyed.

Firstly, if it has anything to do with the Mystery Religions it has to be about the second initiation. If we play about just a little with the phrase 'a comb in her head' we get 'her head in a combe' and it makes much more sense. A combe is a kind of hollow in a hillside – very likely a cave.

Not only this, the comb has other connotations. It is the crest on a cock, a symbol of the sun. The cock heralds the dawn of each new day. In terms of the initiate, this is when the dark night of ignorance makes way for the knowledge of enlightenment. We have already established that the second initiation corresponds to the dawning of Cosmic Consciousness.

But what of combs? Combs also, it seems, have the same significance as a cock's comb. Bayley tells us that the curved combs used in the past were symbolic of the 'Great Father Sun'[3]. They were frequently found in the prehistoric tombs of the Bronze Age and in more recent times they were reserved for burials of spiritual, shining lights in the ecclesiastical world. Apparently a comb was the emblem of St Blase. It is also significant that when the body of St Cuthbert was disinterred at Durham Cathedral, a plain Saxon comb made out of ivory was found on his breast.

The teaching at the heart of the Mystery Religions was that the individual is a spark of the spiritual sun and that the zodiac charted his particular journey through life. He had to both unite his whole being with the spiritual sun and throw off the binding influence of his karma on the Wheel of Necessity. In short he had to be his own solar hero. The catch-phrase in all hermetic circles was 'as above so below'.

Heracles was the archetypal solar hero. He had twelve tasks to purify himself – one for every sign of the zodiac. Even today, astrology still divides the human physiology into twelve distinct parts. Once an initiate has purified his body sufficiently so as to bring about a phase transition from the waking, dreaming and deep sleep states to a permanent state of Transcendental Consciousness, his mind now becomes one with the Cosmic Mind and Cosmic Consciousness dawns.

Returning once more to the poisonous comb, I believe that this stands for perception from the standpoint of ignorance. The view of life from the standpoint of ignorance misses the eternal harmony at the basis of all life, and consequently only sees disorder, confusion and suffering. Once again, I think the wicked queen had a dual role. She was both the ego-driven sense mind and the goddess Demeter in disguise. The latter was on hand to point out the main impediment standing in the way of the enlightenment of the initiate. Once alerted, it would then be simple for purification to take place and for the dwarfs to restructure the physiology without it. Once the poisoned comb was removed the individual would be thoroughly in tune with the Mind of the Cosmos or the large Self. At that point the initiate would have gained Cosmic Consciousness.

Once again the queen looked into her looking glass and asked who was the fairest in this land. Once more the looking glass repeated that Snow White was alive and well and still living over the seven mountains with the dwarfs. The queen was livid and made her final attempt to put an end to Snow White. This time she went to a secret, lonely room where nobody ever came and concocted a very poisonous apple. On the outside it looked very appealing and enticing so that everyone who saw it would want it; but whoever tasted it would die.

When she was ready she made herself up to look like a farmer's wife and went over the seven mountains to the home of the seven dwarfs. She knocked at the door.

'I can't let anybody in,' called Snow White, sticking her head out of the window. 'The seven dwarfs have forbidden me to open the door to anybody.'

'It is all the same to me,' replied the old woman. 'I have some lovely apples in my basket. They will soon be gone. Here, have one!'

'No!' relied Snow White worriedly. 'I dare not take one.'

'Are you afraid of being poisoned or something?' laughed the old woman. 'I'll tell you what, let's share it.'

The old woman cut the apple in two and ate her half. Snow White longed to eat the other half. She could not resist it any longer. She reached out her hand and took the rosy, red, poisoned half and took a bite. Before she even had time to swallow, she fell senseless to the ground.

When the seven dwarfs came home they, once again, found her lying on the ground. But this time there was nothing they could do for her. They washed her with water and wine, combed her hair and laid her upon a bier. They sat around it and wept for three days.

Apples in myths are usually associated with immortality. This is no exception. The third initiation was the one of ritual death. The washing of the body with water and wine and beautifying it is reminiscent of ancient Egypt and it is hard to resist the thought of Mary Magdelene tending Jesus. The dwarfs mourned for three days, the same time as Jesus lay in the sepulchre.

The paring of the apple into two parts is reminiscent of the 'World Egg' in Mystery Religions – namely one part represents the material aspects of life and the other half the spiritual. Similarly, the cave in which the initiations took place: whilst the emphasis of the second initiation was on the floor of the cave, the third was centred on a gap in the vault above it. The symbolism of the initiation cave mirrored the two apertures in the Great Pyramid, one pointed to the escape from the Wheel of Necessity, in the form of the zodiac the other pointed to the pole star, the axis of the universe, the still poin around which all the other stars rotated.

> They were going to bury her but her beauty was undiminished. Her cheeks remained rosy and they couldn't bring themselves to inter her under the dark earth. Nor did they leave her body open to the elements. They had a transparent glass coffin made for her and inscribed upon it in golden letters that she was a king's daughter.
>
> They put the coffin on the peak of the mountain. The dwarfs made sure there was always one of them there to see it came to no harm. The birds also came to pay their respects for Snow White; first an owl, then a raven and finally a dove.

The Great Work was almost completed. The glass coffin symbolises the transparency of a clear nervous system in which all the dross of past karma has been removed. There were virtually no impurities left. In this refined state she was blessed with the language of the birds.

Another indication that Snow White had achieved the state of God Consciousness is that the coffin was placed upon the peak of a mountain. A mountain top symbolised the peak of spiritual evolution. But what about the anomaly of the glass coffin? This obviously symbolised an alchemical glass alembic, whose sloping sides resembled the shape of a mountain.

It must also be remembered that earlier in the book Yogananda was quoted as saying, 'as long as the individual is encased in one, two or three body containers, sealed tightly with the corks of ignorance and desires, he cannot merge into the sea of the spirit'. It is said that when a person reaches Cosmic Consciousness he doesn't need to reincarnate. So unless he comes back to help others evolve he will only need an astral body and a causal body. It follows then that once he has achieved God Consciousness he only needs a causal body. Yogananda said the causal body is 'indescribably subtle'[4] and is at the junction point of mind and matter. Thus, the causal body is the transparent coffin the story is obliquely referring to.

In an Italian version of the story called *Pentamertone*, the similarity to the causal body is even more marked. In that story, Lisa, the heroine, continues to grow in her coffin and the crystal casket in which she was incarcerated grew with her, thus implying that she continued to grow in spiritual wisdom.

In addition to bestowing the language of the Veda upon Snow White the birds have something else to tell us. Whereas today the owl is regarded by most modern western cultures as a bird of ill omen, it always accompanied he ancient Greek goddess Athena as a symbol of wisdom. Similarly, today in Hindu cultures the goddess Laksmi, embodying the fullness of wealth and wisdom, is often accompanied by an owl. Its ability to see in the dark was ymbolic of penetrating the dark night of ignorance.

Like the owl, the raven too was generally thought of as portending ickness and death. However, in Persia ravens were sacred to the god of light. The Greeks and Romans also associated white ravens with Helios and Apollo. n this respect it can be equated with the astral body.

The third is the easy one. A dove perched on the top of a mountain often represented the Holy Spirit in Christian mysticism. Prior to this it person-fied the Good Spirit, because the circles on its throat were taken as repre-senting the seven spirits of God. The ancient Greeks thought of it as the Alpha-Omega, because the Greek word for dove resolved to the same number. It is interesting to note that the Slavs thought the soul took the orm of a dove as it left the body. They personified the soul as leaving the body through the mouth and flying off to the Milky Way, which they called the street of birds'.

One day it happened that a king's son came into the forest and wanted to stay the night in the dwarfs' cottage. He saw the coffin on top of the mountain and was enraptured by the beautiful Snow White inside it. He also read the inscription in gold on the side of it.

'Let me have the coffin,' he entreated. 'I'll give you anything you like for it.'

'She is very dear to us all,' relied the dwarfs. 'We will not part with her for all the gold in the world.'

'Then let me have it as a gift,' mused the king's son. 'I can't live without seeing her. I will treasure her as my dearest possession.'

The king's son was so sincere in the way he spoke that they took pity on him and gave it to him. His servants picked up the bier and put it on their shoulders and began to carry it away. One of them tripped over a tree stump. He didn't drop it but it gave the coffin a hefty jolt. The jolt dislodged the piece of poisonous apple in her throat and before long she revived. She opened her eyes and then pushed up the lid of the coffin and sat up.

'Where am I?' she asked.

'You are with me,' replied the king's son. 'I love you more than anything in the world. Come to my father's palace and become my wife.'

Snow White was more than willing. She went home with the

191

king's son. They were soon married with great pomp and splendour and lived in great joy and happiness ever after.

The dislodging of the piece of poisoned apple from her throat symbolises the purification that has taken place when a mortal achieves immortality – the poisoned half being the entire range of possible flavours of the fruit of the field of good and evil in the relative world. The other half of the apple represents the unmanifest transcendental sphere of life.

The alchemical reason why Snow White awakened to her true splendour and divine status when the prince kissed her is because the gold in the sealed glass vessel has now become living gold – as soon as it touches the lips of an individual soul he or she is rejuvenated and thus restored to their ultimate state of consciousness, bliss and perfect health.

> But what of the wicked queen? She too was invited to the wedding feast. She dressed herself up in her most beautiful clothes and stood in front of her looking glass and said:
> 'Looking glass, looking glass on the wall
> Who in this land is the fairest of all?'
> The looking glass replied:
> 'Oh, queen, of all here, the fairest art thou
> But the young queen is fairer by far as I trow.'
> The wicked woman did not know whether to go or not. Finally, after some hesitating, her curiosity got the better of her. When she recognised Snow White and saw how radiantly beautiful she was, the wicked queen was so incensed with rage that she could not move. Iron slippers had already been put on the fire. When they were red hot they were brought out with tongs and set before her. She was forced to put on the red shoes and she danced, hot-footed, until she fell down dead.

This was not one of those souls flying off to the Milky Way for eventual rebirth. Snow White was destined for the direction of the pole star. She was now supra-cosmic. She had achieved God Consciousness and the king's son had come for her. She would be in Unity Consciousness once the wedding had taken place. But this was no ordinary wedding. It was also an alchemical wedding – hence the iron shoes. Iron was regarded by alchemists as an impure metal, which needed to be transmuted into gold. Also the shoes are on the last extremity of the body, the feet, and as such are nearest to the base earth. A little more heat and the whole physiology of the wicked queen would be purified and she would be completely snow white – pure sattva –

and then everybody would live happily forever after.

---

[1] Quoted in Bayley, 1996, vol. 1, 91
[2] Quoted in Bayley, 1996, vol. 1, 91
[3] Bayley, 1996, vol. 2, 179-180
[4] Yogananda, 1999, 62

# Bibliography

Arunachala, Sadhu (1961), *A Sadhu's Reminiscences of Ramana Maharshi* (Sharada Press)

Aurobindo, Sri (1971), *The Secret of the Veda* (Sri Aurobindo Ashram Trust)

Baggott, Andy (1999), *Celtic Wisdom*, (Piatkus Books)

Bayley, Harold (1996), *Lost Language of Symbolism (1) & (2)* (Bracken Books)

Becker, Udo (2000), *The Continuum Encyclopedia of Symbols* (Continuum Books)

Biermann, Derek (2000), *Samadhi* (Shambhala Publications)

Case, Paul Foster (1947), *The Tarot* (Macoy Publishing Co.)

Campbell, Joseph (1991), *Oriental Mythology – The Masks of God* (Arkana)

Cheshire, Paul (1974), *Eleusis and the Greek Mysteries* (Creative Intelligence)

Churchward, James (1959), *The Children of Mu* (Neville Spearman)

Churchward, James (1965), *The Lost Continent of Mu* (Neville Spearman)

Churton, Tobias (1987), *The Gnostics* (Weidenfield & Nicholson)

Cohen, S. S. (1959), *Reflections on the Talks with Sri Ramana Maharshi* (T. N. Venkataraman)

Cooper, J. C. (1999), *An Illustrated History of Traditional Symbols* (Thames & Hudson Ltd)

Cox, Robert (1997), *The Pillar of Celestial Fire*, (Sunstar Publishing)

Dalai Lama & Howard Cutler (1998), *The Art of Happiness* (Hodder & Stoughton)

195

Eliade, Mircea (1959), *The Sacred and the Profane* (Harcourt Brace Jovanovich)

Eliade, Mircea (1989), *Journal 111*, trans. Teresa Fagan, (University of Chicago Press)

Freke, T. & P. Gandy (1997), *The Complete Guide to World Mysticism* (Piatkus Books)

Freke, T. & P. Gandy (2000), *The Jesus Mysteries* (Thorsons)

Freke, T. & P. Gandy (2002), *Jesus and the Goddess* (Thorsons)

*God, Transcendance & the Brain* – MSNM Newsweek broadcast 3/5/01

Grimm, Jacob & Wilhelm (1893), *Grimm's Fairy Stories* (Routledge)

Guenon, Rene (1995), *Fundamental Symbols* (Quinta Essentia)

Haitch, Elizabeth (2000), *Initiation* (Aurora Press Inc)

Hancock, Graham (1995), *Fingerprints of the Gods* (Heinemann)

Hancock, Graham (1998), *Heaven's Mirror* (Michael Joseph)

Heath, Sidney (1909), *The Romance of Symbolism* (Kessinger Publishing)

Heinberg, Richard (1990), *Memories and Visions of Paradise* (The Aquarian Press)

Graves, Robert (1961), *The White Goddess* (Faber & Faber)

Homer (1996), *The Odyssey* (Viking)

Knappert, Jan (1991), *Indian Mythology* (Aquarian Press)

Knight, R. Payne (1999), *The Symbolical Language of Art & Mythology* (Kessinger Publishing)

Mead, G. R. S. (1908), *The Chaldean Oracles* (Theosophical Publishing Society)

Mackenzie, D. A. (1995), *Crete & Pre-Hellenic Myths & Legends* (Senate)

Mackenzie, D. A. (1996), *Mythology of the Babylonian People* (Bracken Books)

Meyer, Marvin ed. (1987), *The Ancient Mysteries – a Source Book* (Harper Row Publishers)

Nader, Tony (2000), *Human Physiology – Expression of Veda and the Vedic Literature*, (Maharishi Vedic Literature)

Opie, Iona & Peter (1974), *The Classic Fairy Tales* (Oxford University Press)

Paffard, Michael (1973), *Inglorious Wordsworths: A Study of Transcendental Experiences in Childhood and Adolescence* (Hodder & Stoughton)

## Bibliography

Paterson, Jacqueline Memory (1996), *Tree Wisdom* (HarperCollins)

Philip, Neil (1989), *The Cinderella Story* (Penguin)

*Precession of the Equinoxes,* http://cannon.sfsu.edu/~lea/courses/nexa/cwwplan.html

Santillana, Giorgio De and Hertha Von Dechend (1969), *Hamlet's Mill: An Essay Investigating the Origins of Human Knowledge and its Transmission Through Myth* (Harvard University Press)

Saraswati, Swami Satyananda (2001), *The Chandi Path* (Devi Mandir)

Seton Williams, M.V. (1988), *Egyptian Legends & Stories* (The Rubicon Press)

Shearer, Alistair (1982), *Effortless Being* (Wildwood House)

Stephanides Brothers' (1997), *The Gods of Olympus* (Sigma)

Stephanides Brothers' (1997), *The Iliad* (Sigma)

*The Hermetica* (1997), trans. Walter Scott (Solos Press)

*The Panchatantra* (1993), trans. Chandra Rajan (Penguin Books)

*The Way of Hermes* (1999), trans. C. Salaman, Dorine Van Oyen, and W.D. Wharton (Duckworth Press)

*Tripura Rahasya* (2002), trans. Swami Sri Ramamanda Saraswati (World Wisdom)

Yogananda, Paramahansa, (1972), *Autobiography of a Yogi* (Rider & Co)

Yogananda, Paramahansa, (1999), *God Talks with Arjuna – The Bhagavad Gita* (Self Realisation Fellowship Publishers)

Yogi, Maharishi Mahesh (1967), *Bhagavad Gita* (Penguin)

Yogi, Maharishi Mahesh (1965), *The Love of God* (SRM)

Yukteswari, Sri (1990), *The Holy Science* (Self Realisation Fellowship)

Zipes, Jack, (1979), *Breaking the Magic Spell* (Heinemann Educational Books Ltd)

# Index